ANCESTORS
A TALE OF TWO WORLDS

ROB COLLINGE

SilverWood

Published by the author in 2013 by SilverWood Empowered Publishing

SilverWood Books
30 Queen Charlotte Street, Bristol, BS1 4HJ
www.silverwoodbooks.co.uk

ISBN 978-1-78132-096-9 (paperback)
ISBN 978-1-78132-097-6 (ebook)

British Library Cataloguing in Publication Data
A CIP catalogue record for this book is available from the British Library

Set in Sabon by SilverWood Books
Printed on responsibly sourced paper

To my dear wife Helen and my son Stuart
for all their help and support in my family research and in the
writing of this book

Also to Martin Collinge
for supplying much valuable information from his own
investigations into the family history

Contents

Part 2
The Old World: The Cotton Mills of Oldham

Part 3
A Search for Answers

Introduction

The date was 8 May 1900, the place San Antonio, Texas. The event was one of the high society weddings of the year, to be reported in much detail by the local press. Ella Theodora Koerner belonged to one of the leading families of the city, daughter of George Koerner, wealthy merchant and businessman. Wharton Rye Collinge was an Englishman from a cotton mill owning family in Lancashire, at least equal in wealth and social prominence to the Koerners. She was a descendant of early pioneers from Germany in a land where founding fathers were revered. He was a member of a family that had risen to heights of power and prestige during the heady days of the Industrial Revolution.

Soon after their marriage, the couple set sail for England, there to lead a gilded life and to raise a family in a fine manor house, a world of servants and privilege, of comfort and security. But it was not to last – a World War would come and leave behind only the dust and ashes of their hopes and dreams.

They were my grandparents. This is their story.

Part 1

The New World: Pioneers and Exiles

The Texas Connection Family Tree

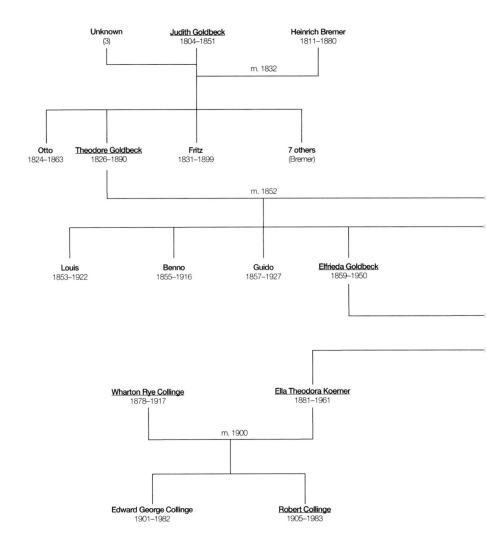

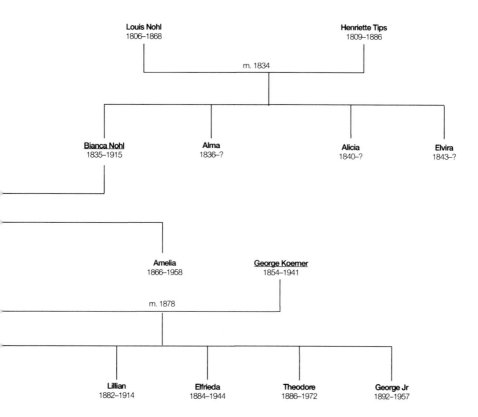

Chapter 1

Judith Goldbeck: A Stranger in Town
Lower Saxony: 1832

Judith had brought some small pieces of bread for the swans. A waste, she knew; she should not be throwing food away. What would the children say, after all her lectures on thrift, of appreciation for every day that they had food on the table? They would remember the days when the table was bare, the hard days in Wolterdingen when only the bitter, grudging charity of Judith's stepmother had kept them from starving. Christian charity, she had called it, accompanied by Christian scorn and Christian contempt.

But the swans were beautiful, so graceful, so serene, so untroubled by the cares of the world. Oh, to be a swan, thought Judith. She leaned forward from the bench by the water's edge and enticed two of the great birds closer with her morsels. She would love to have touched one, touched the smooth feathers, but she knew they would strike her. They said a swan could break your arm. Probably just an old wives' tale, but better not to put it to the test.

Today was Sunday. The bells tolled, the good folk of Verden went about their worship. Judith had not taken up churchgoing in Verden. She would not know anyone there and the curious glances would discomfort her. She had been too familiar with curious glances in Wolterdingen, with muttered words, with turned backs, with the all-pervading village gossip. That was all behind her now. She was here to start again, in a town where no one knew her. She would keep it that way. The children were her life, the only life she needed.

15

She started at a voice beside her. Lost in thoughts of a carefree life, floating on a lake, she had not heard the man approach.

'Do you mind if I share your seat? It's the only one by the water. I often sit here.'

Judith was in no mood to accept advances from strangers. In Wolterdingen, her first instinct would have been to mutter an excuse and walk away. Her reputation as a loose woman there had made her a target for unwanted approaches. In Verden she was determined to make a fresh start for the children's sakes and her own and to avoid any undesirable contacts.

She hesitated a moment, resisting the urge to flee. No one knew her in Verden. She must be a stranger to him, as he was to her. He was a pleasant looking young man, certainly younger than herself, early twenties, neat, well dressed, from a good family by his accent, but not haughty. He would see by her patched clothing that she was not in good circumstances, yet his words had been civil, courteous. He did not need her permission to sit on a public bench in the town park.

She smiled warily. 'Why, yes. Of course.' Inwardly she tensed, ready to follow her instincts if they told her to depart.

'Thank you,' he responded. He seated himself and sat in silence for a few moments, gazing at the lake. Then he motioned to the birds before them, waiting now for more tidbits from Judith's bag of crumbs. 'They are beautiful, don't you think? Have you ever wished you were a swan?'

Caught by surprise, she laughed nervously. 'Why, yes. That was the very thought in my mind when you came.'

He smiled. 'Well then, I will invade the privacy of your mind no further, before your secrets are laid bare.'

Judith glanced at him, wondering if he was mocking her, but he seemed simply intent on light conversation. She shook her head ruefully and replied, half to herself. 'My secrets? Oh, no. That would never do.' Then, not wishing to drive him away with her dark mood, she continued awkwardly, 'You would leave this bench in fright if I told you my secrets.' She was finding already in Verden that she could not suppress the loneliness, the need for human companionship, however she might try, and now she did not want the stranger to go.

She feared that she was making a fool of herself but the man responded pleasantly. 'Ah, but now you have me intrigued. Tell me one of your less frightening secrets, perhaps.' He checked himself. 'Not that I wish to pry, of course.'

In spite of her doubts and fears, Judith found that she was beginning to enjoy this unexpected conversation. After all the years of religious orthodoxy of her childhood, of rigid unyielding dogma, of minds closed to any breath of fresh air, she welcomed an opportunity for verbal sparring with an intelligent adversary. That had always been her problem – an active, inquiring mind, locked in a woman's body, and the daughter of a pastor at that, a man of fixed opinions.

'A less frightening secret. Let me see. Well, I have been in Verden only one month. And I have not been to church today. I might ask why are you not at the service? Do you have a secret too?'

'Yes, I always sit near the side door. If the sermon becomes too boring, I slip out when the others' heads are down. I don't think I am missed. I have never pretended to be devout. I cannot be bothered with pretence.'

She felt an overwhelming urge to share a few confidences with this charming young man. However much she might tell herself that her children were her life, the need for adult company was never far away. Besides, if he was a regular visitor to the park, she might meet him again.

He spoke first. 'Only one month in Verden?'

'Yes, I am from Wolterdingen. You know it – a small place?' He nodded. 'I have three children, three sons. I wanted a better life for them. I have been fortunate. I have a job here, setting the type in Herr Kramer's printing office. He wanted a man for the task, to replace someone he had lost, but I convinced him that I could do it. He is a kind man. I share a couple of rooms with Alma, another of Herr Kramer's workers. She has the children now. They like her. "Go to the park", she said. "Give yourself a break."'

'Your husband is not with you then? Did he stay behind in Wolterdingen?'

This was the hard part. Why did she get into such a conversation as this? She should have foreseen where it must lead. It could only end badly, with embarrassment for both of them.

Her face tightened. 'I have no husband.' And before he could ask, 'Nor am I a widow. I am unmarried.'

He flushed. 'I'm sorry. I have pried into your secrets after all.' He paused, then repeated, 'I am truly sorry.'

Judith saw an expression of genuine concern on his face. 'I must add in my own defence,' she continued, 'that I was wild and foolish in my youth, and far too trusting of men, but I have never taken payment for my services. I am not a whore.' Her eyes glistened and she fought back tears.

His face was red now but he made no attempt to leave. 'I know another of your secrets; you're a good mother. You said you have brought your children here for a better life. You will fight for those children.'

She was surprised at his insight. 'Yes, you're right. They're my whole life now. I will do anything I can for them, anything in my power.'

He relaxed and smiled again. 'Well, let us have something of myself. I have been the apprentice of Herr Heymal, a merchant in herbs and spices, and have now completed my apprenticeship. He's a good master, like your Herr Kramer. I'll stay with him awhile yet, then see about my own little business. I have ideas.'

'A master apprentice then,' she responded. 'A man with a future. I am impressed.'

'Well, the printing trade is a fine one too. Did you know our Herr Gutenberg invented printing? It is a specialty of the German people.'

'Oh yes, I know. Though they do say the Chinese invented it first.' She laughed at the surprise on his face. 'Oh, I'm showing off to you now. I was brought up with books. I have always loved reading. Not that it does me much good.'

He was studying her closely. 'On the contrary, it makes you a most interesting companion. Do we know each other well enough yet for introductions? My name is Heinrich Bremer.'

'And mine is Judith Goldbeck.' She shook his hand.

He took a fob watch from his waistcoat and checked the time. 'I must be on my way,' he said, 'or my family will wonder what has become of me.' He rose to his feet.

'You have a family?'

'Oh no,' he explained, 'just my mother and my brother. Do you have brothers and sisters?'

She laughed. 'Oh yes, indeed. There are nine of us by my dead mother and six more by my stepmother. All dutiful children. I don't think any of them want to know me now.'

He shrugged and spread his hands apart in a gesture of disdain. 'You're well rid of them then. And you are the family rebel, eh? Well, good for you. I like rebels. We must meet again and continue this conversation. Better a talk with you than listening to that damned old parson.' He turned to go, then hesitated and gave her a quizzical glance. 'Would you think to be here next Sunday?'

'As long as you sit by the side door of the church.'

'We have a deal then. Next Sunday.'

Judith nodded and he left. As she walked back to her new home, her step was light. She felt stimulated by the encounter. What a pleasure it was to talk to a person of wit and intelligence, a kind man who did not make her feel dirty or inferior. She would look forward to another Sunday at the lake.

Alma was waiting. 'Oh, you have been a while,' she scolded with mock severity. 'What a handful these children of yours are.' She shook her head. 'And did you have a pleasant time with the swans?'

'Thank you so much. Yes, a very pleasant time. I talked to a most charming stranger. We had an interesting conversation.' She broke off as two small boys flung their arms about her with cries of 'Mama, Mama.'

Alma laughed. She was a pretty girl, about eighteen. 'You watch out for these charming strangers. Some of them are only after one thing. This is not your pious village.'

Judith grinned. 'Oh, they are not so pious in my village, I tell you. Look at this lot, will you?'

'Did he say his name, this charming stranger?'

'Yes, he even shook my hand and requested to continue our conversation next week. His name is Heinrich Bremer. Do you know him?'

That took the smile from Alma's face. 'Ooh, yes I know him.

Good family. The father was a wine merchant. He's dead now but he left them well provided for. Clever lad too, and handsome. He has finished his apprenticeship to old Heymal, the spices man, and done well at it. He would be a fine catch.' She pouted her lips and brushed her hair from her eyes. 'Take me with you next week. You feed the swans with the children and I will talk to Heinrich Bremer.'

'You're such a flirt, Alma. Look at me. Be warned. It could happen to you. I thought I would get a catch out of it but I was the one caught.' She shrugged. 'Anyway, he admired me for my mind. Do you have an admirable mind?'

'No, but I have a good figure.' She cupped her hands under her breasts. 'Do you know any man who is more interested in minds than figures?'

'Yes, I think I just met one.' By now Judith was sitting on one of the two rough chairs in the small sitting room, little Fritz in her arms. She had been less than candid with Heinrich about her three "lads". Otto and Theodore were eight and six but Fritz was not even one year old yet, just taking his first steps.

Fritz's birth had been the last straw to the good folk of Wolterdingen. No matter that the father came from a good family, that his ardent wooing had broken through Judith's defences, that his promises of marriage had been abandoned the moment she confronted him with her condition. He was five years younger than Judith, just a lad they said. No matter that at twenty-two he was surely old enough to make his own decisions. He had been seduced by that wanton Jezebel. Whose son would be next? The shame was more than a weak distant father and a shrewish stepmother could bear. Judith would have to go and go she did, before the year was out.

Another week passed quickly. An arrangement had been made with Frau Kirschner, a housewife with five small children of her own, to mind Judith's three while their mother was at work. That took some of Judith's wage. Then too, some nights at the printing press were longer than others and it was late when she arrived for the children. If the good Frau had already fed them, Judith faced an extra charge. After paying rent little remained but it was a living and she felt happier than she had done for a long time. On Sundays she had the children to herself, though after six long days of work she found them exhausting. Alma's suggestion of an hour in the park alone had seemed a fine idea.

She looked forward to the next Sunday. To have a new friend was a real delight, a man who appreciated her intelligence and seemed unfazed by her domestic misfortunes. Alma did not press her desire to meet Heinrich, but warned as Judith left for the park, 'It's not their minds you have to worry about, it's their hands.'

But Heinrich did not come to the park and Judith returned in a greater state of disappointment than she could account for. It had been a pleasant experience; leave it at that, she told herself. The children were her life now, but that mantra was starting to wear thin already. Was that all the future held?

The next day, Monday, was like any other working day. A brief break for a hasty lunch and back to the task. At least business was thriving and she had no fear of being laid off as long as she could take the pace.

Judith knew how fortunate she was to have found such work. She had told Herr Kramer that the care she would bring to the task, her close attention to detail, would exceed that of any man. Amused by her argument, he had agreed to give her a trial. So far, he seemed satisfied.

It was hardly pleasant work, with the clatter of the printing presses, the ink that stained her hands, the long hours of standing. It was exacting and repetitive and she knew that there could be no margin for error. A mistake with the arranging of the type could ruin a hundred copies if it was not found in time.

Before she could resume at the typesetter, Herr Kramer came to her from the front office. 'A gentleman to see you,' he said in a disapproving tone. Time was precious to the printer, not to be squandered in private visits.

Embarrassed in front of her employer, Judith responded, 'But I don't know any gentlemen.'

'Well, he knew your name. Be quick.'

'Oh indeed, Herr Kramer.' She took off her ink-spattered apron and hurried to the front room of the little shop.

Heinrich awaited her. Judith looked at him in surprise. 'Why, Heinrich – I had not expected to see you.'

He seemed in a serious mood. 'I will only keep you a moment, Judith. I know how busy you are but I am a man of my word and I was not there for our meeting. My mother was ill and I did not go to church. I wasn't able to tell you.'

The importance he seemed to attach to their meeting puzzled her. It had only been a casual proposition between two virtual strangers. She was touched by his concern. 'You need not have worried,' she assured him. 'I just assumed you were busy. I didn't think badly of you. You weren't under any obligation to me. I would have been there anyway – I fed the swans again.'

'Nevertheless, I will see you next time. If my mother is still unwell, my brother can stay with her.'

Somewhat at a loss to understand his concern, Judith responded with a smile, a shrug, a gesture of her hands, 'Well then, we shall meet again.'

'You have my word,' he promised and left the shop, leaving Judith shaking her head in bewilderment. What a strange young man. This was his home; he was surely not short of friends, of conversation. Well, if he liked to match wits with her, she was only too happy to oblige. The relationship was beginning to intrigue her.

True to his word, Heinrich appeared at the park for their next meeting. They talked of many things, of history, of the wars of Napoleon, of Martin Luther, of the prospects for German unity. She found a lot to like about Heinrich. He seemed to have no problem in treating a woman as his intellectual equal. Her past clearly did not trouble him; in fact no further mention was made of it, until as they parted, Heinrich said, 'Why not bring your sons next time? I like children. Let them play in the park. How old are they?'

Judith shifted uncomfortably. 'Well, Otto is eight, Theodore is six, but – well, the truth is…' She hesitated a moment. 'Little Fritz is not quite one year old yet.'

Heinrich showed his surprise. 'Not one year! And you moved to a new town with a baby.' He grinned and cocked his head in a way she had come to like. 'You are amazing. I have had such a safe, simple life. I have a family and friends. I would not have had the courage to do what you have done.'

'Oh, you can't tell. You can do brave things when you are forced to it. The man who betrayed me turned all the blame on me and the townsfolk saw me as a wanton, a menace to all their fine sons. It was an impossible life.'

'I can imagine. Well, you have Alma for a friend, and me, and there will be others. Let us hope this will be a new start for you.' He rose to leave. 'Remember, your sons next time.'

She gave a little salute, as though responding to an order. He laughed as he walked away.

Next week Heinrich was already waiting for her, seated on their bench in the warm summer sunshine. He greeted the two older boys kindly, speaking to each in the tones of one clearly familiar with young children. The two adults sat down and Heinrich took little Fritz on his lap, jigging him up and down and chatting to him in a way that quickly settled the toddler's fears of a stranger. The older boys ran off to chase about the park.

Heinrich stood Fritz on the ground at his feet, one hand still holding him. With the other, he motioned to Judith to pass him some of her bread morsels. With them he enticed two swans towards them. The great birds glided across the water to where the couple sat and Fritz clapped his little hands with glee.

'My,' said Judith, 'how domesticated you are. You do have a way with children.'

'Oh, I have cousins and others. I am not short of relatives in the town.'

Her curiosity got the better of her. 'And do you have a sweetheart, someone who misses you while you talk to strange women in the park – and play with their children?' She hoped he did not feel she was prying.

He took the question casually. 'No – there have been a few...' He sought the right word. 'Liaisons, you might say. All the young ones do. I have no one at the moment. I like to talk, as you see, and I tire of lady friends with little on their minds.'

They were charting a new conversational path now but Judith pursued it, frankly puzzled by the nature of the man. Did he perhaps lack the male instincts of which Alma was so conscious? 'Alma says men do not seek out women for their minds.'

'Well, she would know.' He gave her a sideways look and said in a conspiratorial tone. 'She is not the innocent angel, that one, I can tell you that.'

Judith feigned shock. 'You mean you...?'

Heinrich laughed. 'No, no, not me but others, friends of mine.'

Judith shook her head. 'It's disgraceful – the way you men brag of your conquests.' There was a hint of mischief in her voice.

'And so does your side. We are not alone in that. Anyway, it's not bragging; it's more like gossip.'

'A fine distinction, I must say.'

'Anyway...' He changed the subject. 'I have an idea. I have not told you that I am an actor. There is a little theatre group in Verden and we are staging a play next Saturday. A French play by Molière, a comedy. Have you heard of him?' She nodded. 'It is called *Le Médecin Malgré Lui* – 'The Doctor in Spite of Himself'. It's about a woodcutter who passes himself off as a doctor by reciting Latin. He doesn't know Latin, only pretends, but he impresses foolish people. It's very funny. Would you like to see it...and me?'

Her eyes shone. 'I would love to. But how much is the entrance fee?'

'For you, free, as a friend of an actor. I will take you there early, and get you seated. Later, I will escort you home. We can walk from here. You know the Playhouse, off the main square?' As Fritz became restless, Heinrich passed him across to his mother.

'Oh Heinrich, that would be wonderful. I have not been to a play since I was a child. I will tell Herr Kramer that I must leave in time for me to go out that night. He won't mind. It is Saturday night after all. I will really look forward to that. Frau Kirschner will feed the children – for a fee, of course. She needs the money. Her husband drinks,' she confided.

At home later, little Theodore, ever the thoughtful one, said, 'He was a nice man, Mama. Will you marry him?'

Judith replied in a tone of mixed amusement and exasperation, 'Oh Theodore, I am seven years older than him. I am twenty-eight, he is twenty-one. And I have three children. He will marry someone his own age and have his own children.'

Theodore looked crestfallen and his mother rubbed his hair fondly. 'We will be all right. We can look after each other.'

Later that night she checked her clothes, seeking out a combination that would show the least effects of patching.

The play was enjoyable, a night to remember. Judith was surprised at Heinrich's skill at acting. He had a major role, a nobleman taken in by the charlatan doctor. He was convincing, well rehearsed, indeed so were they all. The standard of the performance impressed her.

Later, Heinrich walked Judith home along the cobblestoned streets, keeping close to the building fronts and out of the way of passing coaches and wagons. She walked carefully in the dim light. The town centre had gaslight, impressive to a village girl like herself, but it was too expensive to extend far and the candle in Heinrich's lantern took them the rest of the way.

As they walked, Judith congratulated her escort. 'You were good, Heinrich, really good. I had a wonderful night. Thank you for taking me out.'

'My pleasure,' he replied. They had reached her rooming house, were standing outside in the moonlight. Suddenly his arms were about her, his lips pressed to hers.

Shocked, startled, she broke away. 'No, Heinrich, no. I may be a fallen woman, but I don't intend to fall any further.' She hesitated a moment, embarrassed and disappointed, then added, 'I don't know where you think this relationship is going, but I have no intention of finding out. Goodbye.' She turned on her heel and was gone before he could respond.

Alma was still awake, a flickering candle illuminating the little sitting room. She saw Judith's concern. 'So he wanted something for his money, did he? They're all the same in the end. Go on, get yourself to bed.'

Next day at the print shop, Judith could not drive the incident from her mind. It had been nice to have a new friend. Now her low expectations of humanity had been revived. As Alma said, 'They are all the same'. She had wanted to think differently.

After work, she collected the children. As she walked them home, Fritz in her arms, her mind filled with dark thoughts. What was to become of these three? She had no money for schooling. They would grow up illiterate, fit only for unskilled work; employed for a pittance in a mine or a factory at ten or twelve, tiny workers destined for lives of hardship and poverty.

She reached home in a grim mood. Alma was waiting for her, dear kind Alma. Well, she had one good friend at least. Alma waved a letter at her.

'Your Heinrich does not give up easily. He asked me to give you this.'

Judith shook her head wearily. 'He is wasting his time with me.' She opened the folded note, sealed with wax, and read. Alma looked on in curiosity.

When she finished, Judith's expression was perplexed. 'What am I to make of this man?' she said, more to herself than Alma. She offered the letter to Alma. 'What do you think?'

A flicker of embarrassment crossed Alma's face. 'I am not very good at reading. I did not have your education. Read it to me.'

Judith read: 'Deepest apologies for my impulsive behaviour. I hold you in high regard and meant no disrespect. I do not know where this relationship is going either, but I promise you that I will never again touch you without your permission. Please meet me again in the park. Your friend, Heinrich.'

Alma grinned. 'He does use big words. You people with your "admirable minds" are too lofty for a simple girl like me. What will you do?'

Judith raised her hands in a gesture of bewilderment. 'Oh, I don't know. I suppose I will meet him again. He has been so kind to me and the children like him. I'll forgive him this once. I don't know what he expects of me.'

'Well, you do enjoy talking to him – that's something. I would like a male friend who just wanted to talk for a change. He's a strange one, your Heinrich.'

At week's end, on Sunday morning, Judith found herself once

more seated in the familiar place at the park. It was odd, she thought, no one else ever wanted to sit there, as though Fate had reserved it for the two of them. She saw Heinrich approach. Just as at their first meeting, he stood formally by the bench and asked, 'Do you mind if I share your seat. It's the only one by the water.'

She realised he was mimicking their first encounter, acting out the part. She responded with a smile that belied the formality of her words. In her best stage voice, she said, 'Why, my dear Heinrich, I think we have played this scene before.'

Suddenly they were both laughing uproariously. As she got her breath back, Judith gestured to him. 'Oh, sit down, Heinrich, sit down. It is a public bench, you know. You don't need my permission.'

In the weeks that followed, as summer drew to a close and autumn beckoned, the friendship grew. An easy familiarity developed. Sometimes with the children, sometimes alone, they would laugh at private jokes, trade confidences, share their knowledge in an endless flow of conversation. He took her to play rehearsals and showed her about the town. He introduced her to others as a newcomer to Verden wishing to become familiar with the place. He had a circle of good friends and seemed entirely comfortable in having her with him. And, as promised, his display of respect for her was never again compromised.

Judith began to see unsuspected depths in Heinrich. He was much struck by the preciousness of life, by the loss of each passing year. He had a desire to avoid the predictable path. He talked of possible emigration to the United States and a life in the New World. In the end they unburdened their souls to each other in a way that Judith would not have thought possible for her to do with another human being.

It was as though she was being borne along on a current, unable or unwilling to turn aside from the course of the flow.

The day came when Heinrich greeted her at the park in a serious mood. He seemed ill at ease, not his usual casual self. 'I have something to say, Judith, and I don't know where to start. Please hear me out.'

He was looking at her with a curious intensity. She felt suddenly conscious of her appearance. Her auburn hair was tied back in a bun and she brushed it absently with her hand. Her large brown eyes widened in surprise, concerned by his mood, wondering what it portended. She nodded at his request and sat silently.

He glanced down for a moment, seemingly at a loss for words, then looked up at her, face flushed. 'I love you, Judith. I want to share my life with you.' The words now came more easily, in a rush. 'I know what you must think; I am years younger than you, you have children, but this is not some young man's fancy, a passing infatuation. I have not met anyone like you before, Judith, and I will not meet anyone like you again. We share so much. We have so much in common. We are two rebels, you and I. We don't care for convention. A chance like this comes only once in a lifetime.' In a heartfelt tone, he repeated, 'I want to share my life with you.'

'What are you telling me, Heinrich?' asked Judith, bewildered by his words.

'I want to marry you, Judith. I will look after you and the children. You may put your faith in me. I will not let you down.'

'Heinrich,' she said softly, 'it is usual to give the lady time to consider a proposal like this.'

He shook his head in embarrassment. 'Oh, of course. I'm sorry. Please, take as long as you like. Ask me anything you will.'

'I have not met your family. What will your mother think? And how would you support us? Where would we live? Are you really willing to be father to my children?' So many questions, her mind a whirl of confused emotions.

'I don't need my family's permission but I think you will like my mother. She is an understanding woman. We would rent a home. I know a place. With your income and mine, we would make a good start. Herr Heymal has asked me to be his partner. It's a good business; we can do well.' He paused a moment, placed his hand on her arm, and added in a tone of conviction, 'I will treat your children as my own and when we have children, there will be no distinction. I will be father to them all. I will never betray your trust in this.' His eyes were locked on hers now, his gaze so intense that her own shifted down uncomfortably.

'Give me a little time, Heinrich. I have been hurt before, you know. I'm scared. I'm scared of being hurt again.' She groped for words, unable to think clearly. 'Why not take this in small steps? I would like to meet your family, your mother and anyone else close to you. I know we don't need permission but I don't want a furtive relationship, a secret from everyone. I don't want to have to run away again from pointed fingers and whispered words.'

'Well, you haven't rejected me. That's a good start.' She sensed relief in his voice. 'I will do whatever you ask. Next Sunday, after church, we will go to my home. Then we will take as many small steps as you wish.'

A week later, Judith found herself sitting on a couch in the parlour of the Bremer family home. She looked up at the painting of the dead Herr Bremer on the wall behind, a distinguished looking gentleman, a man of authority. How could she ever explain herself to the woman before her, she wondered? It must seem a mad proposition to her. Heinrich had introduced his mother to Judith at the door and the older woman had ushered her in. 'Not you,' she said to her son. 'This young lady and I have much to talk about. Give us some time together.' Heinrich had dutifully departed, leaving Judith with the older woman.

'Well, my girl,' Frau Bremer began, 'my son Heinrich has told me of his love for you, but you must realise this is a strange story he tells me. He has only just reached adulthood and you are twenty-eight, with three children and no husband, forced to leave your home town. How do you think a mother should feel? Tell me about yourself.'

Judith liked her immediately and wanted more than ever to win her over, not just for Heinrich's sake but for her own. Frau Bremer was a neat, grey-haired woman, very much in control of the situation, not a person to be taken lightly. And yet Judith sensed a warmth in her that she could only have dreamed of in her own stepmother, or anyone else of influence in her childhood.

Judith told of her rigid, pious upbringing, of the all-pervading gloom, of the strictures that circumscribed her childhood and the rebellious streak that progressively split her from the family.

For some time, the older lady listened in silence. 'There are better ways to assert yourself than to bring unwanted children into the world, Judith,' she observed at one point.

'Oh, I know. I was foolish. I was immature. I had no love in my family and I sought it wherever I could find it and in all the wrong places. I trusted people. I was an easy mark. Then, with Fritz, I was seduced by a cunning rogue, a man who played on all my fears and insecurities and then betrayed me.' She described the disintegration of her life in Wolterdingen and the eventual flight to Verden.

'Did you ever think to leave your children behind?'

'Oh no, not for a moment.' Her face paled and her hand gripped the arm of the couch. 'They are my life. They are everything I have.'

'And how do you know that Heinrich is not just another cunning rogue?'

Judith grinned wryly. 'Because he well knows that there is nothing in it for him in that case. We may meet in the park forever but it will go no further.'

'Could you be holding him to ransom then? A wedding ring for a bed, and entry into a good family?' The mother was looking at Judith shrewdly.

Judith felt her stomach tighten. Here she was in the role of seductress again. She chose her words carefully. 'One of the many things I admire about Heinrich is his independent mind. He thinks for himself. He is nobody's fool. If he wants to marry me, it is all of me that he wants, not just my body. He sees more in me than that and he knows that I have much more to give.'

Frau Bremer smiled for the first time and relaxed in turn. 'Oh, I know. He is not as innocent as he seems. That is the actor in him.' She spoke fondly of her son. 'If that was all he wanted, and you would not give in, he would soon move on. He must see something very special in you.' Then abruptly she asked, 'And do you love him?'

Tears welled in Judith's eyes. 'Yes, Frau Bremer, oh yes. He is a fine, kind man. He has been so good to me. He has restored my self-respect. We enjoy each other's company more than words can tell. I love him very much.' She dabbed a handkerchief at her eyes.

The older lady rose, walked across and sat next to Judith, placing a hand on the younger woman's arm. 'You are a brave lady and you have had a bad life. You stood up to those pious frauds. I know the type. They spread misery in the name of God. They spoil lives instead of saving them. If this is all an act, my girl, then you are a far better actor than my son. I will believe in you.'

Judith put her hand on Frau Bremer's. 'Thank you,' she said simply, tears now flowing freely. 'I will never betray your faith. I will make this family proud of me.'

Later, as she left on Heinrich's arm, Frau Bremer said, 'Visit me again next week, my dear, and bring your children. If I am to be a grandmother, I should meet my grandchildren, don't you think?'

As they walked away, Heinrich observed, 'Well, that seemed to go well. Do you like my mother?'

Judith's barriers were down, her fear of disappointment, her instinctive wariness cast aside. 'Oh yes. She is a beautiful lady. You're so fortunate, Heinrich.'

He was the one now to play his part with caution. 'She will be your mother too, if you wish. That is one small step. What will be next?'

She slipped her arm from his and took his hand. 'Come with me. I will show you.' She led him through streets by now familiar to her and beyond, to the park, to the bench where they had first met. 'Sit,' she commanded and stood before him, gazing down at his perplexed face. 'Do you still want to have me, always, forever? You have no doubts about this?'

'No, none,' he replied, and added, 'always, forever.'

She sat beside him. 'Very well then, Herr Bremer, I accept your offer of marriage. You may put your arm around me now, and...' She could maintain the solemn tone no longer. With a happy laugh, she ended, 'And you may kiss me, if you wish.'

As he took her gently in his arms, Judith felt a lifetime of fears and disappointments fading away into a past that no longer mattered, a crushing burden of insecurity lifting from her shoulders. Her spirit had taken wings, had joined the swans at last.

Chapter 2

Judith Goldbeck: The Pioneers
Lower Saxony / Texas: 1844–1845

Forty years old! Could she really be such an age? Judith gazed around the room, at the happy, smiling faces of her children, at dear Heinrich lighting the candles on the birthday cake; four small candles for forty years. How blessed she was to have such a family. Six children alive, two dead – no, not to think of that now; only happy thoughts today.

They all had presents for her. Little Dorothea with shining eyes, a handful of flowers held in hot hands for too long, starting to wilt. Judith took them from the child and knelt down to hug her before placing them in a vase with some water. Adolph was only two, bewildered by it all, but someone, an older sibling, had given him a gift for his mother. She took it from the little hands. Opening the folded cloth, she saw a piece of wood; a carving, a tiny swan. They all knew the story of Judith feeding the swans.

Tears glistened; the children watched as she wiped her eyes. They knew their mother cried easily. Sometimes it was for joy, sometimes for sorrow. Today it was happiness that brought the tears and they shared the warm glow of a family united in celebrating a special day.

Joy and sorrow; so much of each in a family. Two children had been taken from her by illness. Little Julius was never a healthy child and lived only one year but to lose Catharina at nearly six had been devastating. Judith had vowed to treasure every day that each of her children was with her and never to take their part in her life for granted.

Judith looked around at the family gathered about her, all in their various ways intent on making this day a memorable one. Otto, nineteen now, a baker's apprentice; solid, unimaginative perhaps, but one day to make a good steady husband for Gretchen, his sweetheart.

Theodore, now seventeen – what would become of him, Theodore the impractical dreamer? Heinrich had a special fondness for Theodore, respected his thoughtful nature, excused his lack of any clear direction in life. Heinrich had taken Theodore under his wing, made him his own apprentice in the clothing and general goods store that he had founded. But Heinrich would not always be there to protect his stepson from the difficulties of life. Judith worried about Theodore.

Fritz was twelve, still at school. How fortunate they were, these three. Heinrich had seen to it that they all had an education, would never join the ranks of the unskilled, the poor, the illiterate, the labouring masses. It was up to them now what they made of their lives. Heinrich had given them opportunities that Judith could only have dreamed of for them in those early years. Fritz would do well, happy-go-lucky Fritz, sure of himself, a smart confident child and yet, like Theodore, filled with interest in the world about him.

And then she had her new children – she still thought of them that way – her children by Heinrich. The oldest, Heinrich junior, now ten, kind, affectionate, perhaps a bit of a dreamer like Theodore, but early days yet. Then the awful gap, the two missing children, before Dorothea, turned five only yesterday, a sweet child, and the toddler Adolph, two.

As the day drew to a close, the evening meal over, Heinrich and Judith exchanged glances. The time had come. Judith would explain; best that they hear the news from their mother – and be assured, too, that she fully supported Heinrich in this. 'Children, I have an important matter to discuss with you.'

Something in their mother's tone made even the two little ones look up at her with serious expressions. They were all still seated around the meal table. It had been the best place in the past for a family conference, for family announcements, but this one would be different. There had never been an announcement like this before.

'Your father and I have already spoken to Otto and Theodore. It is time now for all of you to understand what is going to happen soon to this family.' Her words were directed mainly at Fritz and Heinrich junior. Dorothea would barely comprehend, Adolph not at all.

She thought it best to tell them the facts in simple words, hold their attention from the start. 'We, this family, are going to the United States of America. We will start a new life in a new country. Many hundreds of other people like us will be going too. In time there will be thousands. I do not expect that we will live in this country again.'

Fritz was the most shaken. He gazed at his mother, incredulous. 'America! But why? We have a good life here. Why would we go...?' His voice trailed off but the stunned expression remained.

Judith hesitated, searching in her mind for the best reply. This was never going to be easy. Otto had taken the news badly indeed, the night before, as well he might. With Theodore it had been different, the dreamer entranced by the thought of adventure, oblivious to the practical realities of such a decision.

Heinrich caught Judith's eye and a wry grin spoke volumes. How to explain to a twelve-year-old? Well, Judith could only try. 'Your father loves a challenge. Look at you,' she gestured to the older three, 'and me,' pointing to herself. 'What a challenge that was, and how well he has made it work.' A fond glance at her husband and then, 'He has looked after us all, has made a success of himself. He is a good business man; everyone respects him in Verden. But,' looking now at Fritz, 'is that all there is? Will we stay here for the rest of our lives? And grow old and die – so predictable, every year the same. Where is the challenge in that?'

Heinrich joined in. 'There is an old saying, Fritz: "A ship in a harbour is safe, but that's not what ships are for."'

Judith nodded. 'Very true. You see, Heinrich and I prefer the unpredictable path, the difficult one. America is the New World. Everything is possible there. We may be rich, we may be poor, but we will take the chance.' She appealed to the boy's youthful sense of wonder and spoke softly now. 'It will be an adventure, Fritz. You will see things you could never have imagined. It's another world out there, the world of the future.'

Heinrich junior had by now gathered his wits about him.

Displaying an unexpected shrewdness, he was the first to suspect the truth. Perhaps he had seen something in Otto's expression. 'Are we all going, Mama?'

'No dear, Otto will stay. We respect his decision in that. He feels he has too much to leave behind and we understand.'

Alarm now on Fritz's face. 'And Theodore...?' He was very close to his older brother. They had much in common, in spite of the five years between them.

Theodore spoke now. 'I will be going with you, Fritz.' His tone was light, his eyes sparkled. 'It will be an adventure. As Mama says, it is another world. We will be explorers, pioneers.'

If only it was that easy, thought Judith, but she was thankful for Theodore's enthusiasm. It would help to rally the others. As for Otto, he had always been something of the outsider, old for his years, less involved with the family. They would all miss him, but it would fade, even for Judith. He was a good lad, but not much given to displays of affection – and, she well knew, hardly the pioneer, not one for adventure.

'What language do they speak in America?' asked Heinrich junior.

Judith always enjoyed family discussions. She liked to see the children think for themselves, ask their own questions. 'They speak English, Heinrich. We will all have to learn another language, but we will not be alone in this. There will be a lot of us travelling together. There will be plenty of time to learn English.'

'Are we going to New York?' asked Fritz. It was probably the only city he could name in the United States.

Theodore took up the story. 'No, Fritz, we are going to Texas.' He spoke the word as though it had a magical ring to it.

From his tone, Theodore clearly expected a better response than he got. Fritz looked at him blankly. 'Where is that?'

The older brother gave a snort of disgust. 'Texas is the frontier. Texas is the limit of civilisation. There are wild Indian people there. People live in forts, just like here, centuries ago.'

Heinrich stepped in. Theodore's description sounded more likely to scare the younger children than excite them. 'Your mother has a lot to tell you yet.'

Indeed she did. Only a month before, Heinrich had come to her with as strange a story as Judith had ever heard. A prince of the Prussian royal family, Prince Carl of Solms-Braunfels, with a group of influential aristocrats, had formed a German emigration company. The aim was to found a settlement in Texas and he was calling for volunteers. Much good land was to be had there and it was lightly inhabited. True, there had been trouble with the Mexicans and the native Indians in recent times but they would travel in strength and be prepared. A settlement site would be chosen in advance by the Prince before the emigrants arrived. If the settlement flourished, as it should under the influence of thousands of industrious German pioneers, then the company would reap the rewards of controlling the trade between Texas and the German homeland.

Heinrich told Judith that Prince Carl planned for the first shiploads of emigrants to set sail in about nine months' time, perhaps September. They might be in their new homes by Christmas. The scheme was being promoted not only in Prussia but all across northern Germany on notice boards in town squares and company representatives would speak in all the major towns.

One night Heinrich travelled to Bremen to hear a company official report on emigration plans. He returned to Judith with his enthusiasm undimmed. By now Judith shared her husband's fervour. 'We will do it, Heinrich. You will make it work. I have faith in you.'

'It will be hard on you, with small children.'

She gave his arm a reassuring squeeze. 'Oh, Heinrich, I have been through worse. You know me. I'm tough. You didn't marry a weakling.'

He gazed at her fondly. 'No, indeed I didn't. This family will need all your strength in Texas.'

For the next month after the family discussion, Judith and Heinrich made plans. They would sell up everything and convert their wealth to gold sovereigns, as the emigration company had recommended. This would be the currency when they first reached their destination. Two sea chests would carry the possessions they would take with them. All else would be sold.

A few weeks after her birthday, Judith had more news, a mixed blessing indeed. 'Heinrich,' she told him one morning, 'I am going to have another baby.'

He took a deep breath. 'Well, so be it. That is a good thing, but...'

Judith laughed and finished for him, '...but very bad timing. It will likely be born on the ship. And I am not a young mother. That will test my toughness, don't you think?'

Heinrich showed his concern. 'We can delay leaving. Leave with a later group; some time next year, perhaps.'

'No,' she said firmly. 'The family is ready now. We will be in the first ship to set sail. We will found a settlement, Heinrich. Can you imagine that? We will not come later when others have done the work. We will be true pioneers.' Her eyes shone with excitement and then she grinned mischievously. 'Of course, if you are losing your nerve, I will go first with the children and you can follow later when everything is safe.'

He laughed. 'I said I would never meet another woman like you and I was right. We are in this together then, no matter what Fate may throw at us.'

The months rolled quickly by and the day came when the Bremer family stood at the dock at Bremen and surveyed the *Johann Dethardt*, the sailing ship that would be their home for the next few weeks, and home for one hundred and fifty other souls who would travel with them. Two other ships lay at anchor. Four hundred emigrants in all would be travelling to the New World. The adventure was about to begin, a life as unlike the one they had lived so far as it was possible to imagine.

The ship rocked gently, becalmed again – just as well today, the time for Judith's confinement. The children had been ushered out of the cabin that morning and Heinrich had now left to join them. Frau Schmidt, the midwife, had delivered many a baby before, she assured Judith, though never on a ship at sea. The labour pains began again and Judith braced herself. How many times had she been through this ordeal? And yet every time it seemed worse than the last time, as if her aging body was telling her – enough!

At last it was over and Heinrich and the children were gathered around, anxious faces peering at Judith and the new arrival. 'You have a new sister, children.'

Little Dorothea looked intently at the baby, then at the mother. 'What will her name be, Mama?'

Judith gazed up at Heinrich, kneeling beside her, holding her hand. They had discussed names, but her mind felt muddled just now and she was not sure if they had come to a decision.

Heinrich turned to Dorothea, standing next to him beside the cabin bunk that served as her parents' bed. 'Do you like the name Carolina?'

'Oh yes, I like that name.' Pleased, she looked around at the others, clustered close about in the little cabin. The others gave nods and muted sounds of assent, more relieved to see their mother still safe and well than concerned about the choice of a name.

An odd thought struck Judith. 'Where will we tell her she was born, Heinrich? What do we say in the birth record? "In a cabin, on the sea"?'

'They say the island of Cuba is not far away. We will say "On the High Seas, off Cuba". How does that sound?'

Judith smiled, more of a grimace as she shifted her body in search of comfort. 'Oh, Heinrich, I am tired of the sailing life. I long for land beneath my feet again.'

'So do we all, dear; everyone on the ship.'

It had been four weeks since leaving Bremen on the *Johann Dethardt*, four weeks of boredom and discomfort, of bad food and getting worse. They had endured storms, frightening storms with waves higher than the ship's deck, tossing the little craft about. Worse perhaps were the days of no wind, fears that the wind would never blow again and they would stay out there on a featureless ocean and slowly starve.

Then too stories circulated of disease and of fire, of ships found floating with everyone dead of fever or of ships burnt to the waterline. Judith tried to convince her children that these were tall stories, old sailors' tales, but they frightened her too. Whenever a passenger fell ill, everyone's fears would be revived of a contagion sweeping the ship.

Captain Ludering heard these stories too and would remind his passengers that he had made this voyage a dozen times before without mishap. A kindly, reassuring man, he became a father figure to them all and they trusted his word.

The Bremers were fortunate in having a cabin to themselves; privacy for the family at least, if not from each other. It was desperately cramped and little Adolph slept with his parents, sometimes Dorothea too, when the ship rolled alarmingly and she became afraid. Sometimes they were all afraid.

Carolina's birth had been anxiously awaited by all. With little else on their minds, the other passengers had taken a keen interest in Judith's condition. Even Captain Ludering and the crew had followed the course of Judith's confinement.

That Sunday a special service was held to give thanks for Carolina's safe arrival. Judith felt uniquely special, the centre of attention for one hundred and fifty- odd souls, forced to share their little floating world with one another. She stood next to Heinrich and the children, baby in arms, on the poop deck with Captain Ludering, looking down on the throng assembled below. In the absence of any minister of religion on the ship, the captain, Bible in hand, conducted the service himself. He seemed happy to take on any role, serving also as representative of the Prince's emigration company and gathering them all together whenever he had something to tell them.

They were certainly a mixed lot, these emigrants, Judith reflected. Many were desperately poor, farm labourers, mine workers, illiterate folk with nothing to lose and everything to gain from the New World. Others were skilled tradesmen, carpenters, wagon makers, blacksmiths – people whose practical experience would be priceless in the settlement to come.

Boredom was a problem but morale was high. A spirit of hope filled the hearts of the voyagers. Judith saw that only those willing to take risks, those with a natural optimism and a sense of adventure had responded to the Prince's call. Whatever hardships lay ahead, the Bremers would be in good company.

Judith's younger children were not short of playmates. Many of the other families on board had children too and even in such close quarters they found it possible to improvise games, to entertain themselves through the long days. Judith envied them their carefree ways.

One of the families included an older woman, a widowed grandmother, Frau Schlade. She was a woman of some education with the foresight to have brought with her a collection of children's books. She would assemble a group of children and read to a rapt audience tales of fairies and wizards and magical deeds. She became in time every child's kindly grandmother.

Another two weeks remained before they would reach the port of Galveston. There they would disembark and be taken by smaller craft through the shallow coastal waters and barrier islands of the Texas coast to Matagorda Bay. A new port, Carlshafen, had been established for their arrival. There the Prince would meet them with wagons ready to take them to the chosen settlement site. They were all looking forward to meeting this man of whom they had heard so much. It was clear to Judith that Captain Ludering thought highly of him.

A week short of their destination, the captain called them together for another of his talks. He seemed more serious than usual and Judith had a prickly feeling that some bad news had been withheld from them until the end of the journey.

It was a mild day with a light autumn breeze moving the ship along, rippling the great sails above their heads. 'There is something I must tell you,' Ludering began. 'You may have heard of it already. There is a great evil in this land, the evil of slavery.' The listeners fell silent. There had been muted discussion of this subject among them but no one had a clear understanding.

'When we reach port,' he continued, 'you will see black men working at many tasks and you will see their overseers directing them in their work. Some of these overseers – white men, of course – are very cruel and strike the slaves for little reason. You must understand this...' He spoke now with a special intensity, unlike his usual relaxed style. 'Slavery is legal here and the right to it is strongly defended. You must never interfere in any incident between a slave and his owner or his overseer. Slaves are property, like dogs and horses. If you interfere, no one will take your side. If an angry white man attacks you, the law will say you deserved it and will not help you. There is nothing you can do. Being foreigners would make it worse – telling these people how to behave in their own country when you are strangers here, and not even speakers of English.'

His next words carried deep conviction. 'There is one thing you can do. You can decide that you will not take part in this evil and that there will be no slaves in your new settlement. That is the Prince's wish and I am sure that you will agree with him on this.' A murmur of assent swept the gathering.

'Are these white men Christians?' came a question.

'Yes, and they take their Christianity very seriously and would be angry if you doubted them.'

'Then they are bad Christians.'

The captain nodded. 'Yes, indeed.'

Another question: 'Do all the states of this country have slavery?'

'No. In the northern states it is illegal and there is much strong feeling against it. Many good men in the north work to make it illegal in all the states but they are far from success, I fear. It is deeply entrenched in the south.'

A voice from the back: 'Why do we go then to the land of the bad Christians? Why not go to the land of the good Christians?'

The captain shook his head. 'The land is well occupied in the land of the good Christians. It is expensive. In Texas there is much land that is little occupied and can be bought cheaply. The Prince's company could not afford land for all of you in the north. Remember, some of you must work the land and provide food so that the others may make your settlement prosper. That is why the company was formed.'

And so there the matter rested but it left a sour taste in Judith's mouth, a feeling of greater apprehension. This New World was even more strange, more alien than she could grasp just now. Whatever did the future hold for them?

The ship had docked at last. For the first time in six long weeks, the deck was still, motionless beneath their feet. The other emigrant ships, the *Herschall* and the *Ferdinand*, had not arrived yet but the newcomers had no reason to wait. In fact better to get the first shipload on its way along the coast and not hold up the others when they came.

As the Bremers walked down the gangplank, they had their first sight of slaves. The emigrants' sea chests and other cargo were being lowered by rope and pulley to the dockside and straining black men moved it all to waiting carts. It seemed a deceptively peaceful scene. The slaves knew what to do. The few overseers scattered about seemed more bored than menacing but they all carried stout sticks and Judith had no doubt they would not hesitate to use them. The sooner they were all on their way the better, she thought. The children watched the unfamiliar scene in silence, well schooled by the captain's words and their parents' warnings.

Judith saw more evidence of the administrative skills of the Prince and his company. Two small sailing ships with shallow draft were waiting for the emigrants further along the dock. Slaves with wagons brought the sea chests and by nightfall all were on board one or other boat for the final leg of their voyage. No cabins now for families like the Bremers, and not even enough room for all below deck at any one time. Only three days, they were told, and their voyage would finally be over.

It was cold now, and the wind had a bite to it. When their ship's destination came into view on the third day, Judith felt relief. Now the land journey would begin.

The port of Carlshafen was nothing more than a pier stretching out a little way into the sea and a cluster of tents. Beyond the tent lines could be seen some small cabins, one of them for the Prince no doubt. Judith had expected something more substantial. She hoped for only a brief stay in this rather desolate spot before they were on their way again.

A company official came on board to welcome them as soon as the first boat docked. He explained the need to disembark as soon as possible and put up tents for themselves on shore. There would be no slaves to do the work this time. They would unload the sea chests and other cargo themselves. By now the second boat had docked on the other side of the pier.

Small tents were provided for individual families and larger communal ones for the single people and couples without children. The Bremers' tent was as cramped as their sea cabin had been. By the end of the day the men had unloaded the cargo and the family was reunited with its possessions.

Before sundown they were assembled again, this time on the beach by the pier. The location of their new settlement was still in some doubt, they were told, but the Prince would be returning from inland next day and would bring them up to date. Judith had an uneasy feeling that they might be delayed here longer than she had hoped.

That night, they had food enough for all. They had been long expected, these first arrivals from Germany. Supplies of sheep and cattle had been purchased from the local people, and stocks of corn and wheat, but winter was on them now. The cold was becoming bitter and flimsy tents on a windswept coast would not do for long. People would soon become sick, Judith feared, weakened as they were by the weeks of poor food and cramped conditions at sea. It would take a great deal of food to feed so many people and sanitation would soon be a problem. For now though, the emigrants celebrated their arrival in the New World. Great fires were lit and roast meat was soon being eaten in the comforting warmth.

As darkness fell, the Bremer family retired to their tent where Judith read aloud by candlelight from one of their precious books, *Grimms Fairy Tales*, the children's favourite. Books were heavy and took up valuable space but, as Judith had always explained to her children, the Bremers were an educated family and educated people possessed books, even in Texas.

Next morning, the emigrants were assembled for a meeting with Prince Carl, just returned from his journey inland. He stood on the beach by the water's edge, facing the gathering.

The Bremers, indeed all of them, had their chance at last to see the man whose efforts had made all this possible. Judith had built up a flattering image of him in her mind, and in her cautious way was prepared to be disappointed. The Prince however proved up to expectations, at least on first meeting. He was tall and regal, with a polished speaking style and cultivated accent. His dress was plain and practical for a man of the frontier, with long riding boots, grey woollen tunic and a broad-brimmed hat, which he held in his hand as he addressed them.

As an aristocrat, a member of royalty, the Prince could have easily have seemed aloof and superior to the cross-section of commoners before him but he took care to speak to them as a guide and leader, almost a father figure. He was here to welcome them to their new homeland. He told them that over several months he had developed a good knowledge of this part of Texas. He had surveyed many sites for their future home and travelled widely in the countryside.

Judith found the Prince's news somewhat disappointing however. Several attempts to obtain land for the settlement had ended in failure, he said. There had been problems in proving ownership of land in this raw frontier country and he was determined not to become involved in a disputed purchase. Then too some options were in areas known to have hostile Indian tribes nearby or lacking a good water supply. The Prince was frank about the difficulties he faced and apologetic that there must be a delay. He had his eye on a plot of land some fifty miles beyond San Antonio and would be off next day with other company officials to pursue a deal.

It was not a good start. Judith did not like the prospect of living in a tent in winter for any length of time.

The next three months were a trial indeed. They were used to cold winters in Germany but they had not lived in tents before. Snow fell at times and bitter winds blew. Many of the emigrants had not brought enough warm clothes for such an event. They had expected to go straight to a settlement site and begin constructing homes for themselves. Also they had believed Texas to be a warm country – little thought had been given to protection from the cold.

As Judith had feared, deaths were not long in coming; older people and those in poor health. To come all this way and die beside a windswept beach – they had all been prepared for hardship, but this was a waste of lives with nothing accomplished.

One of the saddest deaths was Frau Schlade, the old lady who had read her books to the children on the ship. Everyone came to her funeral. As the body was lowered into the ground, small children cried as they grasped the finality of death. It was so unjust, thought Judith, to have come so far and never reached her goal, never even seen the settlement site.

'Why did the nice lady have to die, Mama?' asked little Dorothea. 'How long will we stay in this awful place? When will we have a home again?' Judith could only try to offer a few reassuring words to the child but she was deeply troubled herself by these unforeseen hardships.

In the end, more temporary campsites were established to ease the burdens of food supply and sanitation and about half the emigrants were taken in wagons to new sites thirty or forty miles away. The wagons were covered with high cloth sides and a roof stretched over hoop frames, open at the back and front except for flaps that could be drawn down. They were unlike the enclosed wooden structures in which the Bremers had travelled to catch their ship in Germany. The children examined them curiously when a dozen wagons were brought to the campsite.

As it happened, the Bremers were among those who remained at Carlshafen. Those coping best with the conditions there stayed behind and the family resigned itself to a further wait. Judith was pleased to see that her children were a resilient lot, prepared to see out their time here with little complaint, able to pass the days and weeks constructively. With horses supplied by the company, Heinrich and the older children began to learn the art of riding, a skill frontier settlers would need. Others too seized the opportunity and soon excursions into the countryside were bringing a measure of relief from the boredom of camp life. Judith herself was handicapped by the demands of the baby, Carolina, but she was pleased to see her family begin the transition to pioneer life.

At the campsite, Judith had befriended a young school teacher, Hermann Seele. He taught a range of subjects but what caught Judith's attention was his command of English. She helped him now to organise regular classes in English for the camp children. Soon classes were held for adults too and Judith and Heinrich began the arduous task of mastering a new language, no easy matter for people who had never before needed such a skill.

At last the day came when the Prince called them all together with good news. All the legalities had been completed, payment made and a settlement site chosen. Thirty wagons, enough for the two hundred of them, were ready. They would leave tomorrow.

The last step of the long journey, thought Judith, a new home, a new life about to begin.

Chapter 3

Judith Goldbeck: The First Founders
Texas: 1845–1846

Judith had been dreaming – more of a nightmare really. She was back on the ship again. The waves were slapping the sides of the vessel and the *Johann Dethardt* was tossing about restlessly, the great sails above catching the sea breeze, driving the passengers onwards to their destination, taking them to Texas, to the New World. After weeks of cramped discomfort, of bad food, foul water, seasickness, it had seemed as if the voyage would never end.

Then a hand was shaking her shoulder. 'Mama – wake up.' It was Theodore, peering at her anxiously. As she opened her eyes, she was conscious of aching all over, her body slumped against the hard boards at the side of the wagon. Gently she eased herself into an upright position.

'Mama, wake up. You were dreaming. How can you sleep like that?'

The wagon was pitching its way along the rough ground like a ship on land. No wonder Judith's sleeping mind had mistaken its movement for the rocking of the waves and the creaking of its wheels for the ceaseless protest of the ship's hull against the battering of the sea. Judith gazed wearily at her son. 'Thank you for waking me. I was on the ship again.' She shuddered. 'All those weeks at sea and then months in that awful camp waiting for the site to be chosen.' She considered his question. 'How can I sleep? I'm so weary of travelling, Theodore. Will we ever have a home again?'

'Oh Mama,' responded Theodore, 'why such a bad mood? We are nearly there now. We will reach the settlement site on the day after tomorrow and then your troubles will be over.'

Judith smiled, buoyed by her son's infectious enthusiasm. To Theodore it was still a grand adventure and all the months of grinding hardship had not dimmed his faith in the future. 'You realise,' she pointed out, 'that we will be the first ones there. It will be just empty fields and forests. We will have to build our own homes, a fort, a church, shops, buildings. We will be starting from nothing.'

Theodore had a ready reply. 'Of course. That is the way you wanted it. Papa offered to wait for a later voyage, wait till after the baby was born, but you said, "No, Heinrich, we will found a settlement. We will not let others do it for us. We will be first." And so we shall be, just as you wished.'

Judith grinned, and responded lightly. 'Ah, but I was young and foolish then. I didn't know what lay ahead of us.'

Theodore laughed. 'Oh, Mama. It was not even six months ago. How could you grow old so quickly?'

Before she could reply, she heard the sound of a baby's wail from the front of the wagon. 'Tell Fritz to bring the baby to me and I will feed her.' Before Theodore could act on his mother's request, Fritz came to her with little Carolina, bundled against the chill spring air.

Theodore acknowledged his brother's presence. 'I'll leave you with Fritz, Mama. I will go and sit up front with Papa.' He moved away towards the front of the wagon, pushing aside the flap beyond which the unseen Heinrich sat with the reins in his hands, guiding the horses onwards. Judith had seen that the countryside was more hilly now, and more wooded than by the coast, the track winding its way around clumps of trees. There was little habitation about, beyond an occasional distant farmhouse.

Judith took the baby in her arms and put it to her breast. She liked the way Theodore and Fritz called Heinrich "Papa". They had been born well before that fortunate day when Heinrich Bremer had come into her life and yet he had treated them as his own, shown them no less affection than he showed to his and Judith's own children. They in turn accepted him unreservedly in place of the fathers they had never known. She felt suddenly guilty to be complaining to Theodore when she had so much to be thankful for.

As the baby fed contentedly, she looked around at those of her brood seated within sight of her, gazing patiently out of the back of the wagon, watching the track recede behind them. She saw Heinrich Junior, eleven now, and Dorothea, five, tending as always to little Adolph, still only three. And then there was Carolina, born on board ship. No more, thought Judith, enough children. Her body was giving out and she was about to help in the founding of a settlement.

They and the two hundred other pioneers travelling with them were the spearhead, the leaders, of the German emigration to Texas. For a moment, Judith's heart quailed. Was she up to the challenge? And then her old fighting spirit returned. She had overcome the calamities of her early life, years of rejection and hardship before she met Heinrich and she had risen above it all. She would not fail now, would not let Heinrich and her family down.

That night she snuggled beneath warm blankets next to Heinrich, her children spread out around them in the dark of the wagon, the flaps drawn. The privacy of a room of their own, space to themselves, a settled life – it had become a mirage, an impossible dream. And yet even now she drew strength and comfort from Heinrich. She was truly blessed to have won the love of such a good man.

When the new day dawned, bright and clear, Judith could detect a mood of exhilaration, of eager anticipation around her. Families called cheerful greetings to one another. They were a resilient lot, these pioneers, plucked from their homes in Germany, lured to this alien place by the promise of a better future in a new world. They had been willing to suffer great hardships and their powers of endurance had been tested to the limit, but tomorrow they would see their reward. The journey would be over; a new life awaited them.

That night a great bonfire was lit and weariness gave way to excitement as families talked and danced to music, for some had brought musical instruments all the way from Germany. They had travelled so long together that Judith was surrounded by familiar faces, happy smiling faces seen in the fire's glow. She felt a resurgence of hope, an impatience to see what tomorrow would bring.

Their leader, the Prince, raised himself on a fallen log and called for quiet. Judith had seen little of him in the journey from the coast. He and his scouts had been out ahead of the wagons, surveying the path for them to follow, but now his dream of a German settlement in Texas was about to be fulfilled.

To a man, the settlers held Prince Solms-Braunfels in high regard. He came from the highest level of aristocracy and they were mostly peasants and humble working folk yet they saw no condescension in his manner. He lived as they did, dressed as they did, shared their hardships. He was their Moses, leading them to the Promised Land, and their faith in him was undimmed.

'Tomorrow morning,' he began, 'you will see the settlement site. It is not the one I first intended. There were problems as you know and I thank you for your patience in these difficult times. I think it is a good place, fertile and well-watered. I think you will like it. My men and I will be there to help you begin your new life.' He paused a moment, gazing at the faces arrayed in front of him in the flickering firelight. Judith heard a softer, more thoughtful tone in his next words. 'You will have the most difficult task of all. Those who follow you will have their work made easier for them but you will be remembered always as First Founders. Only you will have that title – you may wear it with pride.' A cheer broke out and quickly swelled to a roar of approval. Judith's pulses quickened, her heart raced. The Prince's words rang in her ears. This was what she had wanted above all, to be a First Founder, to banish forever the feelings of unworthiness that still plagued her from her early life. This would be her crowning achievement, to be here with her beloved family, to be part of this great adventure, to be first.

The Prince had more to say but Judith missed his words, lost in a haze of memories of the past and dreams for the future. Suddenly Heinrich was holding her in his arms and the children were pressed about her. Judith hugged each in turn, kneeling down for the little ones while Heinrich held Carolina. She felt strangely light-headed. She surrendered herself to the moment, enjoying the love of her family, excited at the prospect of tomorrow.

Little sleep was had that night and in the morning men and women were already busy with their morning tasks at first light. Soon families were climbing into their wagons. They all felt an eagerness now, as if time had suddenly become precious.

Judith sat at the front of the wagon with Heinrich, her arm touching his as he urged the horses on in spite of the roughness of the track. Theodore and Fritz were squeezed beside them. The other children were all up front peering over their elders' shoulders, watching as the trees seemed to part for them as the wagon weaved its way along. And then, mid-morning, the family heard cries from ahead and soon the Bremers' wagon and those around them were emerging into a clearing and pulling up beside one another.

Judith saw that they were drawn up on a bluff overlooking a wide vista. Here was the site for New Braunfels, the Prince's settlement, named after his family estate in far-off Prussia. It was 21 March 1845 – she must remember that date, she thought, their Foundation Day, but then of course they would all remember it. Their travelling days were over at last.

For a long time Judith and Heinrich, with baby Carolina, sat on the grass, surrounded by other families, looking out over the rolling hills before them, the settlement site that spread out from the foot of the gentle hillside, the winding creek that snaked into the distance. Their water supply was assured and the country looked green and inviting.

One by one, the children had joined them and now sat about the couple in silence. Even little Dorothea seemed awed by the significance of this moment in their lives.

Heinrich spoke softly. 'You wanted to found a settlement, Judith, and now you will. You will not follow in the path of others, my brave lady.'

Theodore stepped forward and lifted Carolina from his mother's arms. Judith smiled her gratitude and nestled closer to her husband, her head on his shoulder.

The children heard her words. 'Thank you for everything, Heinrich. I have never been so happy.'

The new year 1846 brought news of the latest shiploads of settlers from Germany. The task of building his new settlement had occupied the Prince's attention since that March day the previous year. Planning at Carlshafen for the next wave of emigrants had been neglected. With greater numbers this time, disaster had struck. Bitter cold, shortage of food and tents and delays obtaining wagons had led to much loss of life. By the time wagons full of wretched survivors began to trickle into the settlement, it was clear that they were bringing an epidemic of fever with them.

Having lost two of her own children to random ailments that struck without warning, Judith dreaded the thought of a silent contagion stalking the streets. Then too, the chilling thought came to her that had they waited until Carolina was born, they would have been a part of the tragic scene unfolding before them.

Before this winter of ill omen came upon them, the Bremer family had adapted well to their new homeland. Nicholas Zink, the company engineer, had seen to it that a fort for protection from the Indians was constructed as the first priority. While the settlers built themselves log homes, shops, a school, all that a new town would need, Zink oversaw the planning of a fine church on the bluff from where they had first looked down on their new homesite. However urgent their other needs, all agreed on the importance of a suitable House of God in which to pursue their faith.

To Judith's eternal pride, the first child baptised in the new church was her own baby Carolina, born on the "High Seas, off Cuba", as Heinrich noted in the first entry in the church register.

Heinrich's old flair for business had not deserted him. Soon he had a snug cabin for his family and a general store, with goods brought in by wagon from San Antonio at first and then from surrounding counties. Judith could only marvel at her husband's confidence in creating a life for his family in a land so different to the one he had left behind.

By the time March came, and with it the first anniversary of Foundation Day, Heinrich shared his wife's concern at the deteriorating health situation around them. It seemed to Judith that every day brought more funerals, their numbers swelling the new town cemetery hastily established across the river. The better health of the first settlers did not always protect from the unseen scourge. One day Theodore and Fritz told of seeing a body in the town square; on another the Bremers heard of close neighbours stricken. Something had to be done.

One night, soon after Easter, Judith called a family gathering. This was always an event for her to take pride in, even in these grim times, when all could contribute their thoughts and be heard. As usual, the parents had discussed the issue first and would now hear out their children. Theodore was nineteen and well able to advance his own views but Fritz, at fourteen, was always the more forceful of the two.

Judith spoke first, as she often did at these times. She knew Heinrich liked it that way, enjoyed her ability to express herself, her bold approach to life, her self-confidence. That was perhaps the secret of success in their marriage; they were partners in everything and proud of the family they had created.

'Your father and I have made a decision, children, that we will share with you.' The younger children listened with apprehension. They could sense another change of direction coming in their lives. Only Theodore knew what was planned.

'Your father loves a challenge,' Judith began. She caught her husband's eye. 'We all know that.'

Fritz saw the look that passed between them and feigned dismay. 'Where to now, Mother? Mexico? California? Is New Braunfels too settled for you?'

Judith smiled. 'Oh, nothing so exciting, Fritz. We had been thinking for a while now of a move to the countryside but with this terrible fever about we decided to move sooner.' She leaned forward and spoke to Dorothea, wide-eyed with anticipation. 'Your father is going to be a farmer.'

The six-year-old's eyes opened wider still and in her piping voice she said, 'But he doesn't know anything about being a farmer.'

Judith looked at the little child fondly. 'Once he didn't know anything about being a shop owner but he learned. And once,' she reached across and put her finger on the child's nose, 'he didn't know anything about being a father but he learned that too. So you see...' She glanced across at her husband. 'You tell them, Heinrich.'

'Well,' he began, 'I have thought of taking up the land offer of the Company that all settlers were offered when they signed for this journey. The longer I leave it, the less choice of good land there will be. This fever, this contagion that the newcomers brought with them is a great danger to us all. Your mother and I think it is time for a new adventure – a fresh life in the country, a new start.'

Fritz again, a touch of alarm in his voice this time: 'Will we be on our own in this?'

'No, a dozen other families will be with us. We will set up farms close together at Buffalo Springs, on the river, the Guadalupe, about twenty miles north of here. We will help each other, work together.' He ruffled his stepson's hair. 'Don't worry, Fritz. You will like the country life. Picnics, hunting, swimming in the river, fresh air.'

'Oh yes, and work from sunrise to sundown, I hear. But I will enjoy the fresh air, even if there is no time for the other things.' He said it lightly, with a grin, and they all smiled. The Bremers would make it work; they always did.

Theodore spoke now, adding his part of the plan. 'I will not be coming with you. I will stay and run the store. I have learned a lot, working with Papa, here and in Verden. I will be my own boss and hire whatever people I need.'

He was making a bold front, but Judith knew he was nervous about the future. Theodore was never the self-confident one. He would stay in the security of the family as long as he could and Heinrich agreed with Judith that it was time for the lad to stand on his own feet, to push him from the nest, as it were, and let him test his wings.

'I will join you, Theodore, in a while,' said Fritz. 'After I have had enough of fresh air and hard work.' Judith blessed his wit, making a joke of it, but giving Theodore a promise for the future, something to look forward to.

A week later saw the Bremers at their new homesite at Buffalo Springs. They endured the cramped confines of the wagon until willing hands had shared the task of building snug log cabins for themselves and their neighbours, scattered among the hills and valleys of a verdant country. A small chapel was built and a vicar from New Braunfels invited to include it in his country circuit.

In time, they planted wheat and corn, purchased beef cattle and dairy cows, established a good life; hard work, as Fritz had said, but rewarding. Judith had predicted to her children that Heinrich would meet another challenge, would once more justify her faith in him.

Sometimes at day's end or on the Sunday day of rest after chapel, they would gather on a bluff near their homesite where an entrancing vista spread out before them. Two mountains, the Twin Sisters, dominated the scene. A rushing stream wound its way through a forest and, closer to view, they saw fields of corn and slow moving cattle, grazing on lush fields, where the hand of man had tamed the landscape.

One problem remained for Judith to address – schooling. As she always reminded the others, the Bremers were an educated family. They had books, true, but education was more than books alone. It required learning under the supervision of a teacher and the nearest school house and teacher were back at New Braunfels. It was clear that Judith would have to take on the task herself.

And so all the children except the smallest, Adolph and Carolina, were required to take instruction from their mother in a specially constructed one-room schoolhouse that Heinrich had had built for them close by the family cabin. Neighbouring families helped too, conscious that Judith was the best qualified of them all for the task and glad of the chance to enrol their young ones with her.

Judith was often to reflect on the curious twist of Fate that had brought her to this far-flung corner of the inhabited world. Thanks to her chance encounter with Heinrich, she had been by turn housewife, mother, emigrant, founder of a settlement and now school teacher and farmer's wife in a country setting far removed from her native

Germany. A life that had once seemed doomed to failure had been transformed into one of good fortune and promise. She had come a long way from the print shop at Verden and the sharp tongues of Wolterdingen.

Chapter 4

Bianca Nohl: A Young Girl's Fancy
Texas: 1849–1852

Bianca's first view of New Braunfels was from the bluff overlooking the town. From here the first settlers had beheld their new settlement site. For them it had been virgin land, untouched by the hand of man but now, four years later, Bianca saw a neat grid of streets and homes spreading out from a central market place. More homesites could be seen across the Comal Creek where the town had outgrown its original site.

Near where they stood a fine church had been built, a commanding structure visible from everywhere in the town. On a steep rise further east stood Fort Zinkenburg, the fort of New Braunfels, named after the company engineer who had contributed so much to the layout of the town. The fort stood there to protect the townsfolk from Indian, or even Mexican, attacks but it had never been put to the test.

Bianca was impressed, yet somehow a little disappointed. She had come with her parents and sisters to the frontier of civilisation, the very edge of the unknown, or so she had believed. Perhaps the stories she had heard back home of the new Germany in Texas had been coloured by an impressionable fourteen-year-old's imagination. True, New Braunfels had a fort, but she could see the grass that grew about its open gates and sense an air of disuse. She had heard the Indians were fierce, a war was being waged with Mexico, life was cheap on the frontier – but the scene before her could hardly have been more peaceful. Not so much as a fence surrounded the town to protect it from marauding Indians; no hint of danger presented itself.

The Nohl family had arrived at their destination after long weeks of oversea and overland travel. Bianca's father, Dr Louis Nohl, was distinguished in his homeland, a writer of learned works on the practice of medicine. The German Emigration Company had lured an eminent physician to its colony in the New World. Lodgings had been prepared for the family in advance and a welcoming committee of town leaders awaited them.

Besides father Louis and mother Henriette, the former Henriette Tips, Bianca had her younger sisters, Alma, Alicia and Elvira, ranging from twelve years old down to six. More relatives were following close behind, both Louis's and Henriette's. Bianca looked forward to seeing Cousin Elise again, Elise Tips, her childhood friend. Though fourteen years old to Elise's eighteen, Bianca's more extroverted personality and greater social skills had bridged the gap in years and made them close companions in the past. They would seek out friends together, have parties, picnics, ride on horseback. It would not be all work on the frontier; Bianca would see to that. An exciting life beckoned in the New World. The cycles of virulent fever that took so many away, the hungry times that came with dry summers or crop failures – she would not let such tales concern her. For now, the future was bright.

Lodgings for the first night were comfortable enough, the four sisters in one room, parents in another, a sitting room with a log fire. Having an important father certainly had its advantages. They were not just another family of wayfarers, left to fend for themselves in a strange land.

As usual, Louis Nohl was full of plans. They would see what homes were for sale in the town, perhaps those of settlers returning to the homeland, or they could look for land over the Comal Creek and build a new home. Louis had sold up in Germany for a good price. All options were open to him.

Bianca liked the idea of a new home, one they could design for themselves, on a good block of land. A room to herself – that would be something. She had never had a room of her own.

The days that followed passed pleasantly enough as mother and daughters explored the town. The roads were wide and straight and dusty, dust that turned to mud when it rained, very different to the narrow cobblestoned streets and alleys of German towns. The marketplace and the main roads had raised plank footpaths that kept one above the mud and the dust, at least until it was necessary to cross the street. Bianca sensed a wide open spaciousness in Texas that was a little unnerving at first.

Nights were dark, even around the centre of town, for New Braunfels was too small yet to afford its own gas plant. San Antonio, it was said, had gas lighting in the streets, but the citizens of New Braunfels had to carry their own candlelight in lanterns if they ventured out after dark.

If the streets, by day and night, seemed at first strange and unfamiliar to Bianca, life indoors was as she remembered it in Germany. The same housing styles, the same layout of rooms, even at night the oil lamps and candles were part of a lifestyle the settlers had brought with them from across the ocean.

Bianca saw too that her father Louis was kept busy as he took steps to establish himself and his family in their new surroundings. A simple hospital existed already, a few beds, a room for surgery. New Braunfels needed better facilities than this. He knew he had the ear of the town leaders and already ideas were springing to his mind, ways to provide a better health service, something more than rough pioneer medicine. He could make his mark here in the New World, in the new Germany in Texas.

A decision was soon made about a home for the Nohl family. Little was available in the original town site and land was cheap further out, across the little river, the Comal Creek. Louis could afford a large block. Builders were found and skilled labour, and soon plans were drawn up for a fine house, a place to entertain the relatives to come, to invite the friends they would make here. Bianca would have a room to herself, her own glorious privacy.

Other elements began to fall into place. Education for the Nohl girls would be in the simple schoolhouse of Hermann Seele, once the town's only teacher, now the leader of a small dedicated band. Begun with one room, the school now had separate classes with rooms of their own. Learning English was the key. Without English, one was confined to the German community, a foreigner forever.

Bianca had always made friends easily and the children here seemed little different to those she had known in Germany. Memories of the old homeland were still fresh among the settlers and she found herself a link to the past, questioned by her new classmates about her life beyond the sea.

Cousin Elise and her family followed soon after and before long Bianca was showing her around town – the market place, the shops, the fort, the block across the river where their house was to be built. 'I will show you the General Store. You can buy anything there. There is a nice boy there too. His name is Fritz. He has been living on a farm with his parents but now he has come to work with his older brother at the store. The brother is the manager there.'

Elise grinned. 'Boys. Is that all you ever think about? You were such a flirt back home.'

'Well, it is no different here – that way, anyhow. German boys and German girls. Just a different country, that's all, but better really, you will see. Here you can go horse riding and have picnics on the farms. I will learn to ride a horse. We can see if Fritz will take us to his farm. We could meet his parents.'

'Do you know him well enough to ask to meet his parents?

'Oh, Elise.' Bianca gave her cousin a friendly shove. 'I'm not going to marry him. I'm just going to see his farm and ride a horse and have a picnic.' She stopped and gestured. 'Here it is – the store.'

To Bianca it was more like a big house than a shop. It had a wide frontage with steps leading up to an open front door. The roof projected over the raised footpath and was supported by sturdy log pillars.

As she led Elise inside, Bianca was once more conscious of an earthy, musty smell. The store was a homely place with a great array of goods, large and small, stacked about, resting on shelves, even hanging from the ceiling. She saw bags of seed, bales of wire, cans of oil for lamps, rat traps and food, local produce of all types, vegetables, corn, fruit. The store was there to serve town and country alike, a veritable indoor marketplace. A long counter separated customer from shop owner, and sales goods and money passed across between the two.

'Come in and meet Fritz and his brother.' Bianca led her cousin further into the building and greeted an older man who came to assist them. 'Hello, Peter, this is my cousin Elise. She has just arrived – two days ago.'

'Welcome to New Braunfels, Elise.' Peter held out his hand and Elise shook it. Bianca knew that the air of easy familiarity here would be new to Elise. In Germany, Peter might have simply smiled, bowed slightly and said some formal words of welcome. Here he obviously thought nothing of shaking Elise's hand. It was pleasant, this frontier informality. Bianca was enjoying herself here and who could ask for a better guide to introduce her cousin to life in the New World?

'Did you come to buy something or are you here to see Fritz?' Obviously Bianca's interest in Fritz had not escaped Peter's attention.

'Oh, Fritz, Theodore, anybody,' said Bianca airily. 'Are they here? I am just showing Elise around.'

'I think they are out the back, in the storeroom. Ah, here is Fritz.'

A handsome, cheerful young man of about eighteen approached, smiling a welcome. Without waiting for an introduction, he held out his hand. 'I am Fritz Goldbeck and you are Cousin Elise, eh? Bianca has told me about you. Welcome to Texas. You will like it here. This is the new Germany.'

'Oh, I like it already. Bianca has told me about you all going out horse riding and having picnics. And your parents have a farm.'

He laughed. 'Bianca knows everything. I warn you – she is a gossip. Don't believe everything she tells you. But you would know that, wouldn't you?'

Bianca was grinning widely. She wagged a finger at Fritz. 'And I will warn you of something. Elise keeps a diary. Anything you say will be written down and recorded forever, so be careful what you say. You have called me a gossip and now it will be written down and people will read it in years to come.'

Elise blushed. 'Oh, Bianca. I only write the big things that happen to me, not everything or my diary would be far too long.'

Fritz moved to finish the conversation. 'I must go. There is always a lot to do here. I will promise to take you both and some of your friends to our family's farm in a couple of weeks – best on Sunday when we are closed. We will give you practice on a horse, Elise, and we will show you something of life in Texas. I will just get Theodore to meet you.' He vanished into the storeroom.

'He's nice,' whispered Elise.

'Yes, we must take up his offer of the picnic. I know others we can invite. We will get a group together. My father has a horse and wagon.' Bianca enjoyed showing off her social network, her familiarity with the world about her and Elise was a willing audience, happy to follow her cousin's lead.

Fritz reappeared with his brother Theodore, a man in his early twenties. Bianca had judged him earlier to be more serious than Fritz, less self-assured but pleasant enough. He greeted them with a welcome to Texas and added to Elise, 'Fritz says we will be taking you to the farm in a couple of weeks. Get Bianca to gather some of her friends and we will show you some countryside. Our parents like having visitors. They will give you a good time.'

In the days that followed, Bianca introduced her cousin to various friends, teenagers young and old. By day Bianca attended the school begun and now led by Hermann Seele. Elise joined the English classes and began the arduous task of learning another language. In the rest of the time, the girls were kept busy helping their families establish new homes in the town.

The Nohl home was under construction and Bianca's dream of a room of her own was about to be realised. Louis had established an office and begun to take in patients. The Nohls and the newly arrived Tips families were soon in regular contact. Bianca's mother Henriette was sister to Elise's father, Johann. Bianca and Elise explained about the plan to visit the Goldbeck farm with a half dozen or so of Bianca's friends.

'Can we borrow the horse and wagon, Father?' asked Bianca one night as the two families sat about the dining table after a meal together.

'And who will take the reins? You, my girl? Are you so skilled with a horse already? And will you all fit in the wagon?' Louis always had a twinkle in his eye when he bantered with Bianca. Bookish and solemn in his way, she knew that he loved her headstrong ways, a perfect foil to his own personality.

'Oh, no. The Goldbeck boys have a horse and wagon too. Fritz can take one wagon and Theodore the other.'

'I see. The great planner has it all worked out.'

Uncle Johann spoke up. 'How far is this farm? Can you go there and back in a day?'

Bianca was unfazed by the elders' doubts. 'Fritz says there are guest rooms for the boys and for the girls and bedding for all. It is all arranged,' she added cheerily.

'Provided we parents agree, eh, Louis?' Johann took the pipe from his mouth and cast a meaningful glance at the other father.

Bianca knew how to deal with parents. A few more questions were successfully fielded and the matter was settled.

Johann had another question. 'Have you met these Goldbeck brothers, Louis?'

Louis nodded. 'Good lads. They do a fine job with the store. The father Heinrich started it but he and his wife moved off to the farm then and left Theodore in charge. Fritz left the farm and joined him later.'

Henriette had something to add. 'Actually Heinrich is their step-father. His name is Bremer, not Goldbeck. Also the lads are only half-brothers.' Her audience looked confused.

'How can that be?' came a question. Bianca listened closely. This was gossip that was new to her, to be noted and filed away in her memory.

'Well, apparently the mother was called Judith Goldbeck and she had two boys, or three they say, by different fathers before she met Heinrich. She is a lot older than him but he married her anyway. They have, I think, five more children of their own. By all accounts, they are devoted to each other and the stepsons and Heinrich are as close as if he was really their father.'

'Well, that is a story, I must say.' Johann shook his head in wonder, then nudged his wife. 'Listen, my girl, if you have any sons

I don't know about, don't think you will be forgiven so easily.' The room erupted in laughter.

That weekend, the Goldbecks closed their store early on the Saturday and the travellers, eight in all, were collected from the Nohl house where Bianca had gathered them. Elise had by now met them all. Bianca saw that Elise was attracted to a youth her own age, Otto Wuppermann, a quiet, pleasant companion with whom she seemed immediately at ease. Bianca, as organiser of the outing, chatted to all, even changing wagons when they stopped to rest.

By sundown they had reached their destination, a farmhouse of generous proportions, with outbuildings and a large separate cabin that proved to be a schoolhouse for the local farms, with mother Judith as school teacher. Bianca was looking forward to meeting this remarkable woman.

Judith and Heinrich were waiting on the front porch to usher everyone inside from the cool autumn air and into a warm room with a log fire. There more Bremer children were waiting, even a baby, Julius, born to the Bremers the previous year, as Bianca later discovered, when Judith was 44 years old. Fritz and Theodore had greeted the Bremer couple with warm hugs before turning to make introductions.

Bianca was watching their host family closely. Judith, the mother, did not disappoint her. A stately middle-aged woman with auburn hair, she had an indefinable presence, an aura it seemed to Bianca, a calm radiance that without effort made her the centre of attention wherever she went. She was the matriarch of the Bremer clan, holding together a large close-knit family.

And yet Heinrich too quickly gained Bianca's respect. In no way overshadowed by his wife, he had an easy self-confidence that matched hers. They had achieved something rare – two strong-willed people had forged a union of equals, a couple whose love and respect for each other could overcome the petty disagreements and differences that bedevilled lesser marriages.

The Bremer children too were a fascinating lot, secure in the family warmth, welcoming hosts to the visitors, even the little ones. Sixteen-year-old Heinrich junior, or simply 'Junior', as they called him, was a confident type who soon caught Bianca's eye, and then four small ones ranging from Dorothea aged ten down to baby Julius.

A fine meal at two long tables in the dining room followed the first meeting. The Bremers were used to entertaining. One table was normally used by the host family, one kept ready for guests but Judith saw to it that the two groups were intermingled. Chandeliers with lighted candles hanging from the ceiling and oil lamps on the tables gave a warm glow to the occasion. Elise sat with Otto. Bianca would like to have sat with Fritz but another girl seemed to have claimed his attention and she found herself beside the eldest brother.

To Bianca, Theodore had appeared reserved, rather bookish, the least impressive of the Goldbeck-Bremers, but his reserve melted in the company of his family. He proved a quite charming table companion, interested in Bianca's background, full of information about life in the new Germany. If he did not have his mother's forceful personality, he was nevertheless a person of depth and character, able to hold Bianca's attention and involve her in conversation. He seemed unconcerned at the difference in their ages and addressed her as an equal, a fellow adult, not as a child. She liked that, to be taken seriously, given credit for maturity and intelligence. When the meal ended and they all retired to the living room with the log fire, she was content to continue in his company.

The memory of that night would stay with Bianca forever, a world removed from everything she had ever known. She had never met a family quite like this one and in some indefinable way she wished to be a part of it, to share in the closeness, the bonding that held this clan so tightly together. Strong-willed herself, very much the odd one out in her rather prim family, she respected strength of personality in others and this family had it in abundance.

By the time the visitors were bedded down in their rooms, Bianca's head was spinning, quite overcome by the drama of it all. She was sleeping in a farmhouse in Texas, in the home of a pioneer family on the frontiers of civilisation. The thrill of adventure coursed through her veins, kept her pulses racing until sleep finally claimed her. Her last thoughts were of the pleasant young man whose company had entertained her that night.

Next morning, the visitors were taken for a walk to the top of the hill overlooking the farm house. The view beyond, to the distant mountains, the Twin Sisters, to forests, to farm lands where cows grazed, held Bianca's gaze for long minutes. She felt that she never wanted to leave this place, this farm, this family. In a few short hours, Texas, the real Texas of welcoming farm folk and vast open country and mountain vistas, had gripped her imagination.

Then Theodore was standing beside her. She heard his soft pleasant voice. 'Wonderful, don't you think? I never tire of it. I love this place.'

Bianca took her eyes away from the view and turned to her companion, a warm smile on her face. She felt there was something right about Theodore, something genuine. He made no conscious effort to impress her with his knowledge of Texas, his greater familiarity with this strange new land. He seemed only to wish to set her at ease and play the gracious host.

There could be no doubt of the sincerity in Bianca's reply. 'I would love it too, Theodore. You are so fortunate – such a fine family and you can come here whenever you wish.'

There was a tinge of envy in her voice and he laughed. 'Well, so can you now. A friend of the Bremers is always welcome here. You will come again, be sure of that.' He gazed at her in a friendly way. 'So you like us farm folk then?'

'Oh, yes, all of you.' Bianca looked across to where Judith stood, talking to Elise and Otto as they too gazed out, entranced by the view. Judith looked so much a part of the scene, statuesque, the breeze ruffling her hair. 'Your mother is a fine lady, Theodore.'

Theodore followed Bianca's gaze. 'She is a wonderful person,' he agreed. 'We are all very proud of her.' Bianca noted the softness in his voice, the gentle smile on his face. Fond though she was of her own parents, Bianca could see that Judith had a very special relationship with her children, a love that none would have been able to express in words.

'Do you know,' continued Theodore, 'that Mama and Heinrich and the rest of us were on the very first ship to leave from Germany for Texas? We were in the first group to arrive at the town site. And

Mama found that she was expecting another baby before they set sail for Texas. That was Carolina over there. She knew that the baby would be born on the ship. Heinrich wanted to change their plans and come later but Mama said, "No. We will found a settlement. We will not go later when others have done it for us. We will be first." And so we were.'

'A baby on the ship,' murmured Bianca. She remembered the long weeks of seasickness, bad food, foul water, monotony. 'What an awful thought.'

Theodore made no attempt to monopolise her company that morning and she had the opportunity to meet all the Goldbeck-Bremers at one time or another. Judith and Heinrich spoke of their different lives in the New World and the Old. As with Theodore, they talked to her as they might to another adult, a person of maturity, not an inexperienced child. Fritz she found charming, more animated than Theodore, more self-assured. Heinrich junior seemed somewhat callow, as did all boys near her own age. The younger children were bright, well-mannered.

Bianca and the other visitors were given their first lesson in horse riding, an intimidating experience but necessary for their future life here. More enjoyable were walks about the farm buildings, discussions about farm life and finally lunch. A long trestle table was set on an open grassy area in front of the farm house. It was soon laden with farm produce – beef, ham, corn, salad, all Bianca could eat. Picnic cloths were laid out and Bianca sat and talked and ate her way through a long leisurely meal.

By the time the wagons were readied and they set off for home, Bianca felt she had had a memorable introduction to farm life in her new country.

The months that followed slid effortlessly by as Bianca settled into the timeless rhythms of small town life. Winter came and then passed into spring. As her schooldays moved towards a close, she focused all her efforts on improving her English, the key to success in Texas beyond life in New Braunfels. She would talk to her family and friends in the new language and especially to Theodore and Fritz in the General Store, a place where she felt quite at home.

Theodore, the thoughtful one, had become a more accomplished English speaker than the easily distracted Fritz. Bianca would drop by the store on her way home from school, or on errands for her mother. Over time, she began a series of English conversations with Theodore until it became a game between them to converse in the new language for as long as Bianca could hold her end of the contest and then they would laugh when she was forced to ask a question of him in German.

One evening, near closing time for the store, Theodore offered to walk Bianca home. They talked in English, Theodore introducing her gently to new words. He was a good teacher, endlessly patient. At the Nohl home, Bianca invited him in. Louis and Henriette greeted him, familiar with him from their visits to the store.

Bianca spoke in English. 'Theodore has walked me home safe.'

Theodore took up the joke. 'We must be careful in the street. There may be bad persons about.'

Louis ushered his guest into a chair and a halting English conversation followed. When Theodore rose to go, Louis said, 'Thank you for walking my daughter home safe,' and they laughed.

After Theodore's departure, the conversation returned to German. Henriette smiled. 'He is a nice man. But a bit old for you, eh?'

'Oh, Mother,' snorted Bianca. 'Of course he's a nice man – that's all.'

Henriette gave a knowing smile. 'I think there is something in the way he looks at you. Have you looked at yourself in a mirror lately? You are filling out. How old are you? Fifteen? You are quite the young lady.'

And there the matter rested for now, but something about her mother's words left Bianca feeling strangely unsettled.

The romance between Elise Tips and Otto Wuppermann blossomed at a pace that quite took Bianca's breath away. Her cousin, so insecure, so lacking in confidence, had transformed herself into a mature woman, decisive, certain all of a sudden of what she wanted from life. And what she wanted was Otto. Fortunately for her, Otto shared this sentiment to the full. It was a union that was greater than the sum of its parts. Two quiet, somewhat ill at ease personalities had bonded in a way that transformed them both.

Bianca was pleased for them and proud too of the way in which they thanked her for bringing them together. 'You are a wonder, Bianca,' said Elise one day. 'Not only do you organise a picnic weekend – something I would not know how to do – but you transform my life at the same time.'

'Well, I did not really plan that,' Bianca said, smiling, 'but I will take the credit, if you like.' In truth, she felt a little disconcerted that Elise had moved forward in her life so suddenly. In an odd sort of way, Bianca felt as if she had been left behind by events. She had seemed Elise's equal in maturity before but her cousin was a woman now and Bianca was still what? – a child?

The relationship with Theodore moved slowly. Bianca was unsure of her own mind. It would have flattered her self-image if there had been some visible competition between Fritz and his brother for her affections but Fritz seemed content to leave the field open to Theodore. On one occasion, when Bianca walked into the store, Fritz called out to his brother, 'Theodore, Bianca is here,' as though there could be only one purpose in her visit.

Bianca slowly came to accept Theodore as a steady presence in her life. She was fifteen, he was nine years older. She sensed that he was moving very carefully, conscious that she might think herself too young, the difference in years too great, for this to be a meaningful relationship. Others too would think the same. And so, for many months, as if by unspoken agreement, they settled into a friendship akin to that of siblings, of an older brother showing fondness and pride in a younger sister. Both were biding their time, waiting to see what the future would bring.

The two had many walks together and conversations in English and German. Theodore clearly felt comfortable visiting the Nohl household. He was well known to Louis and Henriette and always welcome. He would chat about life in the new Germany and offer suggestions from his longer experience here. He was a First Founder, something that still carried weight in these early years. Those who came later had reaped the benefits created for them by those who came first.

Bianca soon detected a special relationship growing between her father and Theodore. The younger man was quiet, thoughtful, respectful, perhaps the son that Louis would like to have had. There could be no doubt that if romance grew between their daughter and Theodore, the Nohl parents would present no obstacle. Even Bianca's more introverted younger sisters found Theodore a welcome visitor. The somewhat uncomfortable thought came to Bianca that Theodore fitted into her household better than she did.

On the evening of 29 September 1850, Elise and Otto were married under a great oak tree in the garden of Elise's parents. They were surrounded by relatives from the old homeland and friends from the new, with congratulations and fond hugs as two families were joined. As relatives, all the Nohl family were present but Fritz and Theodore were also among those invited.

After the wedding service, each of the guests had a glass of wine and the group chatted for some time until word came to enter the house for the evening meal. It was a dinner for Bianca to remember, with a bountiful array of food that reflected the prosperity of their lives in the New World – ham, pork roast, salads, fruits. Many of the guests had brought their own special treats with them – tarts, puddings and cakes.

Later, gifts were given, many hand made, some of practical value, some objects of beauty. Elise's mother pinned a brooch set with diamonds to her daughter's breast, a present from Otto. Louis and Henriette gave a dozen plates and a salad fork and spoon set. After the gifts were given, came music, singing and dancing. Bianca danced with a number of the guests, including Fritz, but was careful to save the last dance for Theodore. When the party ended, the families set out to walk back to their homes, lanterns in hand, a trail of lights in the darkness.

Another winter passed, Christmas was celebrated and the new year, 1851, welcomed. This was the year that Bianca would turn sixteen, a young lady at last, no longer by any measure a child. When the day came in late April, a party was held for her at the Nohl house. It was a festive occasion. All the Nohl family and their relations were there. Birthday presents were given but when it came Theodore's turn, a hush fell as though the guests sensed a significance in the moment.

'I have two gifts for you, Bianca,' he announced. 'This is the first.' He gave her a package wrapped in coloured paper. She opened it, her eyes widened and then she lifted it up for all to see. It was a necklace, a silver chain with a ruby pendant. The red stone seemed to Bianca's eyes to glow with an inner light. A murmur of admiration came from the onlookers. It was truly a special gift.

'Oh, Theodore, it is beautiful,' gasped Bianca. She placed it around her neck, then moved forward, intending to kiss his cheek in gratitude.

Before she could reach him, Theodore said, 'And this is my second gift.' Next moment he had placed his hands on her shoulders and kissed her gently on the lips, the first time he had ever done so. A murmur of approval came from the onlookers.

Theodore drew back a little, holding Bianca's hands. 'As you all know,' he said to those around him, 'I have waited a long time for that moment.' The guests laughed and then Theodore looked at Louis and Henriette and said simply, 'I love this young lady, your daughter.'

Louis beamed. He held up his glass and said, 'I congratulate you both on your excellent taste in partners.' More laughter followed and glasses were raised all around.

Bianca was bemused, bewildered, caught entirely off guard. It was as though her life had suddenly taken a leap forward, had opened a new chapter. She was being swept along on a tide of events seemingly beyond her control. She was the centre of attention in a room full of people who all wished her joy and she was standing beside the man who had publicly declared his love for her. She surrendered herself to the moment and was blissfully happy.

Later that night, Theodore said, 'Would you like to visit my family soon? I can arrange it with Heinrich. He will be coming to the store next week for his provisions.'

'I would love to, Theodore. I adore your family. And I love your farm.'

And so, one Saturday evening a few weeks later, Bianca sat beside Theodore at the front of the wagon as the Bremer farm came in sight. She had been there several times by now, but only as one of a group. Now the two of them were the only guests.

Judith and Heinrich were waiting to welcome them. The visitors were ushered into the sitting room and the four of them sat on sofas. 'So, my girl,' said Heinrich. 'It's a pleasure to meet you again.' Then he leaned forward and his eyes twinkled. 'I had a feeling last time we met that our Theodore saw something special in you.'

Judith spoke. 'Welcome to our household, Bianca. We are very happy for you both.'

Since her first meeting with this couple, Bianca had felt a special bond to them, indeed to this whole family. As a precocious teenager, she had generally taken the company of adults lightly enough, quick to see their foibles and weaknesses, but the Bremers were a special breed, a class of their own.

Bianca's words were heartfelt. 'I love this family. I could think of nothing better than to be a part of it.'

Next morning, the family sat around the dining table after a leisurely breakfast. Judith smiled at her guest. 'Come with me for a walk, Bianca. Let us women leave these men behind for a while.' She gestured airily. 'Let them clean up for a change, eh?'

Bianca nodded, a little intimidated at the thought of being alone with Judith. She felt somewhat in awe of the woman, a feeling few others had ever aroused in her.

As they walked beyond the farm buildings, towards the nearby hilltop, Judith began to speak, slowly, thoughtfully. 'Let me tell you a story, Bianca. When I first met Heinrich, I was a fallen woman. I had three children by different fathers. I had been driven from my home town and my life was ruined. Then Heinrich fell in love with me in spite of everything. The time came when I should meet his mother, for his father was dead. I did not know what to expect. Surely she would think me the worst woman in the world for her son. She would think our union a disgrace.'

She was lost in thought for a moment. 'But you know,' she continued, 'only one thing mattered to her, one question – would

I make her son happy? And I convinced her that I would and she accepted me, just as I was. She was a great lady.'

They had reached the hilltop, where a bench now stood, facing the view. They sat together, gazing out.

Bianca spoke. 'And now you wonder if I will make your son happy?'

Judith nodded. 'I have my fears, just as Heinrich's mother did. Theodore is a lot older than you. He has a good heart, but he is a bit of a dreamer, not a practical man. He depends a lot on Heinrich and me for support and we will not always be there for him. You are a strong willed girl and I admire you for that. I was the rebel of my family and I think you are the rebel of yours but Theodore is no rebel.'

Bianca was unsure where this conversation was leading. 'Do you think I need a stronger man in my life, Frau Bremer?'

The older woman turned to look at her. 'Judith. Call me Judith.' Then returning to the subject, 'I don't know. Tell me what you like about Theodore.'

For once Bianca felt unsure of herself. Judith was forcing her to confront her own feelings about this unlikely romance and she felt strangely unready.

Bianca tried to sort out her thoughts. 'Theodore has always treated me as a woman, never as a child. He is very kind and very patient. If he lacks confidence at times, then I can supply that. I think he draws strength from me. We have a lot in common and we share many interests. We both want our lives to be something special. Theodore came to Texas when he could have stayed behind, like your other son. He wanted to be a First Founder, like you. He has made a success of the store and he is well liked in the town. He is not strong, but he is not a coward. I respect him and I love him.'

Judith put her hand over Bianca's and squeezed it. 'Well said, Bianca, well said. If ever you want my help or my support, you know I will be there when you need me, just as I am for all my family.'

Bianca looked into the other woman's eyes. 'I will remember. I will not let you down, Judith.'

In the months that followed, Bianca and Theodore settled into the lives of a courting couple. Next April, when Bianca turned seventeen, seemed a good time to set for their wedding and early thoughts were discussed with both families about a date.

The Nohl household became a second home for Theodore and he was always made welcome there. Visits to the Bremer farm were by necessity less frequent but once a month or so, Bianca had the pleasure of immersing herself for a day in the life of the family that she would soon join, a family that she had come to identify with better than her own.

'You know, Theodore,' she said one day as they strolled the familiar streets of New Braunfels, 'I think you should have been a Nohl and I should have been a Bremer.'

Theodore grinned at the thought. 'I thought we were bringing two families together, not swapping places.'

Bianca gave him a friendly push. 'Oh, don't tease me. You know what I mean. My parents are more at ease talking to you than they ever were with me. And your family are so outgoing, so full of life and you are the quiet, thoughtful type. Judith calls you a dreamer.'

Theodore took that in. 'Oh, does she now? Well, I will have something to say to her about that. Would you like me to be the man of action from now on – a true Bremer?' He put his arm about her and kissed her.

Bianca laughed. 'No, no. I love you as you are. Don't change.'

Only days later there came dreadful news. Bianca was in her father's office when Theodore burst in, face ashen. Bianca had never seen him so distressed. 'What is it?' she asked, suddenly alarmed.

'Mama has the fever. She is very ill.' He had tears in his eyes.

A tremor shook Bianca's body and a cold hand seemed to clutch at her heart. The fever had struck Judith, the scourge that came every summer to carry away more settlers, as if to punish them for their rashness in coming to this alien land so far from home. Not all died – a hardy few had survived in the past and Bianca murmured a prayer that the woman she had come to love and respect should be a survivor too.

Within the hour, the couple were on their way to the farm in the wagon, accompanied by Fritz. To Bianca, the journey seemed endless. She could not believe that tragedy could strike so suddenly, without warning.

When they arrived it was evident at once that something was badly amiss. All was silent as they entered the house, the activity, the voices, the hubbub of the place was strangely absent.

Heinrich came to them, face pallid, distraught. One look at him and Bianca felt a sudden heartache, a knotting in her chest, a catch of breath.

'How is it?' asked Fritz in a low voice as though it was important not to be overheard.

Heinrich shook his head and tears began to pour down his face. First Fritz, then Theodore embraced him a moment before he found his voice. 'The doctor has been. He says a day or two, no more.'

They found Judith in a semi-conscious state in her bed, surrounded by her family. It was a house of sorrow, so different to the one Bianca had known before. Judith saw the newcomers approach and a weary smile came to her face. She reached a hand out as they knelt beside her and Theodore took it. Bianca saw a look in his eyes, a haunted haggard look, and it stabbed at Bianca's heart. Could she ever hope to replace what this devoted son was about to lose?

Judith died on the second day after their arrival. The two days were a harrowing experience for all those in the farmhouse, from Heinrich to three-year-old Julius, all those for whom the matriarch of the Bremer household had seemed indestructible. Like a candle flame, her life faded away and they could only wait for the spark to flicker out. Bianca could do little to ease Theodore's pain, or any of the family. The enormity of his loss had quite stunned Theodore. He seemed suddenly drained of life, beyond even the relief of tears, mute and helpless.

Bianca had one last chance to speak to Judith as they took it in turns by her bedside. Her voice was faint by now but Bianca caught the words. 'Look after my boy. He loves you so much.' Bianca could only nod her head in silent anguish.

The funeral service was held on a grey winter's day, in keeping with the mood of those who had gathered in the little chapel to say their farewells. All Judith's family was present and other families from neighbouring farms, providing strength and support, sharing the loss. Judith had been much loved and respected in the community and would be sorely missed.

Judith was buried on the hilltop overlooking the farmhouse. From there she had enjoyed the view of the land she had come to love. Near the bench where she liked to sit was a large boulder. She had often been seen to stand with her back against it as she gazed out. She was laid to rest there, at the foot of the boulder, the place marked by a simple gravestone inscribed with her name, the years of her life and the words *'Unsere gute Mutter'* – our good mother.

An eventful life, a life that brought joy to so many, thought Bianca as she listened to the words of the pastor at the service. To be cut short at only forty-seven – how could Fate be so cruel?

Bianca and Theodore were married on 11 May 1852 at the Bremer farm. Theodore wanted the wedding there and Bianca did not argue. Something had died in him that sad day the year before and Bianca wondered if she could ever fill the void in his life. She did not want to live for the rest of her life in the shadow of a lost mother. She felt the first seeds of doubt being sown as to what sort of family head her dreamer might become. Would he be able to take on the responsibilities of a home and a family?

The wedding was a happy and colourful affair. The guests were too numerous to all find lodging in the farmhouse and tents were provided for the others. They were pioneers still in a new land and a night in a tent bothered no one. A wedding in the country was an occasion to enjoy, to mingle with friends and neighbours and escape from town life for a day or two. Friends from nearby farms had come and townsmen chatted with farm folk about the affairs of town and country.

All the Bremers and the Nohls were there. By unspoken agreement, no one spoke of the missing Judith but all sensed that the gathering seemed strangely incomplete. Even now Heinrich was clearly still in a state of shock, however bravely he tried to play the gracious host.

Bianca was too busy moving amongst the guests to let any lingering sadness spoil her special day. She was a social person by nature, a lover of company, of parties and today everyone who mattered in her life was here in this delightful country setting. By contrast, Theodore was less at ease in a group but he made the rounds of the visitors manfully and shared Bianca's pleasure when the gifts were opened.

It gave Bianca special satisfaction to welcome Cousin Elise and Otto, her husband, and receive their warm wishes for her happiness. Yesterday Bianca had been a teenager, a seventeen-year-old, and today she was a wife. How far she had come since the day only three years before when she had welcomed Elise to her new home in Texas.

Judith's schoolhouse provided the setting for the wedding ceremony and Preacher Joung, the pastor who had officiated at Elise and Otto's wedding, gave a moving sermon, exhorting the newlyweds to make the most of God's gifts in their new homeland. Afterwards came food from town and farm in such abundance that Bianca could only marvel at the bounty that pioneer Texas had bestowed upon its German colonists.

Chapter 5

Bianca Nohl: Storm Clouds
Texas: 1852–1861

When Theodore returned home from his day at work, Bianca was waiting at the door. Her face glowed; there was excitement in her voice. 'I have been unwell today,' she said. 'And what do you think might be wrong with me?'

His eyes opened wide in anticipation. 'A baby?'

'Yes, yes,' she said, pride and happiness in her voice, a joyful smile on her face.

'How can you be sure?' he asked

'Oh, Theodore – a woman knows.' She grinned at him and said in a conspiratorial whisper, 'Trust me.'

Theodore embraced her in his gentle way, as though he feared crushing her. 'Well, that is wonderful news.' They moved into the house and he settled her into a chair before sinking into one himself. 'So what shall we call him?'

Bianca laughed. 'I have only just found out and you ask me for a name already. Anyway,' she wagged an admonishing finger, 'it could be a girl, you know.' She gazed at him quizzically. 'So do you have a boy's name ready? Will it be Theodore?'

'No, definitely not.'

She was surprised at the certainty in his voice. 'What then?'

'I think it is presumptuous for a man to name his son after himself. What would you say to naming him Louis? Your father has been very good to us and he would be pleased. He never had a son of his own.'

It continually surprised Bianca how close Theodore had grown to her father. 'Very well then. And if it is a girl?'

'Your choice,' he replied. 'That's only fair. What girl's name do you want? Henriette?'

'No, something different.' She had never felt close to her mother. 'I had a friend once, back home, called Elfrieda. I always liked that name.'

'Very well. That's settled. Now we just have to wait to see if it is a Louis or an Elfrieda.'

After their marriage, Bianca and Theodore had moved into a comfortable home, built for them on the block of land allotted to Theodore in New Braunfels as a founding settler. Bianca enjoyed having a home of her own. Even a room to herself in the Nohl household had seemed a blessing, but this was better still. She helped design the house and choose the furniture and the furnishings. She had a favourite sofa in the sitting room where she would sit reading or talk to Theodore at day's end about their lives together and their plans and hopes for the future. Always fond of social life and entertaining, she would often cook for visitors. At other times she and Theodore would be invited to the homes of friends and relatives.

Their early life together was a happy time but the loss of his mother was still sorely felt by Theodore. Sometimes he would drift into a melancholy mood and on more than one occasion she found him weeping quietly alone. She could only embrace him wordlessly and wait for the mood to pass. She had only known Judith briefly but the memory of those meetings would stay with her forever.

Bianca could understand her husband's grief over his mother but she worried sometimes about their future as a couple. She sensed that as long as life went smoothly, they would be happy together. He was a caring husband and she knew he would be a loving father. Though her personality was much more spirited than his, she knew there was a fun loving side to his nature that she had learned to bring out. She respected his business skills too and had no doubts about his ability to support a family. Her only fear, a fear that nagged at the back of her mind, was that if ever hard times came to them, Theodore would not have the toughness to see it through. His anti-slavery convictions were well known. Powerful forces were at play here and Theodore, she judged, was not the man to handle a crisis endangering his family. She could only hope their marriage would never be put to such a test.

Seeking a break from the responsibilities and long hours of managing the store, Theodore and Fritz had employed others for the task and now tried their hands at different employment. Theodore found work as a clerk at the Law Office while Fritz went through a period of erratic employment, as well as a series of brief courtships.

Theodore was not short of interests. He was an enthusiastic member of the Germania Singing Society of New Braunfels. He had a good voice and sang with his group at parties, weddings or any occasion where people gathered to enjoy themselves.

Bianca liked having a husband who could sing but his abolitionist views were another matter. From his first arrival in Texas, Theodore had felt a deep loathing for the practice of slavery. To own people as property and treat them cruelly without fear of retribution offended him as a Christian and as a man of compassion. He had been to San Antonio for supplies on several occasions and always returned full of indignation.

'They treat their slaves worse than their dogs,' he fumed one day to Bianca. 'If you ill-treat a dog, a dog lover will stop you but no one will stop for a slave. You know Adam Voigt, the glassmaker? He saw an overseer kick a slave until he was unconscious and everyone walked by. When he spoke out in German, then people stopped but they turned on him instead – called him a Yankee lover, told him to go back where he came from. When they catch an escaped slave, they brand him with a hot iron. Can you imagine that?'

Bianca could only cut short her husband's tirades. She saw the issue in more practical terms. 'We have to live with these people, Theodore,' she would argue. 'You will make us Germans seem like enemies to the Anglos. I have heard they call us 'traitors' and 'abolitionists'. There could be war one day over slavery and what would we do then?'

'Would you have me fight for slavery?' he asked, face flushed.

'No, of course not, but you should not antagonise these people. We want to be Texans but how can we be if they see us as enemies?'

It was a discussion that could lead nowhere. Bianca sought a low profile for the family. She felt that to draw attention to themselves was foolish but Theodore was not alone in his convictions. Soon after it was formed, the New Braunfels town council had passed a resolution that owners of slaves could not live within the town, could not purchase property. It was an empty gesture, as Bianca well knew. No Anglo would want to live in a German-speaking community, certainly no slave owner, but the resolution attracted attention in the Texas newspapers. German settlers were seen as unwelcome aliens, suspected of something akin to treason. And now some councillors wanted to repeal the resolution and this triggered more argument.

As the years passed, Bianca and Theodore saw a range of opinions about slavery develop across the German community until a unified stand became impossible. Some, like Louis Nohl, saw it as a matter of Christian principle and common humanity to oppose slavery publicly. Others felt it was more important to be accepted as good citizens. Some were quite indifferent to the issue and argued heatedly that the abolitionist hotheads would turn the whole of Texas against them. To stay on good terms with the Anglos was more important than taking a stand on principle, they said. In any case, as a small group of non-English-speaking foreigners, they were powerless to influence the laws of the state.

This disunity was reflected in the Goldbeck household, with Theodore following the lead of his father-in-law while Bianca counselled caution. As long as Louis Nohl's actions went no further than newspaper articles in German and disputes at council meetings, Bianca was not too concerned. She felt safety lay within the confines of New Braunfels but she feared that her father might yet find a wider audience and get himself into trouble. Worse, he might involve her husband, a prospect she found alarming. Bianca was beginning to distrust her father's influence over Theodore. As time went by, she heard rumours that Louis was communicating with a wider anti-slavery movement in the north. She heard talk of membership in a Free Society, an abolitionist group. Bianca had an uneasy feeling that her meddlesome family was playing with fire and that she was not going to escape the consequences.

On a more cheerful note, the birth of their son Louis was a happy event for the couple. Theodore was delighted at fatherhood and Bianca enjoyed not only the pleasures of being a mother but also the attentions of a wide circle of friends and relations. Her parents especially doted on their first grandchild. Only 18 still, she had been a wife for a year and a half and now a mother. Life was moving quickly indeed.

Early in the new year, 1854, Theodore unveiled a plan to his wife. Bianca rather admired the restless streak in her husband. He did not like to stay in one place or follow one lifestyle for too long. Without a change of direction from time to time, he would begin to find life dull. It was time to move on.

Fritz was a part of the plan. He was a frequent visitor, always welcome, a devoted brother to Theodore and a lively, witty companion to Bianca. He had a relaxed manner with his sister-in-law, treating her much as he might a sister his own age, sharing jokes, bantering with her. His outgoing personality matched Bianca's own and she sometimes wondered idly whether she had married the wrong brother. And yet Bianca saw an unstable side to Fritz that she mistrusted. Theodore planned his moves while Fritz acted on impulse, seemingly adrift in life, taking work wherever he found it with little thought for the future. On balance, her serious-minded husband was still the better choice but it would have been easy to fall in love with a charming rascal like Fritz.

That evening, Bianca sat on her favourite sofa, breast-feeding little Louis. She heard Theodore come into the house. He strode immediately into the living room. Clearly he had something to tell his wife. 'Fritz is here. Do you mind if he comes in?'

Bianca grinned wryly. 'Oh yes, let him in. I'm sure he has seen a woman feeding a baby before.'

Fritz strolled in at that. 'Well, not exactly feeding a baby, but...' There was a roguish smile on his face.

With mock indignation, Bianca pointed a finger of condemnation at him. 'Enough. I don't want to know.' They laughed together as the menfolk settled themselves in chairs. 'So,' she said, 'and what have you two been planning? I expect I am the last to know, as usual.'

'Have you heard of a place called Comfort?' began Theodore.

'Yes, a German settlement, about fifty miles west of here, on the north road out of San Antonio. A group from Fredericksburg started up there just a few months back and I think a few from New Braunfels.' She frowned. 'I hope you are not thinking of going there. I am happy here and we have a baby.'

'Do you know why they called it Comfort?' Fritz posed the question.

'No, but you are about to tell me.' Bianca could not resist Fritz's wiles.

'Well, the settlers were so pleased with their choice when they first went there that they called it Camp Comfort, and then just Comfort. It has rolling farmland, good soil, a secure water supply. It is a beautiful place. I have been there.'

'And they need a general store,' Bianca finished for him.

The two men swapped glances then nodded agreement to her words.

The plan was unveiled. Comfort was in good farming country near the Guadalupe River and the settlement was growing. It needed a general store, a place where goods could be brought in in bulk from San Antonio or further east and made available to the settlers and the surrounding farms. The brothers would sell their interest in the New Braunfels store and build one at Comfort. A change of scene and ownership of a store once again, a role for which they both felt nostalgic by now – it all made sense, to the brothers at least.

Bianca shook her head in a spirit of resignation. 'You could have chosen a better time, but I suppose you have made your minds up.'

It was only a token resistance. And so within a short span of months Bianca found herself in a much smaller town than the one she had come to regard as home. Only about one hundred German-speaking souls were settled here and more on surrounding farms. It was New Braunfels in miniature; raised footpaths, wide dusty streets, a cluster of houses, a central square, a chapel, a blacksmith – the basics of a community. Even the same river, the Guadalupe, but further upstream here, more easily forded. No saloon as yet – they tended to attract the rougher Anglo types and pious Germans saw no need to invite trouble.

Rolling farmland was all about the little settlement with hills and streams and copses of trees close by. Bianca was much more conscious of nature, of the countryside all about her, not like her last home with the town outskirts perhaps half a mile away.

For the first time Bianca lacked the security of a large German-speaking population to provide a buffer between her family and the Anglos. It was indeed a beautiful setting but she found an unfamiliar society all about her, with its own language and customs. Bianca had not realised how exposed she would feel. She had been some years in Texas by now but she had been well cocooned from the realities of life here. Now she would have to come to terms with being a true citizen of Texas – and so would Theodore.

By selling their interest in the New Braunfels store and renting out Theodore's home, the brothers raised the money to build the new Comfort general store. At first they would all live at the back where rooms were provided in the plan for living space. After the store was open for business, Theodore and his family would move out while Fritz would stay behind, living alone in the rooms at the back.

With careful financial management and some help from Louis, Theodore was able once again to acquire a home of his own, one that he designed himself and had built by local craftsmen. It was none too soon. Bianca's patience with living behind a store with a baby was fast running out. After six long weeks, Theodore was at last able to move his family into their new home.

Now Bianca could begin to take in life in her new surroundings. The house plan was similar to their first home in New Braunfels and she had no cause for complaint on that score. Their fellow townsfolk, though few in number, were all first settlers here and eager to socialise with one another. For a gregarious person like Bianca, it was another chapter in her life unfolding and she made new friends quickly.

When first built, the store seemed cold and uninviting but the industrious brothers had soon laid in a surprising variety of merchandise. Within weeks the musty smell and homely clutter of the New Braunfels store was being reproduced in its new location.

A general store was a focal point in a town and all the citizens had reason to go there at one time or another. Bianca enjoyed being a storekeeper's wife and she spent a lot of time there, baby nearby, helping Theodore and Fritz, chatting to the locals, helping to make the store a popular place for the people of Comfort.

One day, following a trip to New Braunfels, Theodore arrived at his home with startling news. 'We have been invited to a wedding,' he announced.

Something in Theodore's tone suggested that this was not just another mutual acquaintance taking the step into matrimony. His face was serious, even perhaps disapproving. Puzzled, Bianca looked up at him from her sofa and asked 'Who is it, Theodore?'

'Heinrich.'

It was a common name in the German community. For a moment, Bianca cast around among the Heinrichs she knew and then suddenly realisation came. 'Heinrich Bremer?' He nodded.

Bianca brightened, her voice full of surprise. 'Why, Theodore, I think that's good. He has been alone for nearly three years now – Judith wouldn't want him to spend his life like that. He's still only in his early forties.' She spoke carefully. She knew how sensitive the subject of his mother was to Theodore.

He relaxed at her words. A ghost of a grin crossed his face. 'Yes, you're right. Heinrich says Mama told him "Remember me but don't mourn for me too long. Find another wife. Don't be lonely."'

Bianca smiled. She had always thought well of Heinrich. 'Well there you are then. He has Judith's blessing. And who is the lucky lady? Is she a widow or is she unmarried?'

Theodore laughed now. 'Oh, very definitely unmarried,' he said in an emphatic tone.

Bianca gave him a puzzled frown. 'What do you mean?'

'Do you know the Keilmanns – Carl and Frieda? They have a farm not far from the Bremers?'

Bianca nodded, unable to see the connection for a moment. Then suddenly light dawned. 'Not Caroline, surely? He couldn't possibly. She is younger than me.' She had jumped to her feet in surprise.

Theodore was amused at her reaction. 'Yes, she is eighteen. And more than that, she was Heinrich Junior's sweetheart and his father took her off him and now Junior is furious with jealousy. He has left home and will not speak to his father.'

'Oh well, that's no loss. I never liked him. He thinks too much of himself. Caroline has made the better choice.'

Theodore grinned at his wife's outspokenness. 'You always speak your mind, don't you? But you are right, as usual.'

A week later, the couple were guests at a small gathering at the Bremer farm. As soon as she saw Heinrich, Bianca rushed up to him. He greeted her warmly and she flung her arms about him and kissed his cheek. Before she stepped back, she whispered, 'Good for you, Heinrich. Good for you.'

He smiled his appreciation. 'Not everyone agrees with you, Bianca, but Judith always said you were a rebel. We rebels don't care what others think, eh?'

'No, indeed we don't,' she replied. 'And where is the bride? I must meet her.'

She liked Caroline immediately. She was tall, dark-haired, pretty and self-assured with a ready laugh and the two became instant friends. 'I was married here, just like you,' Bianca told her. 'You're a lucky lady. Don't let anyone tell you otherwise.' Caroline acknowledged Bianca's words gratefully – as Heinrich said, not everyone approved of the union.

After the ceremony was over, Theodore and Bianca spent the night in the farmhouse before the journey back to Comfort. To Bianca, this was always a special place, a house full of memories, many warm, some bittersweet. She lay awake for some time, reliving the past.

Back at Comfort, it was not long before another event occupied Bianca's attention. A grouping of German settlers from singing societies all over the United States had formed for the purpose of holding an annual Saengerfest, a Song Festival. This year, 1854, was the second and was to be held in San Antonio. There would be contests and prizes for singing groups and individuals, for church music, for traditional German songs and more.

Theodore had enjoyed being in a singing group in New Braunfels.

He had a fine voice and Bianca enjoyed hearing him, encouraging him to sing old German melodies to her.

She soon came to grasp, however, that more than harmless fun was involved in the festival. The arrival of many Germans from the North brought heavy political overtones. She heard that at the first Saengerfest, in the North, in Kentucky, political resolutions had been passed on such subjects as constitutional reform, voting rights, foreign relations and, inevitably, slavery. More ominously, to Bianca, was the news that her father Louis was a major organiser and planner of proceedings and that Theodore would be his assistant.

'Theodore,' she said one night, shortly before he was to set off for San Antonio. 'Listen to me. Stay out of the political talk. Don't get involved. These Yankee Germans can say what they like and go back to their safe homes but we have to live here. We Germans already have a bad name for not supporting slavery. At least we could be quiet about it. If the abolitionists make speeches we will all be held to blame. And if you make yourself known, the Anglos will not forget you. They watch us. They don't trust us. They write in their newspapers about us.'

Theodore had a maddening habit of being evasive when he did not want to confront an issue with Bianca. He acknowledged the wisdom of her words and added 'You must trust to my good sense.'

'That is just what I fear,' she said acidly. 'My foolish father will get himself into trouble and you will be dragged into it.'

It was no use. Theodore would not commit himself one way or another. Fritz was going to the Saengerfest too and was equally close-mouthed about his intentions. She suspected that neither of them knew what to expect and had no plans as to how they would conduct themselves. When the time came for her to say goodbye it was in a spirit of deep foreboding.

Her mood was not helped while she tended the store in their absence. She had struck up a good relationship with a local Anglo farmer, Tom Ferguson, who came in for stores from time to time. A son of his had married a girl from Comfort and he took an interest in the German community. He had even learned some German words and with Bianca's faulty English, they would joke together in a mixture of languages.

Ferguson was not a slave owner himself. He saw it as a bad practice already abandoned in every other civilised country. He could only hope it would fade away over time without the need for war. He sat on the county council and was a mine of information for Bianca on local issues. One day, before the end of the Saengerfest, he came to the store in an agitated state.

He displayed a newspaper, *The Western Texan*, to Bianca, laying it on the counter between them. Bianca's command of written English was even less than her ability to speak it and Ferguson explained the lead article to her carefully.

There had indeed been political resolutions at the festival as well as song contests. One resolution criticising the practice of slavery had aroused a storm of protest across Texas. Every German was now suspect. 'Those Yankee Germans have got you all in trouble,' the farmer avowed in his gravelly voice. 'See this.' He read slowly from the newspaper, underlining the words with a finger. '"German settlers who wish to be accepted as citizens of Texas must learn to support the laws of this state. If these laws do not satisfy them then they should leave Texas and find a place that is more to their liking. They were not invited to live here and they are not welcome in our great state."'

The message was clear enough but Ferguson had more to say. 'Your father is Louis Nohl, isn't he?' Bianca nodded. 'Someone should tell him there are spies for the slave owners at the festival, German speakers who support slavery. They are noting everyone who plays a part in these resolutions. They are drawing up a list. They plan to make trouble for people on the list. They see war coming one day and they want to know who the traitors are. You tell your husband he is playing a dangerous game, being seen associating with Louis Nohl.'

Bianca thanked him for his advice. She could see the advantages of having an informant in the enemy camp, so to speak. The very thought that the surrounding country held "enemies", people with lists who aimed to cause her family harm, was a frightening thought.

Theodore and Fritz returned to a tense welcome from Bianca. She told them of the farmer's words but they had already seen newspapers. Fritz was uncharacteristically subdued, seemingly wishing to dissociate himself from the festival, but Theodore still had a touch of defiance left in him. 'What can they do?' he asked. 'We have broken no laws.'

Bianca gave in to a flash of anger. 'They can burn the store down if they want to, and our house too. Do you think you can complain to the law? The slave owners are the law. No one will help you. Do you think the people of Comfort want to get involved in your little war? How many slaves have you set free with your efforts, eh?'

The brothers were taken aback by her words. Theodore could only say in a low voice, 'I hear what you say. I will be careful.'

'I hope so,' said Bianca wearily, her anger fading once more into deep concern for their future. She forced herself to change the subject and asked about the song contests they had taken part in. That was the point of the festival, after all.

The first test of suspect Germans by the local slave owners came quickly. One morning, several days later, the store was entered by a hard-faced young man accompanied by three slaves. Bianca was at the counter, talking to a local couple about a purchase. Seeing trouble approach, she called sharply to her husband.

Theodore was in the back office with little Louis. The urgency in Bianca's voice brought him to the shop front in moments. It was the first time he had faced such a challenge. Only a few local Anglos like Tom Ferguson visited the Comfort store and they presented no problem. 'We do not serve men with slaves,' said Theodore. 'This is not a slave-owning community.'

The smirk on the man's face showed that he had expected such a reaction. Bianca was conscious that a trap was being sprung. She sensed that the man's visit had little to do with purchasing stores.

'Well, that's where you would be wrong, Mr Goldbeck,' he responded in a nasal twang. 'This is a slave-owning community. This is Texas. Maybe you think you're living in some other state.' The man's sarcastic tone contrasted with the impassive faces of the slaves. Bianca wondered if they knew that their presence here was part of a charade intended to provoke an incident.

Before Theodore could reconsider the wisdom of standing his ground, the man turned on his heel. From the doorway, he barked out, 'Captain Morgan will be very disappointed at your lack of hospitality, sir. And we did so hope that you foreigners would be good neighbours – and good Texans.' The man had arrived in a wagon. He climbed up and seated himself and was swiftly driven away by his black servants.

Bianca and Theodore stood on the planking outside and watched the wagon disappear into the distance, the dust cloud billowing behind. Bianca's English did not enable her to understand all the man's words but the message was plain enough.

'You should not have done that, Theodore. That was what he wanted you to do. He will be back with others. You must not defy these people.'

Theodore was still shaken by the suddenness of the incident. 'Don't you think there is a principle at stake?'

It was not what Bianca wanted to hear. Her voice took on a shrill note. 'Damn your principles. Do you think your principles make any difference? If they burn this store down do you think the law will take your side? No one will help you if you make enemies of the Anglo farmers.'

As she took her husband to task outside the store front, Bianca had not noticed that word of the incident had quickly spread and that townsfolk were gathering about them. Fritz appeared, puzzled at the commotion.

One of the neighbours spoke for the others. 'This is our town, Bianca. We will stand by you if these people come here to make trouble.'

Before Theodore could take heart at this show of support, Bianca raised her voice. 'Thank you, Otto. Thank you all, but listen to me. That man was right. We are citizens of Texas and we have no right to fight its laws. If we turn this town against the Anglos, it will be like a war and we will lose.'

Theodore stood silent, a defiant look on his face. Bianca's anger surged. Why did she have to take the lead at such a time? 'Do you want to drag all the people of Comfort into this?' Her eyes flashed fury at her husband.

Fritz spoke up. Like Bianca, he took the side of practicality over principle. 'She is right, Theodore. We can't let this matter get out of hand. When those people return, we must do as they say. If they just want to make purchases, let them have what they want. We play into their hands if we let them make trouble.'

Theodore conceded defeat. 'You're right, both of you.' He raised his voice to the dozen or more citizens gathered about. 'Thank you for your support but I must not get you all into trouble with the Anglos. I will bury my principles for the sake of peace.'

A murmur of assent told Bianca that the situation had been defused for now. A thought came to her. 'That man spoke of Captain Morgan. Does anyone know who he is?'

A voice answered her. 'Frank Morgan has a ranch over towards Kerrville. He heads the volunteer regiment around here. He was in the war with Mexico. He is not a man to pick a fight with.'

Theodore looked at Bianca, then the others and said, loud enough for all to hear, 'I hear what you say. If this man has finished his war with Mexico and wants a war with Comfort, I promise to give him no more cause.' A little subdued laughter followed and then the group drifted off back to their homes.

The next turn of events was not long in coming. Early the following morning, shortly after Theodore opened the store, six horsemen rode casually down the main street, followed by an open wagon manned by slaves. The group was led by a middle-aged man with a broad-brimmed hat and trimmed beard, wearing a long grey coat. He seemed unarmed, except for the riding whip in his hand, but a number of the others had guns in holsters. The young man of yesterday rode beside him.

Theodore and Fritz stepped out onto the street to meet the horsemen. They were trying, Bianca knew, to look more in control than they actually felt. The man in the lead stopped before them and spoke to the brothers. His voice had a sharp ring to it, a tone of authority, and the whip in his hand added a touch of menace to his demeanour.

'I am Captain Frank Morgan, First Texas Volunteers. My son James here tells me that he was refused service here yesterday. I don't see the point in a store that will not serve its citizens. Which of these men refused you, James?'

The young man pointed to Theodore. 'That one.'

Morgan leaned forward and looked down at Theodore. 'We do not intend to be turned away today, sir. But first, my son is owed an apology for yesterday's insult.'

Theodore's limited store of courage was fast deserting him. He feared that at any moment the man would unleash his whip at him.

Bianca had stepped out onto the footpath outside the store. The other two had warned her to stay inside but she was not one to hide from danger, nor did she trust her husband to swallow his principles enough for them to survive this threat to their livelihood and perhaps their lives.

But Theodore was by now thoroughly cowed, drained of all defiance, first by Bianca's wrath and then by Morgan's. Bianca could see that her husband was focusing on his English and trying to conceal the attack of nerves that threatened to reduce him to a foolish stammer. He spoke directly to James Morgan. 'I apologise for my actions yesterday. You are welcome to visit my store whenever you wish.'

James glanced across at his father who nodded, apparently accepting Theodore's response. The men then dismounted, hitching their horses to rails along the edge of the footpath. The black men drew their wagon alongside the store front.

Captain Morgan stepped onto the footpath, taking in Bianca's presence for the first time. He took off his hat, nodded to her and strode into the store. Several of the men followed him, the others remaining outside. Bianca wondered what course this little drama was going to take next.

Morgan walked around the store briefly, giving its contents a cursory check. He selected some items, a horse blanket, some baling wire. He pointed to a saddle. 'How much?'

Fritz was nearest. 'Twenty dollars.'

'I'll give you fifteen.'

Theodore gestured acceptance. The last thing on his mind was haggling with his unwanted customer. He had been afraid they might take what they wanted without payment but Morgan was clearly intent on keeping up his side of the formalities.

Payment was made. Black men were summoned to carry out the goods to the wagon. That done, Morgan turned to address Theodore, who was still standing behind the counter.

'Now you listen to me, Mr Goldbeck. If I ever again have to come this way on such a mission, I will burn this damn place down. You abolitionist foreigners came here of your own free will. We own slaves here in Texas, Mr Goldbeck. If you take the Yankee line on that, then get the hell out of this state. Mark my words, there will be war with the Yankees one day and you will be called to fight for Texas. I'll come for you myself and I will make a soldier of you, damn it. Don't think to run away – they hang draft dodgers in a war, same as deserters, so keep that in mind.'

Bianca was struck by the strange mix of civility and menace in the man's behaviour. He had doffed his hat to Bianca and addressed her husband as Mr Goldbeck while at the same time threatening to hang him as a draft dodger.

Having made his point, Morgan strode towards the door, passing close to Bianca as he did so. Much as she blamed her husband for the whole affair, the humiliation of it all had left her quivering with rage. As Morgan passed, she burst out in her heavily accented English, 'You are a bad man, Mr Morgan.'

He turned sharply, gave her a piercing stare and snapped, 'Oh indeed I am, madam, as you may well learn to your cost one day.' The glitter of malice in his eyes chilled even Bianca's combative soul.

After they had left, Fritz chided Bianca gently. 'I thought your advice was not to antagonise them any further.'

Never one to admit a mistake, Bianca responded irritably, 'It should never have come to this in the first place. You two are marked men now. If war comes, Morgan will be after you and you know what he said – he will hang you unless you fight for Texas – and for slavery,' she added as an afterthought.

And so there the matter rested, but it had brought a shadow into their lives that would darken as time went by, an element of uncertainty about the future that was never far from their thoughts.

Theodore had learned a hard lesson. He promised to keep a low profile on the subject of slavery from now on but occasional visits to Free Society meetings with her father Louis in New Braunfels kept Bianca in a state of apprehension. On matters of principle, discretion came much more easily to Bianca than it did to Theodore.

In spite of concerns about slave owners, life in Comfort had its advantages over New Braunfels. In such a small setting, it was possible to become leading figures in the life of the town, to play a variety of roles. When the need for a post office became apparent, Theodore applied to the Texas government for authority to provide this service in his store. Authorisation came, and with it the role of postmaster.

Encouraged by his newfound importance in the life of the township, a brief study of the law rewarded Theodore with the title Justice of the Peace and the right to sign legal documents and even officiate at weddings. Singing too still played a part in his life and he enjoyed training the chapel choir.

It may have been a small stage and a small audience but during their time in Comfort, Bianca enjoyed the ways in which the town had expanded their lives. Storemaster, postmaster, choirmaster, justice of the peace, leading citizen – Theodore had developed a rewarding life for them both. It was in fact rewarding in more ways than one, for his new roles also meant new income. Bianca could indulge herself more freely with shopping trips to New Braunfels and even to San Antonio.

One amusing incident that was long remembered came when Theodore was asked to officiate at the wedding of a German couple from a nearby farm. On the appointed day, the prospective bride and groom found themselves on the opposite side of the river to Theodore and a gathering of wedding guests. Heavy rain lately had raised the river level and the couple and other guests, all those from farms on the other side of the river, faced a turbulent flow in place of the usual placid stream.

As the two groups faced each other across the divide, Theodore shouted across an offer to conduct the ceremony right where they stood. The offer was accepted. The couple were anxious not to delay the day so long awaited. Theodore called out the words he would normally have spoken in the peaceful enclosure of the Comfort chapel and the couple responded in the spirit of the event. After the bride shouted 'I do', Theodore pronounced them man and wife. He could have waited for his fee but the grateful groom wrapped the money in a cloth and threw it across the river to the opposite bank where Theodore retrieved it.

Early in the new year, January 1855, Bianca's second child, a son, Benno, was born. With her first child, Louis, only thirteen months old, Bianca had her hands full. Now that his wife was less available to help out at the store, Theodore had more need of hired help for Fritz was finding small town life confining by now and was often away.

Another year passed pleasantly enough but by year's end, Fritz had moved on in his life and left Comfort behind. He moved to San Antonio, the big city, at least by Texas standards, forty miles to the south of Comfort. It was a city of Anglos but many of the more adventurous Germans from New Braunfels and elsewhere had drifted there in recent years. With size came opportunity. It was a bustling place, still with a frontier sense of risk-taking, of seizing the chance, of building for the future.

Fritz found work in the field he knew best, as a store clerk. It was a clothing store, not a familiar environment but he adapted quickly and his new manager soon saw value in him. If it was at first a city of strangers, an intimidating place after life in Comfort and New Braunfels, it had also a dynamic feel about it that clearly appealed to Fritz. His English improved rapidly and a circle of friends began to grow.

On visits to Comfort, Fritz was not slow to extol the virtues of city life to Theodore and Bianca. As a settled and house-proud mother of two, Bianca was in no mood for a further shift but she could see

Fritz's words were falling on fertile ground as far as Theodore was concerned. Too long in one place, with one lifestyle, and Theodore had once again become restless. It had happened in New Braunfels and now again in Comfort.

Bianca had mixed feelings. She was conscious that it would be hypocritical of her to oppose her husband's urge to take on a new challenge. It had once been her fear that over time he would become dull, unadventurous, happy to lead a quiet life. And yet behind his scholarly demeanour, to the surprise of those who did not know him well, was a desire for new experiences, to move on, to begin a new chapter. Bianca had sensed this quality in Theodore from the start – it had been an appealing part of his personality. She could not in good conscience be the one now who thwarted that drive, who acted as the brake on his ambitions. And in all honesty, though she had not even admitted it to herself yet, life in Comfort had rather outlived its novelty.

And so the day came, just as it had in New Braunfels, when Theodore and Fritz came to Bianca with a proposition. She was seated on her favourite sofa, the one brought from New Braunfels, feeding little Benno, now more than a year old, from a bowl as he sat in his baby chair.

The brothers seated themselves opposite her and Theodore opened the conversation with, 'There is something we would like to discuss with you.'

'I have been waiting for this,' replied Bianca with a resigned sigh. Then she laughed. 'Why do you wait until I am feeding the baby before you come to me? Do you think I am more easily convinced when I am distracted?'

Fritz grasped her meaning first. 'New Braunfels, remember?' he said to his brother. 'She was feeding the baby, feeding Louis.' Theodore grinned and nodded.

'So when do we leave Comfort?' she asked. 'Will we have our own store – and our own home?'

Fritz looked at her in mock exasperation. 'Bianca, we have spent all morning rehearsing our speech to convince you and now we can't use it. Would you like to hear it anyway?'

Bianca gazed at her brother-in-law fondly. 'No, thank you, but keep it. You may need it in the future, when you want me to go to California or Indian Territory.'

Theodore chipped in. 'We may try those places later, but for now we have San Antonio in mind.'

And so, after a little over two years in Comfort, the Goldbecks moved on. The store was sold and a profit made for the brothers to share.

Before they left, the family had many farewells to make. One was with Tom Ferguson, who had unsettling news. 'Many think war with the Yankees will come. The army reserve has a list of Yankee sympathisers – collaborators they call them – to be rounded up when war breaks out. I've seen the list. Your name is on it, Theodore, but not Fritz's. If war comes, you had best get out of Texas as fast as you can. You won't last long in a prison camp.'

The three of them, Theodore, Fritz and Bianca, took in their visitor's grim news. 'Where could we go?' responded Theodore. 'It's a long way to Union territory.'

'Yes, and they will be watching the roads. You could try for Indian country but they would hardly welcome you. With a war distracting the army they will probably start attacking outposts and stealing horses. And it would be no place for a woman.'

'Mexico?' suggested Theodore. The border was about one hundred and fifty miles to the south of San Antonio, several days ride on rough roads.

Tom nodded. 'It's probably your best chance. They don't like Texans – after all, we had a war with them and stole their territory – or that's how they see it. But if the Texas army was your enemy they might see you as being on their side. It would depend on how you played your cards. Take my advice and start planning your escape when you are in San Antonio. If you get supplies in from Mexico for your store, try to make contacts down there.'

Fritz saw problems of his own. 'Even if I'm not on the list, I don't want to die for slavery.'

Tom had advice for Fritz too. 'You might have a chance to join the volunteers for Indian territory – guarding the forts out there and the settlers. It would be a lot safer than fighting Yankees. Somebody has to do it. They can't just leave the frontier wide open.' Before Theodore could speak, Tom added, 'That won't work for anyone on the list. They won't let Indian duty be a way out for traitors, you can be sure of that.'

And so once again the matter rested but it was always there, in the back of their minds, a black cloud on a distant horizon. As Bianca could not help but point out, Fritz had somehow avoided being blacklisted – why could her husband not have had the sense to stay out of trouble?

San Antonio proved to be a challenge indeed. Not content this time with a simple streetfront store, the brothers had rented a warehouse. They brought in merchandise in bulk and supplied stores throughout the city. Though by the time they arrived in San Antonio, they had ample funds for their new venture, the deals they were making now were on a bigger scale than in the past. A few unwise purchases, goods that would not sell, buyers that would not pay, employees who stole from them and their fortunes might turn around sharply. They had to be seen to be honest and reliable and they had to work hard at establishing a good reputation.

Home for Bianca and Theodore was a pleasant rambling house in a good part of town. Friends from New Braunfels and Comfort would drop in and they in turn would visit their old haunts. Both enjoyed trips to the Bremer farm, north of New Braunfels, where a daughter had already been born to Heinrich and his young bride. Visits to the Nohl family were always a little unsettling to Bianca who saw her father as a bad influence on her impressionable husband. Theodore's links to the anti-slavery movement were not clear to Bianca but she had heard from more than one source that the movement was thoroughly infiltrated by Confederate spies. Theodore's infuriating response to Bianca's warnings was to declare, 'Well, if I am on the list of Yankee sympathisers already, what more do I have to fear?' To Bianca's bitter gibe: 'How many slaves have you freed?' he would reply, 'They will never be freed if everyone accepts the situation.' It was an argument that led nowhere.

Life in San Antonio was certainly different. In the past, Bianca had been used to seeing familiar faces every day but in a city this size she would see only a multitude of strangers when she ventured out. The city centre and the wealthier parts had gaslight now, the first Bianca had seen since leaving Germany. One could walk the streets at night without the need to carry a lantern. The streets were wide and busy with wagons and carts and coaches and bustling crowds were always about.

Black men too were a frequent sight and while Bianca did not see any ugly scenes of brutality of the type Theodore liked to describe, the sight of slaves always made her uneasy. It was an issue that dominated the relationship between North and South and Bianca had a feeling of gathering storm clouds, of calamities to come that would not leave the Goldbecks unscathed. Tom Ferguson's hope that slavery would just fade away over time seemed less and less likely. Its preservation had become an icon of Southern pride.

Late in the year that they arrived in San Antonio, 1857, Bianca had a third child, a boy once again, whom she named Guido. She and Theodore had discussed using Anglo names but they agreed that they were still German at heart, still spoke the language among themselves and though neither put it into words, they still felt like foreigners in this alien society.

Another year passed uneventfully. Bianca was kept busy with three little boys. Theodore was a loving father but his demanding life as a merchant left him with less time than he would have liked to spend with his family.

One evening, Theodore looked across the dinner table at his wife and said simply, 'Well, this is the one, just as we thought.' He had a twinkle in his eye.

For a moment, Bianca was at a loss as to his meaning, and then, 'Oh, you mean Fritz. Well, it's about time. I thought he would go from one affair to another forever. Is it Natalie?' Theodore nodded.

When they had first met Fritz's latest love, a tall attractive young woman, Bianca had instinctively felt that this one was special. When Fritz had brought her to meet them over a dinner at Bianca's home, there had been something a little more thoughtful about his manner than before. With others, his casual, flippant style had told Bianca that it was just fun, nothing serious, but Natalie was different. She had a calm confidence about her, a poise, a gravity that suggested that she possessed a will of her own, that she would make her own decisions, that this prize would not be easily won. Fritz would have to woo her with all the charm he possessed. He was twenty-seven, she was twenty. She had plenty of time to find others if she decided Fritz was not the one.

Bianca had been much impressed and she and Theodore had played the part of gracious, welcoming hosts to the hilt that night. Fritz was a part of their lives and they had long wished to see him find a partner. Now after many false starts, they saw success within reach, if Fritz could only play his part and take the matter seriously enough to win out. And play it he did. Not three months had passed since that first dinner and already Theodore had good news.

'Fritz has asked for her hand and she has accepted.'

'Wonderful,' breathed Bianca. She had come to think of Fritz over the years as the brother she had never had and his welfare was dear to her heart; but somewhere, deep down, she felt a little pang of jealousy. What would life have been like with the impulsive, unpredictable Fritz in place of the steady, reliable Theodore? Now Natalie would be the one to find out. 'Have they set a date?' she asked.

'February the twenty-seventh – what is that...?' He calculated. 'Four months'

Bianca was all action. 'We haven't even met her parents. We are his family. We are all he has. We must make a success of this. You know what Fritz is like. He never takes anything seriously.'

Theodore laughed. 'Oh, this time is different. My little brother has grown up suddenly. His whole attitude is different. That is true love for you.'

'Is that how you felt when you first met me?' she asked teasingly.

'When I first met you,' he replied, 'you were only a child. I thought you needed a good spanking.' Marriage to Bianca had sharpened his wits.

Natalie Muller married Fritz Goldbeck on 27 February 1859 in the Lutheran church of San Antonio. Theodore was best man for his brother, an Anglo custom, a role he greatly enjoyed playing. His customary reserve melted on this special day. It was a large crowd, Germans from the city, New Braunfels, Comfort and beyond and Anglos too, friends through business, neighbours, social acquaintances. Fritz was a gregarious man and was widely popular. The Mullers too were a well-established merchant family and had their own guest list. It was through Herr Muller that Fritz had met his bride.

The reception afterwards in a large hall festooned with decorations was a memorable event for Bianca. She loved a crowd and circulated happily, meeting old friends and making new ones. Fritz and his bride were the centre of attention, and a number of guests noted to Bianca how well suited they were, the confident wife already taking charge of her easily distracted husband. If only, thought Bianca, if only life could always be like this, and yet she knew that she would miss the days of having Fritz as the unattached soul so much a part of her life.

Bianca and Theodore returned home after a late night. With the children asleep and the babysitter taken home, a lazy Sunday morning was in order. At the first sound of small children stirring, Bianca awakened her husband. 'This morning,' she announced imperiously, 'you can feed the children and bring me breakfast in bed. I have had a late night. I need the rest.'

Used to his wife's whims, Theodore went off obligingly to fulfil her orders. Later, as he sat beside her, he observed casually, 'I had a late night too. Why should I not have breakfast in bed?'

'Because,' responded Bianca between mouthfuls, 'I am going to have a baby and you are not.'

Theodore looked at her in surprise. 'Well, that's always good news. Perhaps an Elfrieda this time.'

Bianca gazed at him with mock sternness and spoke in an authoritative tone. 'Elfrieda or not, four is enough. I will not be one of these women with a dozen children who exist only to breed. I want more from life than feeding babies.'

'Oh, but I agree with you,' he replied. 'I don't want to come home forever to crying infants. I think we both want more from life than that.'

A little taken aback by his easy acquiescence, Bianca added, 'That means self-restraint from you, you understand? I don't want to have to lock you out of the bedroom.'

Theodore grinned. 'No, that would never do. I will learn to behave myself.'

Later that year, in September, their desire for a daughter was fulfilled when Elfrieda Goldbeck joined the family. Both felt a sense of completeness. As Bianca said, four was enough. It was time to move on.

Fritz and Natalie's first child, Hermann, was born at the end of the year. The cycle of life's renewal was beginning for Fritz and ending for Theodore.

By the start of the new year, 1860, the storm clouds that Bianca so feared were gathering fast and becoming rapidly darker. Powerful anti-slavery forces were asserting themselves in the North and the San Antonio papers were filled with ominous news. The Republican Party candidate for President was Abraham Lincoln, a staunch abolitionist, or so he was seen in the South. More and more, Bianca heard the declaration that if Lincoln was elected, the South would secede.

There came a night when Bianca determined to have a discussion about their future. With little interest in business affairs, she had not inquired before into what Theodore planned to do if the worst came but she could not let the issue drift on any longer.

Theodore heard his wife out gravely. When she finished, he settled himself back in his armchair and began to talk. 'You fear the worst, Bianca, and you have good reason. Lincoln has not said he will forbid slavery in the South but he will fight to stop it spreading to new states. He hates slavery and the South doesn't trust him to leave it alone once he is President.'

'Is he likely to win?'

'Yes, very likely. And the South will certainly secede. It is believed that Lincoln will not allow the dissolution of the Union and that can only mean war.'

'What then? You know what Tom Ferguson said. You're a marked man.'

Theodore pressed his fingertips together as he did when deep in thought. 'We own this house but we only rent the warehouse. I have built up a store of wealth in gold coins. If we flee to Mexico, these coins are convertible to any other currency but if they are stolen then we have nothing. We must not let this knowledge get out. Say nothing to anyone. I have a wagon ready that we can all ride in, with good horses. I have contacts in Mexico, in Saltillo, not far beyond the border. We buy clothes and blankets from a factory there. I have met the manager. He understands our situation and he will help us. We must go as soon as I get word that they are coming for me. We may have to leave very suddenly. If we wait too long, you may never see me again.'

His words, his whole manner, sent a shiver of naked fear through Bianca's body and she gave an involuntary shudder. For the first time, she began to grasp the full enormity of what was happening to them. Theodore, the Dreamer, as Judith had called him, was describing a nightmare, a living nightmare, that was rushing to consume them, a force so vast, so monstrous, that it all but defied belief. War between the states was coming and the Goldbecks would be caught on the wrong side of the battlefront, traitors to the cause of the South, to the land of their adoption.

'What of my parents? What of Fritz and Natalie?' Her mind was spinning.

'Louis must make his own way with Henriette. We might be able to meet up later. His daughters may stay behind – I'm not sure if he will take them.'

'Will they be watching the roads?'

'I don't think so. Not if we go quickly enough. There will be too much happening when war breaks out. As for Fritz,' he added, 'he is not on the list. He has a baby, a sick baby – have you heard?' Bianca nodded. 'He can stall for time. He will apply to join the Territorials to defend the frontier out West, as Tom suggested. We have contacts. We know who to pay off. We have planned it all together. We must not wait too long and yet if we run away too soon and war doesn't come, then what? We are in Mexico for no reason and we will look really guilty then. All we can do is wait, and be ready to run if we need to.'

'When we need to,' corrected Bianca gloomily. Theodore could only nod and shrug his shoulders resignedly.

The year 1860 was a year of ill omen indeed. As the political situation grew ever worse, tragedy struck closer to hand. Fritz and Natalie's child was clearly not long for this world. A sickly boy, little Hermann died that November, before reaching his first birthday. Months of nursing a dying baby, their first child, placed a terrible strain on the parents. Bianca could only admire how the two drew strength from each other to weather the crisis. Having never lost a child herself, she could scarcely imagine how one would cope with such a loss.

On the night after the funeral, Bianca saw to it that the couple were not alone with their grief, insisting that they stay the night with herself and Theodore. She would remember long after the sight of Fritz sitting beside Natalie with little Elfrieda in his arms, as if replacing the child he had lost, and saying, 'We will have more children and some day there will be no more fear of war. Some day all this will be behind us, like a bad dream. The clouds will part and the sun will shine again.' Bianca had noticed before a poetic streak in Fritz and tears welled in her eyes at his words. How long, she wondered, before the sun shone in their lives again?

Only days later, word of Abraham Lincoln's election as President of the United States was headlined in the local newspapers. After that, events moved with lightning speed. Before the year was out, South Carolina had seceded from the Union and other Southern states soon began to follow. Texas left the Union in February and life took on an air of unreality. The Goldbecks were no longer citizens of the United States. Wherever would it end?

The weeks that followed Texas's secession from the union were eerily calm. Bianca still prayed that war would not come but Theodore told her that Confederate forces were seizing federal property throughout the South and conflict was now inevitable.

Louis and Benno were old enough at seven and six years to realise that their parents were under great strain, that their family life was unravelling. One night, Bianca and Theodore sat with them and tried to explain the danger that faced the family, the likelihood that they would have to flee suddenly to a distant city in a very different land, to leave behind their home and virtually everything they owned, to be exiles in a strange country, perhaps for years to come, perhaps forever. If it was frightening for adults, it was doubly so for bewildered children.

The weeks of nervous waiting ended in April. All in a rush, war between the states began and the South mobilised. General Lee, military commander of Confederate forces, ordered conscription – all men eighteen to thirty-five to report to their nearest recruiting station. Captain Morgan's words rang in Bianca's ears. 'They hang draft dodgers.'

That night as darkness fell, all was in readiness at the Goldbeck household. All that they could take with them was packed, the precious gold coins hidden unobtrusively among their possessions. When there came a tap on the front door, Theodore moved to answer it immediately. Bianca heard low voices, a brief discussion. Someone was risking his life to help a collaborator. Bianca took one last look around at her living room, at her home. Would she ever see it again?

Theodore closed the door. 'We go now,' he said tersely. With those words, the Goldbecks ceased to be citizens of Texas and became fugitives, fleeing for their lives to an uncertain fate.

Chapter 6

Bianca Nohl: Bitter Exile
Mexico: 1861–1866

The road seemed endless, mile after mile of rough track winding into the distance. The far south of Texas was a wide brown land, with few trees and little habitation. As the wagon rolled on, Theodore held the reins while Bianca sat beside him, little Elfrieda held tight in her arms. The closer they got to Mexico, the worse the road became. Sometimes large rocks protruded from the stony surface and as the wagon lurched over them, it was thrown from side to side. The three boys behind were tossed about but they endured the rigours of the ride with stoic silence, even four-year-old Guido.

It was the second day of their flight. If they could make fifty miles a day, Theodore had predicted, they would reach the Mexican border early on the third day, and Saltillo several days after that. Never the most communicative of men, Theodore had lapsed into a morose silence that had begun to chafe on Bianca's nerves. How much was he withholding from her, she wondered, and determined to start asking the questions that needed to be answered.

'What do you know about Mexico?' she asked abruptly. 'What will it be like there for us?'

Theodore shrugged, then shook his head wearily, as though disillusionment with life had penetrated his very soul. 'It is a country in turmoil,' he began. 'There are uprisings everywhere. There is no real government. The country is bankrupt. It owes a lot of money to the European powers and there is talk of them invading Mexico to make it pay its debts.'

Bianca waited for him to say more, then prompted him: 'Who is uprising against who? What is the trouble about?'

'Well,' he resumed, 'the common people, the poor peasants and townsfolk, have a very bad life and they are full of resentment. All the wealth and power is with the army, the big landowners and the Church. The people have formed their own armies – well, armed bands in different parts of the country – and they fight for their rights.' It was obvious from his tone on which side Theodore's sympathies lay. Other forms of injustice existed in the world besides slavery and Theodore's instinct would always be to side with the underdog.

A thought came to Bianca. 'Does Mexico have slavery?'

Theodore's response was a bitter, sardonic laugh. 'No, they abolished it long ago. We may think Mexico is so backward but they are ahead of us on that score at least.'

Since their furtive night-time flight from San Antonio, they had seen little wagon traffic on the road, certainly no sign of Confederate forces sent to capture deserters and suspects. They had food enough for the journey to Mexico but what then, Bianca wondered? How could they hope to feed themselves and their children in a land stricken with civil strife, a land of poverty and injustice? So many problems, so many fears – who could ever have imagined such troubles? And they had four little ones to feed and care for, a mother's worst nightmare.

'Do you speak any Spanish?' Bianca questioned her husband. She knew his talent for learning languages, though modest enough, was certainly better than hers. To this day, her mastery of English lagged behind his. The thought of learning yet another language intimidated her.

'I know a few words,' he replied. 'You remember Eduardo at the warehouse? He used to help me dealing with my suppliers in Mexico.' She nodded. 'I used to pay him a bit extra to teach me some Spanish in our spare time at work. I can make some simple talk but I have a long way to go.'

'And not much time to catch up,' she finished for him. 'Tell me,' she added, 'why we are going to Saltillo? Isn't Monterrey closer?'

'True, but my best contact is in Saltillo. There is a Senor Rodriguez there who has a textiles and carpet factory. I've dealt with him for a long time. He came to San Antonio a couple of times, for business with me and others. He speaks fair English. He is an educated man.'

'I remember him,' interrupted Bianca. 'You brought him home for a meal. He had dark hair and a moustache.'

Theodore laughed for the first time that day. 'Well, they all have dark hair and moustaches, but yes – that was him. I think we made a good impression. I had drinks with him afterwards and told him of my problems with the Confederacy. He said that if I had to flee Texas I should pay him a visit and he would see what he could do for me.'

Bianca sighed wearily. 'Well, if we ever needed a friend, we need one now.' She thought a moment, then gave Theodore a sideways look, a glint of humour in her eye. 'Promise me something.'

'What is that?'

'Don't try to free the peasants. Freeing the slaves has got us into enough trouble.'

Theodore gave her a fond look and stretched one arm to bring her closer. 'How you do love to tease me. I will let the peasants look after themselves, I promise you. I have enough problems just looking after us.'

They chatted on, taking their minds off the slow, jolting ride and the uncertainties that lay ahead. They discussed other German settlers they knew who might be escaping the Confederates but Theodore had little knowledge about the situation, even in San Antonio. Fear of informers had kept people close-mouthed about their plans. Louis and Henriette Nohl were believed to have a contact in Monterrey. Theodore would try to link up with them later.

Early the next morning, after another uncomfortable night in the wagon, they reached the border. They had feared difficulties with suspicious Texan border guards but the two young soldiers they met there seemed entirely unsure as to their role now that war had been declared. They had been primed to watch for gun runners and wished to search the wagon. Afraid that they would discover his cache of gold coins, Theodore made excuses – he had sick children and they were asleep. He was taking a load of trade goods to sell in Mexico and anyway, why would gun runners take guns into Mexico when the war was on this side of the border? The guards let the matter drop, more intent on pumping Theodore for information on the war situation. They felt they had been forgotten in the tide of events in which Mexico was only a distant backwater. Theodore sympathised with their plight and bade them, and Texas, farewell.

The Mexican border guards a hundred yards further on were of more concern. They would no doubt be armed. If they insisted on searching the wagon and found the gold coins, they might well murder the Yankees and steal the money. Bianca understood full well the danger. She had by now no illusions about the state of law and order in Mexico. How long since these men had last been paid? She knew that Theodore had a loaded gun in the wagon for use as a last resort, but he had little practice with weapons and a shoot-out was a grim thought indeed.

The two Mexican guards who stepped out of the small guard hut were, inevitably, dark-haired, moustached and swarthy. They had furtive expressions, Bianca noted, and rotten teeth. She felt the tension mount. Theodore climbed down and the men gestured at the covered wagon, clearly asking about its contents. The children were clustered at the entrance, looking down at the scene. It was now in the family's interests to tell the truth, that they were fleeing from the Confederates, from the war. Theodore had explained to Bianca his hope that fugitives from the Texan army would win some sympathy in Mexico, where defeat at the hands of the Anglos had robbed Mexico of vast land resources in years past, including Texas itself.

Theodore made it clear by words and gestures, including holding an imaginary gun to his head, that the family were fleeing for their lives and sought sanctuary in Mexico. One guard pointed to the trunk that lay nearest the wagon front and Theodore lifted it down and opened it to reveal only clothes, crockery and saucepans. He then reached into his pocket and brought out some Texan paper money, about fifty dollars, along with a packet of cheap cigars from the trunk. The guards clearly had no qualms about accepting a bribe to let the travellers on their way, but the money aroused little excitement. They were at least shrewd enough to realise that this money would be worthless if Texas lost the war, as must have seemed likely to even the most ignorant Mexican. Theodore did not dare offer them gold coins for fear they would suspect that the Goldbecks had more of them in the wagon.

Bored and hot standing in the early morning sun, the guards waved the family on its way and retreated to the shade of their hut. As Theodore took the reins and resumed the journey, Bianca reflected that they were now in a foreign country, one that she would never have thought to visit under normal circumstances. She was filled with a feeling of ill omen, almost of dread. Would they have been better off hiding out somewhere in Texas or taking their chances in Indian territory? Well, it was too late now. They must make the best of things.

The rest of the day's travel did nothing to lessen Bianca's anxieties. The condition of the road grew worse and the going slower. They passed through some small villages, poverty-stricken places with dilapidated homes, ragged children and lean hungry-looking stray dogs. Nothing was sign-posted and only with the aid of a map and occasional questions of locals did Theodore stay on track for Saltillo.

They wound their way south for two more days. In her depressed mood, the countryside seemed to Bianca to be uniformly bleak. It was dry and desolate, with peasants' shacks scattered about and rows of brittle cornstalks in dusty fields.

When Saltillo at last came into view, Bianca's low expectations of their sanctuary city were soon justified. The outskirts were a succession of poor homes on dusty side tracks from which townsfolk surveyed the Goldbecks with silent reserve. Did anyone ever smile in this forsaken land? Bianca wondered. How could her family hope to survive in a land where centuries of tyranny had given way to lawlessness and chaos?

A truly huge cathedral came into view in the distance and Theodore steered his way towards it. They entered at last into a square of noble proportions, one that in colonial times, Bianca reflected, must have been an imposing sight. Now everything seemed in a state of decay, the square empty but for the ever-present stray dogs and a few locals in ragged shawls.

'This is the Plaza de Armas and there,' he pointed, 'I think that shop should be Senor Rodriguez'.' Bianca followed his direction to a shop front on one side of the great square. 'Where is everybody?'

Bianca looked around at the grimly alien world all about her. 'Is it Sunday today?' she ventured.

'Yes, so it is. But the church seems empty.' He looked at the huge edifice opposite them. 'In fact, it seems boarded up. The Church is very unpopular for siding with the landowners,' he added. That was not news to Bianca but the sight of the great church before her in such an obvious state of disuse brought home the depths of animosity between the factions in this strife-torn land. Had they traded one civil war for another?

Theodore stood before the closed shop. He saw a door and a window with drawn curtains at ground level, and another floor of living quarters above. It had a sign over the entrance but Bianca could only recognise the name Rodriguez. 'I wonder if anyone lives above,' thought Theodore out loud and knocked on the carved wooden door. The sound echoed across the plaza but it brought a quick response. A window opened above and a middle-aged man looked down at the newcomers. He spoke in Spanish, something along the lines, Bianca guessed, of 'Who are you? What do you want?'

Theodore responded with a mixture of limited Spanish and sign language, trying to convey the message that the Goldbeck family from Texas was seeking Senor Rodriguez. The man soon reappeared, opening the door and stepping onto the Plaza in front of Theodore and the wagon.

After more talk and signs, Theodore spoke to his wife as she looked down on the scene from her seat on the wagon. 'This gentleman is Senor Castillo, the manager of the shop. He lives above the shop. Senor Rodriguez lives somewhere else, further out. He will be here tomorrow. We can sleep in the shop tonight.'

The Goldbecks' first night in Saltillo was spent sleeping on the wooden plank floor of the shop, using the bedding from the wagon with the gold coins still secreted among their baggage. The horses and wagon were moved to a courtyard behind the shop, safer there from thieves, as the manager explained. Bianca was gratified at the patience of her children. Even little Elfrieda seemed to grasp that nothing was to be gained by bewailing their situation.

They had used up the last of the food and drink from Texas. Tomorrow they would have to make a start on their new life, confronting the future, whatever it might bring.

In the morning, soon after sunrise, Senor Rodriguez appeared, striding into the shop with a purposeful air. He seemed pleased to see Theodore and recognised Bianca. He shook hands with the couple and smiled a welcome at the children. His English was good, better in fact than Bianca's, and he bade them call him Manuel. Bianca's memory of the man returned from their sole meeting in the past. He had a refreshingly informal air about him. A cautious feeling of hope lifted Bianca's spirits a little. Senor Rodriguez might just be the friend they so desperately needed at this low point in their fortunes.

The shop manager set about opening the store for business. It was basically a clothing shop, with a range of other odds and ends on offer such as curtains and rugs. Manuel explained that he had several enterprises in the city, of which this shop was one. He checked daily on each of his businesses but spent most of his day at his textile and carpet factory, the one of which Theodore had spoken.

'This war of yours is bad for my business, Theodore,' Manuel said. 'Now I have lost you in San Antonio, I must deal with others. You and Fritz were my best customers. But,' he shrugged, 'life must go on. Shops will stay open. People must buy clothes even in a war – unless the battlefront comes to Texas. Do you think that may happen, Theodore?'

They chatted on awhile and a plan for the immediate future began to emerge. Manuel owned a house that was presently vacant – the Goldbecks were welcome to use it for a modest rent. 'Not a house such as yours in Texas but it will serve you for now – better than living in the wagon.' He focussed his gaze on Bianca. 'Your husband is a clever man, Senora. He can help me with my business.' He smiled reassuringly at her.

Bianca felt a surge of gratitude. 'Thank you, Manuel. Thank you.' She felt a weight lifting from her shoulders. A temporary home at least and even the prospect of employment – a promising start, good news such as she could not have expected so soon after their arrival.

'And Theodore,' Manuel continued, 'beware of thieves at all times. Nothing is safe here. If you have gold with you, tell no one. If you want to change gold to local money, do it through me. The money here is not much use anyway. We exchange goods – do you call it 'barter'?' Bianca did not know the word but she understood the message. Life here could never be easy, even if the problems of home and employment were successfully sorted out.

The house offered by Manuel was gratefully accepted but by any standards Bianca had ever known, it was little better than a shack. It was a typical local home, Theodore assured her, but a dirt floor, a filthy iron bowl in the fireplace for cooking, an old bucket in the corner for sanitation, one bedroom for them all – for a person used to life in Texas, or for that matter Germany, it was clear that living in Mexico would be a trial indeed.

Bianca surveyed the scene before her with dismay. 'My God, Theodore, how long must we live like this?'

'Let us hope for a quick victory for the Union. Once the war is over, we can go back.' Neither noticed the irony of hoping that their adopted land would be defeated in battle as expeditiously as possible.

'And how long might that take?' queried Bianca wearily, her mind scarcely registering what she was saying as she contemplated the prospect of life as a pauper in this benighted city.

'A few months, perhaps only a few weeks. The North is much stronger and wealthier and has far more men.' His words did not sound convincing.

But Bianca was barely listening as she overcame her first wave of revulsion and began to search in her mind for practical steps to make their enforced poverty bearable. She suspected they might be here for a long time. The children needed their mother to keep her wits together and not go to pieces under the strain of their misfortunes. As Judith had told her long ago, Theodore was 'a bit of a dreamer', not the most practical of men and Bianca could not rely on him to be a pillar of strength for the family. She must take on as much of the load herself as she could.

And so from these inauspicious beginnings, the Goldbeck family slowly created a life for themselves in an alien land. Manuel Rodriguez was much impressed by what he had seen of Anglo society and business skills. The fact that Mexico had not succeeded in centuries in achieving the living standards that were taken for granted in Texas suggested some lifestyle secret that had eluded his people. With Theodore as an employee, adviser and informal junior partner, he sought to improve his own ways of doing business.

Bianca and Theodore were soon made aware of the gulf that separated rich from poor, the powerful from the powerless. Even in this stronghold of popular forces, where the oligarchy of army, landowners and Church had had their grip on society prised from their fingers by repeated uprisings, that gulf remained. A man like Manuel had to tread a fine line to maintain a relatively wealthy life without arousing the envy of the poor. Hunger and malnourishment, unemployment, illiteracy, all this and more was the lot of the vast majority. Texas, and for that matter Germany, had their illiterates and their hungry and their homeless too but at least to outward appearance those were prosperous societies. Mexico seemed to have no middle class, only extremes. The numbers of the poor were quite overwhelming.

Over time, Bianca learned in many subtle ways to blend in. The Goldbecks were careful not to give any appearance of wealth for fear that they would attract the legions of thieves and robbers so feared by those who were not themselves penniless. As Theodore began to earn a meagre wage, Bianca learned to supply the family's basic needs from the local market. She bartered their Texan clothes for food and replaced them with Mexican garments, the better to avoid attention. She learned to take a live chicken home, kill and pluck it, and provide a meal on the table. Only by slowly trading in their gold coins with Manuel's aid did they avoid hunger and sickness and keep themselves clothed. As for schooling the children, Theodore and Bianca could only provide for that themselves, with the aid of the few books they had brought with them. What would happen if the gold coins ran out, Bianca did not care to speculate.

Nothing was heard of Bianca's parents or of other German fugitives. What little news flowed in from the North was deeply discouraging. Brilliant Confederate generalship more than made up for Union strength. Victory after victory came to the South. The prospect that the Confederacy would win the war, slavery would be retained and the Goldbecks would spend the rest of their lives in Mexico seemed a grim possibility. Rumours filtered down of a party of sixty German men trying to escape conscription who were ambushed by Confederates and slaughtered at the Nueces River. Wounded men were hung from trees. How could the Goldbecks ever go back to face such hatred?

As the months went by, Bianca realised that things would not get better for them. Poor food, patched clothes, the rough home she so detested, this was their lot now. Theodore, with his book-keeping and business skills, had proved his worth to Manuel, but the poor had little money to spend and so customers were few. The flow of goods to Texas was squeezed by the war now and Manuel was forced to reduce Theodore's wage even further.

It was a year before contact was made with Bianca's parents. One day they arrived unannounced on horseback. Bianca welcomed them warmly but it was in the back of her mind that if Louis had not been such an enthusiastic abolitionist, they might not be here now, might in fact be in a frontier fort with Fritz and Natalie, a much better prospect. Louis had established a medical clinic in Monterrey but customers who could pay for his services were few and it was a thin living. Theodore was delighted to see them, as Bianca rather cynically noted, and then next day they were gone and the isolation returned.

Even now, Bianca knew hardly anyone in the city. Boredom and loneliness were everyday burdens. She loved her children but she longed too for adult company. Theodore seemed to have become more reserved and taciturn, perhaps overwhelmed by guilt at having reduced his family to such a poor state. A few tactless comparisons with Fritz's better fortunes had not endeared Theodore to his wife.

Bianca's Spanish was at least serviceable by now but the local people seemed wary of a foreigner. Attempts to meet people at the market or in shops met with little success. The common folk had no reason to show an interest in her and the wealthy disdained a poor Yankee fugitive.

Her parents' visit gave Bianca an idea. She had assisted her father in his clinic and was familiar with the workings of a doctor's practice. Could there be a job for her with a local doctor here in Saltillo? A second source of income might get the family into a better home at least. She set out to investigate.

Theodore still owned the two horses and the wagon. The horses stayed in a field next to the house, their feed supplemented by hay bought from time to time, a further drain on their finances. The couple feared losing their only means of returning to their homes in the North, however remote that prospect seemed. Theodore rode one horse about on his rounds for Manuel and Bianca could use the other. She was not a skilled horsewoman, but the animal was placid and it was not practical to go everywhere on foot.

With time she located the city's doctors. Some were rough unskilled men with a smattering of medical knowledge who catered to the poor but Bianca was repelled by the conditions in which they worked. Besides, they had no need for her services and could not have afforded them anyway.

It was not easy to locate doctors, or any other service in Saltillo for that matter. One had to ask about and it became clear that a doctor wealthy enough to afford Bianca as an office worker or nurse or as any type of assistant would cater only to rich customers, people with whom Bianca did not come into contact.

Theodore took an interest in his wife's quest and asked about among the people he met. Several visits to newly discovered doctors yielded nothing. Bianca's Spanish was not good enough to field abrupt questions from busy physicians. She had difficulty describing what she had to offer or even that she was not a patient herself. She became discouraged. It was now 1863. The war had raged for over a year and a half and seemed no nearer resolution. Was this dismal hardscrabble life to be hers and her children's forever?

One day, Theodore came home with another name – Dr Carlos Leon D'Aguilar. He was wealthy, educated by all accounts and catered to the rich folk drawn from a large area in and around Saltillo. Patients would hear of him through word of mouth and his name would be unknown to those, the great majority, who could not afford his services.

And so one day Bianca found herself dismounting from her horse, dressed in the best clothes she could muster, outside an imposing house front in a better part of the city, an area she had not visited before. She had left the older children to look after the younger ones. Only the rationalisation that she had nothing to lose impelled her to go on. If she made a fool of herself again, well, so be it. Bianca had never lacked the courage to accept a challenge, though the justification for this one was wearing thin.

At her knock, a maid answered the door. In her careful Spanish, Bianca asked, 'May I speak to Dr D'Aguilar, please?'

'Is he expecting you?'

And now the little prepared speech. 'No, I am seeking employment. I am Senora Bianca Goldbeck. My father is Dr Louis Nohl and I have much experience in working as an assistant for a doctor.'

The maid opened the door wider. 'Please come in.' That was a good start, thought Bianca. She had had more than one door closed in her face. 'Please wait.' The maid pointed to a chair in the entry room and spoke some more words, apparently to the effect that the doctor was busy and would see her when he was free.

Only one other person was waiting, an elegantly dressed middle-aged woman. As Bianca had imagined, the good doctor's scale of charges would ensure that only the wealthy would be found in his waiting room. If only that could include her family, she thought. That shrinking hoard of gold coins was all that kept them from sinking further into poverty.

Time went by slowly. Another patient left and the elegant lady was conveyed to the unseen doctor by the maid. Bianca wondered how far the maid's duties extended. Would the doctor have any need for another assistant? And then the patient left and the maid returned. 'The doctor will speak to you now.'

Bianca followed her into an office lined with book shelves on which weighty tomes rested. Behind a large ornate desk sat a man of about forty. He was clean-shaven except for a neatly trimmed moustache, slim, good-looking, with dark wavy hair, expressive brown eyes and an alert expression. He was wearing a white shirt under a neat well-pressed tropical jacket. Bianca was immediately impressed. He had an air of educated sophistication about him that she had not encountered in anyone else in this turbulent country.

He had stood as Bianca entered. The maid ushered her to a chair facing the desk, then left. The doctor seated himself again and looked at her quizzically. He was silent for a moment and then he asked, 'Do you speak English, Senora Goldbeck?'

He had spoken the words in English, much to Bianca's surprise. She responded with relief, more comfortable in that language than Spanish. 'Oh yes, I do,' she replied.

'And you are the daughter of Dr Louis Nohl?'

'Why, yes,' she replied in a puzzled tone. 'Have you heard of him?'

For answer, Dr D'Aguilar rose and took a book from a shelf, then offered it to Bianca across the desk. 'Do you recognise this? I have others.'

'Oh yes, this is one of my father's books. I know it well.' This was not too much of an exaggeration. Bianca had taken a keen interest in her father's work, always proud to have an eminent physician for a father, an author of learned books.

Dr D'Aguilar put his fingertips together and gazed at Bianca thoughtfully. 'You seek employment, Senora?' She nodded. 'So you are from Texas? You escape from the war?' She confirmed his assumptions. 'Well then, there may be ways you can help me.' Bianca's heart leapt. At last, a promising response.

A series of questions followed. The doctor's English was more limited than hers and the conversation was somewhat halting but it seemed that he was determined to persist with the unfamiliar language. He asked her about her experience with her father, about the extent of her medical knowledge, and explained ways in which she might help him. The maid Panchita could be present when he examined female patients but she had no medical knowledge. He had too few patients to share his practice with a fellow physician. Then too, most medical books were in English and he needed help in understanding them. Had Bianca seen her father use ether as an anaesthetic? Yes, she assured him, a wonderful advance in medicine, now a regular practice in San Antonio surgeries.

When the visit ended, Bianca felt greatly encouraged. 'Come back tomorrow, Senora,' he said. 'Think about what we have said. I think we can help each other.'

That evening, Bianca greeted Theodore enthusiastically and told him of her visit to Dr D'Aguilar. He responded in his cautious way and Bianca felt a sense of annoyance. Was he offended by the thought of needing his wife's help in supporting the family? At times like this, her spirited ways clashed with his more withdrawn personality. She knew he felt ashamed that his actions had brought them to this place and that he could not provide adequately for them – knew too that her own sharp tongue had wounded his pride at times. Well, they would never get out of this pigsty if they waited on him. She would do whatever was necessary to create a better life for her children and if that embarrassed Theodore, then so be it.

And so began a new life as doctor's assistant for Bianca. Her salary, though humble by Texan standards, was enough to enable them to rent a better house, with a board floor, a separate kitchen, a bedroom for the boys and even a small room for Elfrieda – all simple living still but a big step forward. Money now could be found for schooling beyond what Bianca and Theodore could provide and the children could increase their skills in Spanish.

Employee and employer were soon on a first name basis, Bianca and Carlos. She found much to admire in the doctor. Though his prospects were limited by the backwardness and turmoil of his country, his dedication to his profession went beyond merely making a living. He had about him an air of quiet dignity, a calm self-assurance that appealed to Bianca. Over time their friendship grew and they began to discuss their lives and their problems. The medical profession was not highly regarded in Mexico, most doctors being poorly trained. In a male-dominated society, young women had little chance to marry against their family's wishes. More than once Carlos had embarked on romances that led nowhere when families intervened and so he remained a bachelor.

Another year dragged slowly by. News of the war came in spasmodically as random travellers from the North brought word of events, of great battles and terrible bloodshed. The Union was winning at last. Gradually but relentlessly the Confederacy was being ground down. Theodore lived in an agony of impatience. It was clear that the Goldbecks could not return to Texas as soon as the war ended. They would have to wait till the bitterness of defeat began to subside and order was restored. To return too quickly as traitors who had fled their country in its time of need could be a mistake indeed.

One evening, as Bianca prepared the family meal, there came a knock on the door. Theodore rose from his chair and moments later, she heard his excited voice, 'Bianca, Bianca, we have a visitor.'

She heard an urgency in his tone that impelled her to abandon her task and rush to the entryway. Theodore was embracing the visitor. Bianca's eyes opened wide. 'Fritz, oh, Fritz,' she cried and a moment later his arms were about her. 'Oh, do come in,' she said as he released her. 'Have dinner with us. It is so good to see you.' The children ran in and Fritz hugged each in turn, exclaiming at how they had grown.

Over dinner, Fritz filled his hosts in on his life since they had last seen him, before the terrible night when they had fled the city. He and Natalie now had three children with a fourth on the way. Natalie was well. For a long time, they had passed a tolerable existence in frontier forts out West but in the end Confederate desperation led to the conscription of anyone who could bear arms, from teenage boys to old men. Defending the frontier became a matter of little consequence. Hired thugs roamed the countryside hunting down deserters and draft dodgers. In the dying days of the South's lost fight for independence, lawlessness was rampant and Fritz judged it time to make his escape with his family. They reached Monterrey safely and Fritz found work with a local merchant as a store manager. It was a thin living but it would do for now. He had linked up with Bianca's parents and brought their love and good wishes. The war could last a few more months at most and by the end of 1865, allowing a decent interval for emotions to cool and life to return to normal, it should be safe to return.

The talk lasted deep into the night. Fritz slept at last on a couch and at daybreak he bade them farewell. Theodore was much heartened by the visit and the talk of a final end to their long exile. Another twelve or fifteen months perhaps – a long time but still an end in sight.

Bianca too was much affected by the visit, but in ways that she could not fully rationalise to herself. She was very fond of Fritz. As he swung into the saddle and rode away, she noted what an expert horseman he had become, a frontiersman indeed. She had always felt him to be a kindred spirit, with a streak of wildness in him that appealed to her, that contrasted with the cautious Theodore.

In fact, the differences between the two brothers struck her more forcefully than ever. She faced the fact that exile in Mexico had not strengthened their marriage, more the opposite. She wished for a stronger partner, a better support for her and the children through the hard poor years. Now that she was a vital source of income for the family, Theodore seemed less sure of himself than ever and the relationship between them grew ever more distant.

For a long time, Bianca would not acknowledge to herself that she had another problem to face. Slowly, inexorably, she was falling in love with Carlos and he with her. She could not tell when she had begun to feel this way. Perhaps it was the day that she had gone with him to a young woman's house, a woman dying in childbirth. Bianca had helped Carlos for hours that day to no avail and she had shared his disappointment at the loss of a young life. Perhaps it had started before that, even at their first meeting. Neither spoke of their feelings for each other but it was there, in moments when their eyes met, when they smiled at one another, when they shared a joke.

Fritz's visit crystallised her feelings. She realised with a start that she no longer yearned to leave Mexico with Theodore. The dislike for life here had been overridden by a stronger emotion. She did not want to spend the rest of her life with her husband, but rather with another man, and yet what to do about the children? Could she abandon them for Carlos? The very thought was enough to chill a mother's soul. It was an impossible dilemma and yet somehow it must be resolved before the end of the Goldbecks' time in Mexico. With the defeat of the Confederacy, a return to Texas was now inevitable.

And so events drifted on and the months passed slowly by. Bianca noted with alarm that Theodore seemed to be becoming aware of her diminishing love for him and to suspect that her relationship with Carlos had something to do with this. One night the issue came to a head and a minor argument exploded into rage.

Bianca had never seen Theodore so angry.

'What sort of wife are you?' he shouted. 'You're so cold with me now. Are you cold with your doctor, eh? I bet he sees the warm side of you. Would you rather live with him? I need a real wife. The children need a real mother.'

As the frightened children hid in their room, Bianca's rage matched his. 'A real father is what they need. I went out and worked to make more money. You couldn't provide for us. And now you're so damn sorry for yourself – moping about all the time. We need a real man to lead this family.'

'A real man – like Carlos?'

'Yes.' She fairly screamed the words. 'A real man like Carlos.'

Pent-up fury on both sides erupted in charge and counter-charge until abruptly Theodore stormed out into the gathering dusk and disappeared.

Still shaking with emotion, Bianca entered the children's room. She tried to calm them. 'Your parents have had a fight,' she said. 'All parents do, sooner or later. We are people too and sometimes we lose control of ourselves but you know we both love you always.'

The boys sat stunned and silent but Elfrieda, six years old now, was crying inconsolably. 'Why are you so cruel to Papa?' she asked bitterly. 'He is a kind man. Why do you not love him? I love him very much. I would never hurt him.'

Elfrieda had always had a close relationship with her father. Bianca had not realised that the child could take sides in this way, could see her so plainly as the one at fault. In no mood to tackle the issue now, she bade them all go to sleep and retired, leaving Elfrieda to put herself to bed in her own room.

Later that night, as she slept fitfully, she was awoken by the door to the bedroom being opened suddenly. A slurred voice spoke, the words unintelligible – an intruder, drunk. Panicked, Bianca fumbled to light the lamp but rough hands gripped her and forced her onto the bed. 'Who is it?' she gasped.

'It's your husband,' rasped the voice.

Suddenly angry, Bianca burst out, 'Oh, Theodore. What are you doing? You frightened me. You're drunk.' She had never seen him like this before. He had never been a drinking man.

'Yes, I am drunk. Did you hope it was your damn doctor?' She could barely understand his words and suddenly she was very afraid of her mild-mannered husband. He was possessed of a strength she had never known in him before and as he tore off her nightgown, her desperate struggles were unavailing. After he had forced himself upon her, he rolled over and passed into a deep sleep, snoring loudly. She lay awake for a long time, shaking uncontrollably.

In the morning, she awoke to find Theodore standing beside the bed, fully dressed. Seeing her eyes open, he spoke in a strangely unemotional voice. 'I apologise for my behaviour last night. It will never happen again.'

For the first time ever, she felt somewhat cowed by his presence. In a subdued voice, she responded, ' I would hope not. You have never treated me like that before.'

'You have never given me cause,' he replied and left the room.

Several weeks of uneasy calm ensued in the couple's relationship. Each was guarded and wary with the other, unsure whether, after thirteen years of marriage, they still had a future together. And then one day, Theodore returned home to find his wife seated on a chair, her face drained and pale. 'What is the matter?' he asked. Once he would have taken her in his arms but now he stood apart, looking down at her.

'I am going to have a baby,' she said simply. There was despair in her voice. She felt utterly weary.

Bianca saw a swirl of mixed emotions in her husband's face. In the past this had been joyful news, a cause for celebration. Now it was a disaster in their lives, a bitter blow to any remaining hopes of Theodore's for a quick end to their exile, another complication in their tattered marriage.

Bianca had already told Carlos of their fight and now of this further calamity. 'Elfrieda was to be my last child. She will be seven when this baby comes. I cannot go through all this again.' She was desperate now, panicking. What if Carlos turned her away? What if he did not care to maintain his feelings for her through all the months of her pregnancy with another man's baby? She could not lose him now, could not face all the blows of Fate that were combining to defeat her.

By now Carlos had become her source of strength, the one to rely on when she needed emotional support. Ever the gentleman, he had never made any advance before but now he knelt beside her and put his arm about her shoulders, held her close as she suddenly loosed a flood of tears. 'Have this baby, Bianca, then we will see what to do next.'

She nodded. They had developed a way of expressing their thoughts in which words had deeper meanings. He was suppressing any thought in her of terminating the birth. He was saying that later, after the birth, she must make a decision – to return to Texas with her family or to stay with him alone but that decision could wait for now. One thing at a time.

The months that followed were an ordeal for Bianca. To endure an unwanted pregnancy was bad enough but to know that she would in all likelihood have to give up this child and the other four cut to the very heart of a mother's instincts. Whenever she looked at them now, she felt as if she was on borrowed time. To say goodbye to them forever, never to see them again after all these years of motherhood, and the baby too – how could she do it? And yet what choice did she have? She could think of no other future now than to be with the man she loved, and that was no longer Theodore.

To make matters worse for Bianca and her embattled conscience, Theodore, ever the fondest of fathers, became once more the solicitous husband she remembered from their early happy years together. He wanted their family life to work again, with a new baby to draw them together. How could she tell him that this was not to be, that they had no future now, that even their children could not hold them together? She knew that Theodore would never give the children up and in any case, she could not force another man's children onto Carlos, a man with no experience as a father. It could only be a clean break – there simply was no other way.

Amelia Goldbeck was born on 25 July 1866. All talk of a long overdue return to Texas had been delayed until after the birth and Bianca insisted that she should nurse the baby for three months before there could be any consideration of a long rough trip by wagon. While Theodore waited in a state of bewildered anticipation for a signal from his wife that they could at last leave Mexico, she secretly trained the infant to accept cow's milk from a bottle and taught the uncomprehending Elfrieda how to feed her little sister.

After Bianca told Carlos of her decision to stay with him, he held her in his arms for a long time. He had won the fight for Bianca's affections and Theodore had lost but clearly Carlos understood full well the sacrifice that Bianca was making, the greatest that one could ever ask of a mother, to abandon her children forever.

The day came that she had long dreaded. The night before, she had had a nightmare. She had relived her meeting with Theodore's mother, Judith, on the hilltop lookout at the Bremer farm. 'I will not let you down, Judith,' she had said. And she remembered Judith's last words to her as she lay dying. 'Look after my boy. He loves you so much.' Now she would break all her vows to Judith, and her marriage vows too. Theodore loved her still yet she would leave him and all their children for another man.

It required all the courage that Bianca could muster to confront Theodore on his return home. 'I have something to tell you.'

She could see the alarm on his face and for a moment her heart went out to him but then she steeled herself to continue. 'I am leaving you now, Theodore,' she said softly. 'You will not see me again. The children will stay with you.'

His legs seemed to give way and he sat heavily back in a chair.

Sensing something amiss, the children had drifted into the room and watched as their father held his head in his hands and began to sob, his shoulders shaking.

Louis, the eldest, looked up at her and said gravely, 'Are you leaving us now, Mama?' He had tears in his eyes yet there seemed little surprise in his voice. She realised that they had suspected what was to come, perhaps more clearly than Theodore. Little Guido began to cry softly, tears running down his cheeks.

The three boys gathered about Bianca while Elfrieda remained beside her father, her hand on his arm. The baby slept in its crib in the corner of the room.

Bianca knew this must be done quickly. Dragging out the inevitable would only make it worse for all of them. First she stepped across to the crib and touched the sleeping infant gently on the cheek. She gazed down at her little daughter for a moment. Then she knelt to hug each boy in turn. 'You will be going home now, with your father,' she said. 'You will live in Texas again. That is better for all of you.'

She straightened up and motioned to Elfrieda to come to her but the child put her arm about her father's shoulder. Still he sat with his head in his hands, unable to look up at his departing wife.

'I love Papa,' the little girl cried out, tears glistening in her eyes. 'I will never leave him. Never.'

Bianca's tone took on a note of impatience. 'Come to me now and say goodbye.'

Elfrieda's composure crumbled and she screamed at her mother in her shrill child's voice: 'No. Go away. I hate you.'

Without a word, Bianca turned on her heel and walked out of the room. She did not look back as the door closed softly behind her.

Chapter 7

Elfrieda Goldbeck: A Family Lost and Found
Texas: 1866–1899

They had travelled this road five years before, the winding rutted road that led from Texas into Mexico. It had been a time of fear and desperation then and yet the return journey was little better. Now despair had replaced fear. At least they had been a family then, facing the future together. The loss of the wife and mother who had been at the very centre of their lives had left a gaping void that time could never fill.

Theodore sat at the front of the wagon, holding the reins, and Elfrieda sat beside him, nestled up against him. From time to time he would acknowledge her presence with an arm around her shoulders but for long periods he sat silent and stony-faced as the wagon rolled slowly on. Elfrieda feared for her father, feared that the depth of his grief would leave him mute and expressionless forever. She had lost a mother and now the thought of her beloved father lapsing into a form of living death terrified her. At only seven years old, she found the need to comfort another in his grief when her own heart was breaking was too much to be endured.

Elfrieda felt the tears coming again and cursed her own weakness. She could not bring comfort to her father if she could not even control herself. The problem was, as she realised in a half-formed way, that this was worse than a death in the family. If Bianca had died tragically, they could at least remember the good times and mourn for the loss of a loved one. But how to deal with a mother's betrayal?

Was hate the answer? Over and over the terrible scene in the little room in Saltillo played itself out and her own words echoed in her mind: 'Go away. I hate you.' Did she really mean it? What should she have said? Such thoughts tormented her endlessly.

A baby's wail came from the back of the wagon and Elfrieda awoke from her reveries. A dull feeling of resentment had lately been building within her. Had she not enough misery of her own to contend with? How could she hope to bring consolation to her father and act as little mother to baby Amelia at the same time? It was too much to expect of her. She had three older brothers – why could they not do more?

'Bring the baby to me and I will feed her,' she called to those behind her. Benno quickly responded with the baby in his arms while Guido brought a jar of the baby food that Elfrieda had prepared before they left. Elfrieda had only Bianca's rough training on looking after a baby to guide her. She hated having to take responsibility for the child. What if it sickened and died? Would she have that on her conscience as well?

She noted that Louis had not helped with Amelia. He seemed as immobilised by grief as Theodore. Guido was little better but at least he was only nine. Louis was 13. Benno was the most help and it seemed to Elfrieda that she and Benno were all that was holding the family together at this moment.

At last they arrived at the Texas border and prepared to put the sad poor countryside of Mexico behind them. They felt no joy in re-entering Texas after so long away, no sense of returning home. From brief comments of Theodore's, Elfrieda had learned to fear what Texas might hold for the Goldbecks. It was a defeated land, a lawless chaotic place occupied by a hated foe. How easily the Goldbecks could be seen as traitors returning from their safe haven, ripe targets for vengeance.

The Mexican border guards waved the wagon through, little interested in poor wayfarers leaving their country. The Texas post was manned by Union troops in smart blue uniforms. Theodore explained their situation frankly and the Union officer shrugged. He seemed not unsympathetic. 'Be careful,' he advised. 'There are cutthroats everywhere. The cities are under government control but the countryside is not safe. Best stay on the main roads and get yourselves home as fast as you can.'

Theodore thanked him for the advice and they resumed their journey. The frontier town of Laredo had first to be crossed to reach the north road to San Antonio. The town seemed as much Mexican as Texan, the people a mix of both, but already the loss of the state's prosperity was apparent. Elfrieda watched nervously around her as Theodore negotiated his way down the main street. She sensed an air of defeat that was almost palpable. There were many beggars about, lean hungry-looking men, some with war injuries clear to see. The occasional group of soldiers in Union blue was the only indication of law and order.

By the time the Goldbeck family emerged from the town, nothing would indicate to the casual eye that they were traitors returning from Mexico. They could be a homeless family on the move for a thousand reasons in this time of despair and turmoil, on their way to anywhere or nowhere, too poor to be worth robbing. Elfrieda watched ragged men on foot or horseback pass them by on the road north. By law of the occupying army no one was allowed to carry arms, but guns would be easy enough to hide. In any case, some of the men they passed looked so sinister to the child that she was sure they could kill all the Goldbeck family without the need for a gun.

On one deserted stretch of road, a lone rider approached them. He gazed at them intently before abruptly seizing the reins of their nearest horse to bring the wagon to a halt. Elfrieda felt a chill of fear. The man was as villainous a character as any she had seen in their travels. He had a lean face with a week's growth of stubble. 'What you got in that wagon?' he asked Theodore menacingly.

Theodore was surprisingly calm or perhaps past caring about anything now. 'I've got kids, hungry kids. You got some food for them?' he demanded. The three boys had by now shown themselves, seeking to find the reason for the sudden halt. Theodore spoke again, anger in his voice. 'We've got nothing but the clothes we're sitting in. We've got no money. Now will you get out of our way?'

Theodore's weary irritable tone carried conviction. The man hesitated, then gave the family one last venomous stare before swinging his horse away and riding on. Elfrieda was not sure if they had just had a close shave but it was at least another unpleasant event to add to their tribulations.

It was true that they had very little food and little money to buy more. At each day's end, they had less to eat than before and sleeping on an empty stomach was not easy. Elfrieda feared most for Amelia. She could not eke out the baby food much longer.

It was becoming a race against time to reach New Braunfels before real hunger set in, before the food was gone and the money with it, but first they had to pass through San Antonio. Elfrieda had no memory of the place, being only two years old when she left it, but it seemed a sad beaten city now, grimmer and poorer than Laredo, ragged beggars and crippled war veterans at every turn.

And then at last the day came when they were entering the outskirts of New Braunfels. Theodore had become more articulate as his home town approached. 'We will go to the Nohl house first,' he told the children, 'and hope they can help us.'

Moments later Elfrieda and the others were climbing down from the wagon as an elderly couple ushered them into their house. Soon they had warm drinks and warm food to fill themselves and Elfrieda felt her tattered nerves begin to relax for the first time in months.

Henriette Nohl's main concern was her new grandchild Amelia. 'The poor little dear,' she clucked as she fussed about tending to the baby.

Louis Nohl was an intense little man, never more so than now. 'I can't believe it,' he said to Theodore. 'My poor boy, that my own daughter would abandon you, abandon her family, even the baby, for another man. What sort of a mother could do that? You are not a drunk. You did not have other women. You provided for your family. What more could she want?' It was clear to Elfrieda that Bianca's father had taken Theodore's side entirely in the family break-up. It was comforting to see her father vindicated, and by her mother's own parents at that.

Theodore was encouraged to stay with his family at the Nohl

residence until he had restored some semblance of order to his life. Elfrieda's nerves slowly calmed under the influence of her kindly grandparents.

The day after the family's return, a visitor came to the door and called for Theodore by name. Elfrieda watched as her father reacted joyfully to the sound of the voice. The children rushed with their father to the door and watched the two men in a warm embrace, a heartfelt reunion.

Elfrieda had only seen him once before, in Saltillo, but she knew her uncle Fritz and how important a figure he was in her father's life. Both men had tears in their eyes. Then Fritz drew back a little, his hands on the other's shoulders. 'Welcome back, brother,' he said in a voice hoarse with emotion. 'Welcome home.'

Theodore was almost too overcome to speak. 'It's good to see you, Fritz. It's so good to see you. It's been a long time.'

Suddenly Elfrieda was crying copious tears. It was the first time she had seen her father show real happiness for many a long day and the joy of such a moment seemed to release a well-spring of pent-up emotion in the child. Hope could at last replace despair. They were with good people now, kind loving people. Life could begin again. They were home at last.

Louis and Henriette were enjoying the sight of the brothers' reunion as much as the children. Then Henriette said suddenly, 'Oh Fritz, your family is waiting outside. Bring them in. Do bring them in.'

The house was soon crowded with visitors. Theodore's children were introduced to their aunt Natalie and their four small cousins, four boys, the last born in Mexico and little older than baby Amelia. It was clear to all, looking at Natalie, that a fifth was on the way. The boys were all younger than Elfrieda and the house seemed full of children of all ages all chattering animatedly together while adults fussed about arranging an unplanned meal from what was available. It was a day to remember, a new beginning.

Fritz brought the news that Theodore's old home was vacant and with a little maintenance would be ready for the family to occupy. He had news about himself too. The Union administration had asked him to take on the role of Mayor of New Braunfels and he had accepted. The Union occupation might be hated by the defeated Texans but German settlers like Fritz were already outcasts in Confederate eyes so what was there to lose? New Braunfels was his home town and he had ideas for making it a better place, helping it to recover from the ravages and turmoil of the war years.

Within days the family was safely ensconced in a snug home of their own, one that had once been Theodore's but that Elfrieda had never seen before. Another special family came to visit soon after to a warm welcome from Theodore. This was the Bremers, Heinrich and Caroline, Theodore's much-loved stepfather and his young wife. There were more young children for the Goldbeck family to meet and once again Elfrieda could enjoy seeing the pleasure her father gained from being reunited with long-lost loved ones.

In the days that followed, Elfrieda watched her father begin to pull the strands of his life together again. Finding work was the first priority but with Fritz's help, Theodore found ways to make a living, involving himself in the town's administration as well as turning his hand to various practical tasks. One such task was saddle-making and with time this became a useful sideline.

As if by unspoken agreement, from that time on no mention was ever made of the missing Bianca. She had become the ghost of the family, the unseen presence, the unmentionable subject, but there were times when Elfrieda would see a look of inexpressible sadness on her father's face. Then she would know that the ghost had returned to haunt him again and she sensed that it would haunt him forever, that he would never be free of it. His heart had been dealt a blow from which it could never recover.

No one could replace Theodore's lost love but Elfrieda had resolved ever since that terrible day in Mexico that she would always be there for him, that she would never see him left friendless and alone with his memories.

Elfrieda's own memories were more than enough of a burden. At nights, in her dreams, she would hear her mother's voice again.

'Come to me now and say goodbye,' and the look of bitter rejection on her face as Elfrieda shrieked, 'Go away. I hate you.' Once more, Elfrieda would see the door close on her mother forever and she would awaken from the nightmare trembling.

A year passed by and the Goldbeck family gradually readjusted to a settled life. The four children went to school, made friends, came to see New Braunfels as home, familiar territory. One aspect of her life was special to Elfrieda. Her role as little mother to Amelia had become a central fact of her existence, a responsibility she wore willingly, unconsciously took for granted. She watched as her little sister took her first steps, spoke her first words, became a toddler fussed over by all.

Some six months after the family's arrival in New Braunfels, Louis Nohl accepted a posting as a physician in San Antonio and he and Henriette departed. Elfrieda had become very fond of her grandparents. She was sad to see them go and sadder still when word came less than a year later that her grandfather had died.

Without grandparents, it became difficult to find a carer for Amelia while the Goldbeck children were at school and Theodore was at work. Elfrieda could only do so much and she became increasingly worried as Theodore began to show concern over Amelia's welfare. Still, she was caught by surprise when the matter suddenly came to a head.

One evening, after the family had finished eating, Theodore spoke softly to Elfrieda. 'I have something to discuss with you. Come for a little walk with me. The boys can clear up.'

Elfrieda had a sudden feeling of foreboding. Something was not right. 'Yes, Papa,' was all she said.

As they walked, Theodore chose his words carefully. 'I wanted to talk to you first and then the boys after.' He paused, gazing down at Elfrieda a moment, before continuing, 'Do you know Mr and Mrs Loeb? Hugo and Barbara? They are nice people, don't you think?'

Where was this leading? Elfrieda's heart was pounding. 'Papa, what are you trying to tell me?' she asked desperately.

'Elfrieda, I cannot look after Amelia properly. The four of you can take care of yourselves but there is no one to look after Amelia.'

Panic surged in Elfrieda's breast. 'I can look after her, Papa. I can be with her all the time that I am not at school.'

Theodore's voice carried great sadness. 'She needs a settled life, Elfrieda. Mr and Mrs Loeb are childless. They will love Amelia as their own and they will never keep secrets from her. She will always know that you are her sister and I am her father. You may see her whenever you wish.'

Elfrieda was by now crying helplessly. Theodore knelt and put his arms about her small body. 'You have been so strong for us all, Elfrieda. You have helped me to live through terrible times. You have been the little mother for Amelia. This family owes you so much but you must believe me now that this is best for Amelia.' He was crying gently now too.

They clasped each other for a long time until Elfrieda's body stopped shaking and her sobbing ceased and then Theodore led her slowly home.

Elfrieda was in a disturbed state when she returned home from work. 'Papa, the young man at the grocery store told me that I always look sad. Do you think I always look sad?'

Theodore lowered his newspaper and looked up at his daughter from his armchair. His eyes twinkled behind his glasses. 'Well,' he ventured cautiously, 'Perhaps if you smiled a little more, the man might realise that you really like him.'

'Oh, Papa, you are impossible.' She shook her head in exasperation and walked off to her room. Theodore chuckled to himself as he raised his newspaper again.

Elfrieda knew that her father had noticed her visits to the grocery store, surely more frequent than necessary. When she returned from her room, he spoke up as though there had been no break in their conversation. 'His name's George, isn't it? He's a very bright young man. He came out here from the old country when he was only seventeen, all on his own. That's courage for you. He's saving to buy his own shop or maybe a trading business of some sort. He will go far, that lad.'

Elfrieda took all this in, eyebrow raised. 'Do you always investigate young men who talk to me so carefully?'

Theodore cocked his head, thought a moment and replied, 'Only the more promising ones.'

'And I take it that he has passed the test,' she inquired coolly.

'Oh indeed, with full marks.'

It had been ten years since their return from Mexico, their fifth in Austin. Old friends had found Theodore a job as Spanish translator for the city council and when he lost that post with a change of administration, he found work as a clerk at the courthouse. Benno and Guido accompanied their father and sister but Louis stayed behind working in New Braunfels. Amelia had remained there too – a happy and much-loved child, even a little spoiled as Elfrieda was forced to concede.

Now that Elfrieda had found work in a draper's shop, all four of them were employed. The household was thus in a comfortable financial state and Theodore still had three children to keep him company, to provide him with a family life but it could not last forever. Already Benno was courting Adele Kuss and it was likely the family would be reduced before long.

What would happen to Papa when they all left him, Elfrieda wondered. She had vowed long ago never to leave him lonely but she had a life to lead too, as Theodore himself had reminded her more than once. He had made it clear that he would not let any child of his grow old looking after him and miss out on a home and family for his sake. If only he would remarry, Elfrieda thought, but she knew in her heart that he had lost the love of a lifetime. Bianca could never be replaced.

The comment of George, the grocery store clerk, about her sadness had stung her. The trauma of her early years had left a deep impression and she realised that she must come across to others as both shy and serious but the notion that she carried with her an air of permanent sadness was a concern. She had made no close friends in Austin and at seventeen, an age when she should be enjoying a social life and being out and about, she was rarely away from home. She mulled over George's remark and realised that she must make a conscious effort to be more outgoing. If she was seen by others as a figure of gloom, she would never have a life.

Elfrieda decided to challenge George about his judgement of her next time she saw him. She could not deny Theodore's claim that she liked him. George Koerner was in his early twenties, perhaps five years older than herself. He had made the same impression on her as he had on Theodore. She found him intriguing. The first impression was of intelligence. He was by turns thoughtful, jovial, charming, a many-sided personality but whatever he had to say to Elfrieda was always interesting. He was not one for idle small talk. As she turned her contacts with him over in her mind, she resolved to get to know him better. Her father's approval of George pleased her. She paid close attention to Theodore's judgement in all matters.

A few days later she found herself in the grocery store once more. She was returning home from work and dropped in to make a small purchase. She pretended to be making up her mind until George was free, not wanting to deal with anyone else, then walked to the counter.

George smiled and took the item from her. As he did so, she said, 'I told my father that you said I always looked sad.' She tried to sound disapproving.

'Oh. And what did he say to that?' George was looking at her with an amused expression.

She hesitated, feeling rather foolish. 'He said that I should smile more often and then people would not say things like that.'

George folded his arms and looked at Elfrieda directly. 'Well,' he said, 'I'm waiting.'

His grin was so infectious that Elfrieda suddenly burst out laughing.

George laughed too. 'Oh, that was good. I like it. You see what you can do when you try. Not just a smile but a laugh – even better.'

Elfrieda was not sure how to take this, lacking the self-confidence to simply take his words in jest, fearing that she had made a fool of herself. He seemed to read her mind and continued reassuringly,

'I'm not making fun of you. You look so nice when you smile.' He continued then in a cautious tone, suddenly a little ill at ease himself, 'Would you let me walk you home?'

No one had ever made an offer to her like that before. Her heart leaped. 'But you have to work,' she responded and instantly regretted her negative reaction.

George was unfazed. 'It's nearly closing time.' Then he called out to the store owner. 'Mr Jones, is it all right if I walk Miss Goldbeck home?'

Mr Jones did not even look up from his ledger book. 'Sure, take yourself off.'

George pulled on his coat and escorted Elfrieda to the door, opening it and ushering her out. As they walked, he chatted pleasantly, setting Elfrieda at ease. 'I've talked to your father about his trading business back in San Antonio before the War. He is very interesting. I think he can teach me a lot. Do you think he would mind if I came to see him sometime?'

It brought pleasure into Elfrieda's heart to hear someone speak well of her father. 'Oh, he would like that,' she responded enthusiastically. 'He told me that he had an interesting talk with you. I know he would be glad to help you.'

They chatted on as they walked and Elfrieda's customary caution with others began to melt a little. 'Your father said he lives with his children. Is your mother dead?' asked George casually.

Without warning, Elfrieda began to cry. 'No, no,' she managed to say, cursing her own weakness. 'She is not dead.'

George was clearly embarrassed at having struck such a raw nerve. He motioned her to a bench they were passing and sat down beside Elfrieda, offering her his handkerchief. 'Tell me, if you wish, and I will not mention it again.'

Haltingly, Elfrieda told the story of that harrowing day. 'And the last words I ever said to her were "I hate you". None of us have ever spoken her name again.' She was by now crying freely, unable to stop.

George was contrite. 'I have made you cry when all I wanted to do was see you smile again. I'm so sorry.'

'Oh, it's not your fault.' She tried to smile through her tears, to set his mind at rest. 'You were not to know. I am all right now.' She looked at him directly, overcoming her natural instinct to cast her gaze down when she was nervous or embarrassed. She wanted very much to keep him with her, not to drive him away. 'You were right about me. I am always so sad and serious. I must smile more. Thank you for making me laugh at the store.'

She felt as if she was sounding foolish, like a child, but again his kindly tone calmed her fears. 'I've upset you enough for one walk home but I promise you I'm going to make you laugh again – you'll see.'

When they reached her home, Elfrieda thanked him for taking the time with her.

'Well, I didn't do a very good job of cheering you up but I would like another chance. May I see you again?'

She felt a wave of relief that she had not embarrassed him with her tears. 'Yes, that would be good. And you can talk to Papa too.'

'I'll look forward to it.' Elfrieda detected a warmth, a kindness in his tone that lifted her spirits and overcame her customary shyness. She smiled a goodbye as he turned to walk away.

In the weeks that followed, George Koerner became a frequent visitor to the Goldbeck household. He would hold long conversations with Theodore, seeking the older man's guidance on his plans for the future. He made friends with Benno and Guido and began courting Elfrieda. He had no relatives of his own in Texas and the Goldbecks became his family.

The year passed pleasantly. Benno married Adele and moved out to a home nearby. Elfrieda enjoyed George's company. She admired his ambitious nature and she knew that he had a great desire to have his own business, to be his own master.

One day George told her that he had discovered an opportunity in a town called Brazoria, far to the south, near Galveston. It was a small trading store, a wholesale business, buying goods in bulk and selling at a profit. With a little careful borrowing, he could buy the store. He had talked it over with Theodore.

Elfrieda's heart sank. 'How will I see you again?' she asked, trying to suppress tears.

'Would you miss me?' he countered.

'Oh George, of course I would.' She felt suddenly fearful. She could not face another cruel twist of Fate in her life. 'I don't want to lose you.'

He placed his hands on her shoulders. 'Well then, what would you say to marrying me?'

She gazed at him for a moment in stunned disbelief and then flung her arms about him and buried her face in his shoulder.

He held her close and said softly, 'I take it that was a "Yes",' but Elfrieda was crying now and in no condition to reply.

After she regained her composure, she drew back a little and looked at him with tear-stained face. 'I just want to be with you, George, always.'

'We have your father's blessing. You are only eighteen and I thought it would be the right thing to do to seek his approval first.'

'What did he say?'

George grinned. 'He said that I had made a brilliant choice and he congratulated me on my good sense.'

'I take it that was a "Yes",' mimicked Elfrieda and the two burst out laughing.

George had more to tell. He had made careful plans. After their engagement was announced, he would go to Brazoria and as soon as his business was established, he would send for her to join him and they would get married. He would invite all her family down and maybe by then he would be in a position to have Theodore live with them in Brazoria. He might even be able to employ her brothers.

It sounded too good to be true but Elfrieda's cautious nature came to the fore. 'Papa would not want to be a burden to us. He would want us to have our privacy.'

George responded reassuringly. 'We could have him live near us without being in our house. I know you fear him being lonely but he's become like a father to me and I worry about him just as much as you do.'

Elfrieda could only sigh contentedly and rest her head on his shoulder.

Next week Elfrieda said a sad farewell to George as he boarded the train for San Antonio. From there he would make his way to Brazoria and his new life as a self-employed man, a businessman, the fulfilment of a dream.

Elfrieda's natural pessimism took control. George would forget about her. He would find another woman. She would never hear from him again. Only the engagement ring on her finger gave her hope. When a week later a letter had still not arrived she was so concerned that Theodore said in amusement, 'He has to run a business, Elfrieda. It takes all one's time, you know. I've been there.'

A few days later, when Elfrieda came home from work, Theodore greeted her at the door with an envelope in his hand, a grin on his face.

Feeling sheepish about her needless anxiety, Elfrieda took the envelope from him. As she did so, he said, 'Of course, it could be bad news. He may have met someone else already and he wants the ring back so he can give it to her.'

'Oh Papa,' she responded in exasperation, 'don't even joke about such things.' Then she could maintain her seriousness no longer and she smiled back and shook her head. 'What am I to do with you? You do make fun of me.'

'Well, it makes you smile. Someone has to do it now that George isn't here.'

It was the first of many letters. As the weeks passed into months, Elfrieda heard how George's trading business was progressing well. He was paying off his debt and was enjoying success, justifying his faith in himself.

At last George sent word that he had a home established suitable for a married couple and proposed a date for their marriage, 15 April 1878. It could only be a simple ceremony. He had a few friends in Brazoria by now but the only family members would be the Goldbecks. He asked Benno to be best man. Adele would be maid of honour. Arrangements were made for them all to take leave from work and travel as a family for Elfrieda's wedding.

The last leg of the journey to Brazoria was by stagecoach from Galveston. When Elfrieda at last saw George waiting for them at the station, she could barely wait for the coach to stop before she was out and running towards him. Her customary shyness in public was cast to the winds as she hugged him for the first time in months.

George greeted Benno and Adele and Theodore and Guido as if they were his own family, as they had indeed become. Accommodation for all was arranged in the town's best hotel – paid for by himself, as George made clear.

As George had said, the wedding could only be a simple affair, with scarcely a dozen people involved, but Elfrieda had never been happier. Everyone who mattered to her in her little world was there. She had once feared growing old and alone and yet here she was, still only eighteen and about to be married. It was a dream come true. When the couple stood at the altar of the little church in their rented wedding clothes, she feared that she would cry tears of joy. When it came time to say 'I do' she said the words with such breathless fervour that those around her smiled at one another.

Only in fleeting moments during the wedding did the memory of a lost mother come to Elfrieda, a mother who would never see her children marry, would never hold a grandchild in her arms, a mother whose name, like some terrible curse, must never be spoken.

True to his word, George invited the Goldbecks to join him in Brazoria as his business expanded. By the time a year had passed, George and Elfrieda were living with Benno and Adele as neighbours on one side and Theodore and the unmarried Guido on the other. Theodore found work at the courthouse. Benno and Guido worked with George, helping him with his business, often travelling about in Texas and Mexico to obtain merchandise – cigars and tobacco, coffee, salt, foodstuffs such as cheese and fruit and much else, some sold direct to the public but most bought in bulk for selling to other traders elsewhere in Texas. Elfrieda too helped in the office with the paperwork. It was indeed a family business in these early days. As Theodore, well experienced in such matters, told his daughter one day, 'He is good, Elfrieda. He is very good. Brazoria will not hold him for long.'

On the last day of 1880, Theodore received sad news in the form of a telegram from New Braunfels. Heinrich Bremer had passed away in his sleep, one month short of his seventieth birthday. Theodore was greatly upset. As Elfrieda well knew, the unlikely marriage between the young man of good family and the older single mother of three was Goldbeck family folklore. Heinrich had in all likelihood rescued Theodore and his brothers from a grim fate as illiterate labourers in the old country. He had been a kindly caring stepfather. He had vowed to Judith that he would treat her children as his own and he had never failed to keep his promise. Theodore was away from Brazoria for a week attending Heinrich's funeral. In the days that followed his return, Elfrieda noted that he was more silent than usual. She made sure to include him in all the family activities and worked at taking his mind off his latest loss but by now she was far advanced in an event of her own, pregnancy.

After nearly two years of marriage, George decided to employ a housekeeper, Emma Boeke, to spare Elfrieda from housework. It was partly an act of kindness. Elfrieda had befriended Emma who had come alone to Texas from Germany, as George had done. George admired her courage. Her English was poor and she had difficulty in finding employment.

Elfrieda suspected another motive in finding her a housekeeper beyond doing an immigrant a favour. She knew that George was keen to start a family and she guessed he felt that lightening her already modest workload might help the process along. If that was indeed the plan, it seemed to work. Soon after, Elfrieda had fallen pregnant, much to the couple's delight.

Ella Theodora Koerner was born in Brazoria on 13 February 1881. Elfrieda at twenty-one was now a wife and a mother.

As Theodore had predicted, Brazoria was not big enough to contain a man of George's talents and ambitions. In 1882, George moved his business interests to San Antonio and took up office space in the heart of the city. Theodore moved back to Austin and lived for a while with Louis, who was then living there, and with Benno. Later he moved to San Antonio, close to Elfrieda, and on the day he died

142

in 1890 his last act had been to visit the Koerner's office to collect his mail. Elfrieda had kept her promise to her father, to stay by him always, right to the end.

Ella burst into the sitting room, eyes shining. 'Oh, Mama,' she cried out, a little breathless, 'Elsa is going to get married and she wants me to be her maid of honour.' She waved a letter, the source of the news, at Elfrieda.

Elfrieda smiled at her daughter's exuberance. Seventeen now, Ella Theodora had grown into a lively, vivacious girl, a contrast to her mother's quiet ways. 'I know, dear,' said Elfrieda, 'I have a letter of my own, from her sister Matilda.' She displayed pages of writing in her hand.

Ella was crestfallen for a moment. 'So you know already?' Then she shrugged, too excited with her news to be deflated for long. 'She is going to marry that Englishman she has been seeing. He owns gold mines in Gillespie County. He comes down from Austin to see her. His name is Robert Collinge and she says he is tall and handsome – and very rich. His family owns cotton mills in Lancashire.' She looked a little doubtful. 'Where is that? Is that in Scotland?'

Elfrieda applied some gentle logic. 'Well, if he is an Englishman, it must be in England.'

'But isn't Scotland part of England?'

Geography wasn't Elfrieda's strong suit either so she tactfully changed the subject. 'The wedding is still a long way off – about nine months, August 6 next year. Matilda says they want to get to know each other better and be sure of what they are doing. It's very difficult with her in Fredericksburg and him in Austin. And so,' she finished, ' you will have plenty of time to decide what to wear.'

Elfrieda enjoyed her children, three daughters and two sons. No doubt sons were a blessing, especially to fathers, but you could not take them shopping, try on dresses, swap gossip. She knew her girls were a little spoiled, that the good things of life had come too easily but after her own deprived early life she wanted only the best for them.

Elfrieda had learned over the years that motherhood required skills that did not come easily. When Ella was younger there had been difficult times, friction between a possessive mother seeking to direct her daughter's life and a headstrong girl unwilling to be led along paths not of her choosing. Elfrieda had come to realise that she could not let her own traumatic childhood influence her in dealing with a child who had never known fear and hardship, a child possessed of a natural self-confidence far removed from the chronic self-doubt of her mother's early life. With time, each came to realise that there was something to be learned from an opposite personality and a bond was established between mother and daughter that transcended their differences.

Life had been good to the Koerners in San Antonio. George had built up a thriving business. "Wholesale Grocer and Commission Merchant" his advertisements said, "Dealers in Fine Cigars and Tobaccos" and much else. He was recognised in San Antonio as one of the city's leading businessmen and his family was much in demand at social functions. They had a fine home in the best part of town and all the trappings of success were theirs to enjoy.

Elsa Eisfeld was the sister of Hale Eisfeld, George's store manager. Hale came from Fredericksburg, a day's trip west, in Gillespie County. Their family ties were complicated indeed. They were German Texans, like the Koerners. Elsa and Hale had many siblings, some still in Germany. A much older sister, Matilda, was married to the town doctor in Fredericksburg, Albert Keidel, and Elsa was part of their household. She had arrived from Germany at fifteen to join Matilda. Her widowed mother and another sister had emigrated more recently. Other relatives were scattered about. Dr Keidel was a leading citizen and his household was a focus of social activity in the town.

The Koerners had developed close ties with the extended Keidel family and Elsa, though four years older than Ella, had struck up a special friendship with Elfrieda's spirited daughter. The two families had visited each other a number of times and the choice of Ella as maid of honour was a special compliment to the families' friendship.

Elsa's letter had more to tell yet and Ella continued on. 'Elsa wants to come to stay with us and bring her fiancé with her so that we can meet him.'

Elfrieda laughed. 'I know, I know. She is obviously proud of him. He does sound a very interesting man. He is only twenty-four and Matilda says he is a cotton merchant. He has had high positions in the cotton trade in Lancashire and in Austin and he has mining interests near Fredericksburg. That's how he met Elsa.'

Ella fairly bubbled with enthusiasm. 'And I will be their maid of honour. Isn't that exciting, Mama? When can we have Elsa here? I haven't seen her for weeks and I do so want to meet this man of hers. All the way from England. Can you imagine?'

When the Keidel family and Elsa arrived to stay, three weeks later, the young English cotton merchant was the focus of attention as Elsa introduced him around. He was indeed tall and handsome, as promised in Elsa's letter, with a confident air, a ready smile and a cultured English accent that fascinated his Texan hosts. Elfrieda sensed a genuine warmth about him, in his voice and in his smile. He was in no way pompous or aloof as his accent might have suggested.

Elsa introduced him to Ella with the words 'Robert, this is Ella, my maid of honour.'

'My pleasure, Ella. I've heard a lot about you. I'm very pleased to meet you.' The Englishman seemed irresistibly charming and Elfrieda could see that Ella was instantly smitten.

George too was clearly impressed with the visitor and as they all sat together in the sitting room before the evening meal, Elfrieda could see that the two men of different generations had struck up an immediate rapport.

'So who will be best man, Robert? Anyone we know?' George was assuming, as Elfrieda had, that being so far from home, Robert would have to take one of Elsa's relatives unless he had someone from Austin in mind.

This had been the subject of speculation already. Elfrieda noticed that Elsa had been curiously reticent on the subject. It seemed she was leaving this particular announcement to her fiancé. Ella would be especially interested to know who her male counterpart would be at the wedding.

Robert smiled. He looked at George, then at the others. 'I have a little secret that Elsa and I have been keeping from you. My best man will be my own brother, Wharton Rye Collinge. He is four years younger than me and he's been working in Austin with me for several months now. He is a real adventurer. He travelled to Texas on an old cargo ship – all through the Caribbean. I asked him if he would take on this role and he was delighted. Elsa has met him already.'

Elsa leaned over towards Ella and said in a stage whisper, loud enough for all to hear, 'He's just great. You'll love him.'

They all laughed at that and George responded, 'There you are, Ella. Something to look forward to, eh?' Ella flushed, half way between excited and embarrassed. Meeting the best man had suddenly become an event for all to anticipate.

The months of Elsa's engagement ticked slowly by for Ella and even Elfrieda and George found themselves often discussing the wedding. It was flattering for their daughter to have been invited to play such a part. George tipped off his contacts at the *Daily Express* to the coming event but a reporter had already been assigned the task of journeying to Fredericksburg that day. This wedding would involve families well known in society circles in two cities and the fact that the groom was a titled English aristocrat made it all the more appealing – not to be missed, the editor assured George. As he later recounted to Elfrieda, it was the first he had heard of Robert being a 'titled aristocrat' but the wedding was clearly taking on a mythology of its own and he held his peace. Why spoil a good story?

The next big day would be some three months before the August wedding, a meeting of all the main parties involved. They would be greeted at the Evangelical Church in Fredericksburg by Pastor Roehm who would officiate at the ceremony. In particular, the maid of honour would meet the best man for the first time. Ella could hardly wait, overcome with curiosity. Wharton Rye Collinge – what an exotic name, she told her mother. A younger version of Robert – who could ask for more than that? Elfrieda smiled indulgently but in fact she was looking forward to meeting this intriguing young Englishman almost as eagerly as her daughter.

The day of the wedding preparations finally came and the Koerner family travelled to Fredericksburg in their coach. Moses Johnson, their black coachman, had the reins. He was as excited as any of them, Elfrieda noted. They would all stay the night with the Keidels and attend the church in the morning when Robert and his brother would arrive from Austin.

On the following day, Elsa and the Keidels and their Koerner guests arrived early at the church and were soon grouped around the Pastor in the reception hall. The coach from Austin would arrive within the hour. In the meantime they all had plenty to chat about. Elsa and Dr Keidel departed to await the coach.

It seemed to Elfrieda that only a few minutes had passed before they heard Elsa's voice calling, 'Ella.' Elfrieda was standing with Ella. They turned around at Elsa's call. She was walking towards them with Robert and a young man who seemed almost his double, a junior version, as Robert himself might have looked a few years before. The resemblance was striking.

Without waiting for the trio to reach them, Ella broke free from the group and moved swiftly towards the newcomers, extending her hand in welcome to Wharton. Elfrieda had a sudden eerie feeling, a premonition, that she was witnessing a significant moment in the life of the Koerner family.

Painting of Judith Goldbeck, aged 28 (1832).

George Koerner with Elfrieda (1879).

GEO. KOERNER,
WHOLESALE
Grocer and Commission Merchant,
COR. NAVARRO AND COLLEGE STS.

Dealer in Fine Cigars and Tobaccos. Country Merchants Will Find it to their Advantage to Write for Prices.

TELEPHONE 312

Advertisement in San Antonio city directory (1896).

Edward and Emma Collinge, with baby Wharton (1879).

Lieutenant Wharton Rye Collinge in World War 1 officer's uniform.

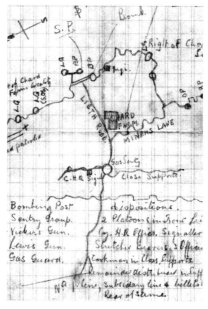

Map of local trench network found in the possession of Wharton Collinge at the time of his death in World War 1. Believed to be by his own hand.

Ella Theodora Collinge as a young woman. Photograph found in the wallet of her husband, Wharton, at the time of his death in World War 1.

Part 2

The Old World: The Cotton Mills of Oldham

The Collinges of Oldham Family Tree

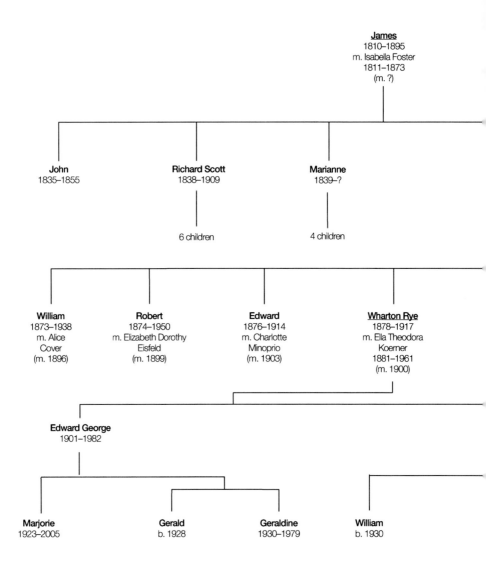

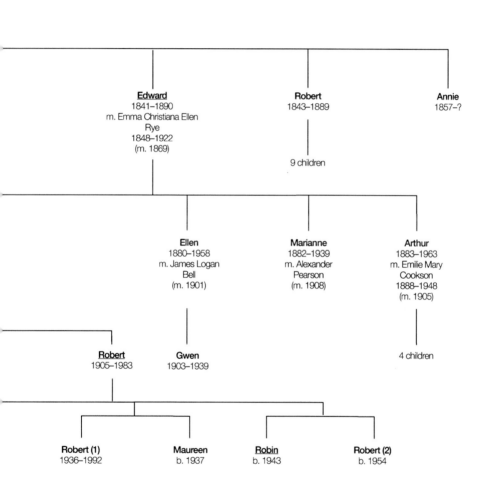

Chapter 8

Wharton Rye Collinge: A Privileged Life
Lancashire: 1888–1895

Wharton always remembered the day his father took him to the cotton mill. It had etched itself into his mind. He was only ten years old but his father wanted to teach him about his heritage from a young age. One day this would be his living. Edward Collinge took his responsibilities as a cotton mill owner seriously indeed. His father James, Wharton's grandfather, had founded the firm of James Collinge & Sons of Oldham and had seen to it that his three sons grew up to be businessmen in his own mould. There would be no wastrels in the Collinge family, no idle rich giving their occupations as 'living on own means' or merely 'gentleman' as if that qualified them for a life of spending money that they had never earned.

Wharton loved his father, knew that behind that stern demeanour was a kind heart. His father had known great sadness. A first son, James, named after Edward's father, had died at ten months, victim to a horrible death that had only been described to Wharton as "water on the brain".

After this shattering loss, it had come natural to spoil their second child, William, who had grown into a most disappointing son. William was the epitome of the lordly "gentleman of means", shrewd enough to see that a life of ease and luxury could be his without the need for undue effort. He had been born into the Upper Class, with all the privileges that a high position in society could bestow on him. Why work as if he had been born poor when the trappings of wealth were all around him to remind him of his good fortune?

Edward had determined to have no more Williams in the family. Three more sons had followed, Robert, Edward junior and Wharton Rye, all imbued by their father with the sense of responsibility and business skills that a cotton mill owner of Oldham needed to stay ahead of the competition and increase his wealth, not just live off it.

Their grandfather James, Edward reminded his sons, had not been born to wealth. As a young man, he had attracted the attention of his uncle, founder of one of the first mills in Oldham in 1817. Under his uncle's patronage, the hard-driving nephew had learned the business and had inherited ownership of the mill when his uncle retired. The original Commercial Mills on Glodwick Road had been expanded and expanded again until it employed over one thousand men and women in a vast multi-storey building, a citadel of brick and iron.

Under James's leadership, the firm of James Collinge & Sons had prospered. By the time he in turn retired to his farm in Cheshire, he knew that he was leaving the business in good hands. His three living sons, Richard Scott, Edward and Robert, had learned all that he could teach them and each was ready to work long hours in the role of major employer and leading citizen.

Wharton was a serious and thoughtful child, attributes that he had realised early in life appealed to his father. Seeing the thinly disguised contempt that Edward felt for William, Wharton worked hard to win his father's approval. The differences in the four brothers were indeed marked. Robert was clearly Edward's pride and joy, a bright, outgoing lad, interested in everything about him. Next came Edward junior, a sickly child, eager to please but prone to letting poor health hide a tendency to laziness.

Wharton also had three younger siblings. Sister Ellen was next at age 7, two years younger than Wharton. He found her somewhat cold and reserved, with a streak of sarcasm that proved less than amusing at times. By contrast, five-year-old Marianne was a delight, a bright, happy child loved by all. Then came four-year-old Arthur, a cheerful boy, ready to accept the attentions due to the baby of the family.

When they arrived at the mill on that dark winter's morning, Wharton felt a strange mix of excitement and foreboding. He had seen the mill outside before, several times, but never the inside. The mill was not a place for a mill owner's child to visit unsupervised. It was a hive of industry, operating twelve hours a day, six days a week, from six in the morning to six at night. It was a place where a thousand people worked hard, very hard indeed, for long hours amid row upon row of machinery that could inflict terrible injuries and sometimes did.

To a child, it was an intimidating place, vast and grim. Its exterior lacked any trace of ornamentation. It was a factory that produced cotton cloth for sale, a place that served no other purpose but that, and Wharton knew it only too well. One day he might help in the management of this place. One day these people could be working for him.

On arrival at the mill with his father, Wharton saw that all about in the side streets and in the empty space in front of the mill men and women in their hundreds, and children too, were gathered in eerie silence. They were waiting for the mill to open and the work day to begin and woe betide anyone who arrived late. They were not forbidden to talk but Wharton could see that out here in the cold and the dark there was simply no incentive for conversation. Another long day in the mill lay ahead of them and then back at last to the tenement home nearby for a night's rest before another early rise. The whole family would most likely be at the mill. Wharton saw children no bigger than himself. He knew that the law now forbade the employment of children under twelve but in years past every child from seven years old would have been out there waiting for that six o'clock start.

That first day at the mill had been an unforgettable experience. Wharton had not been prepared for the noise. Great unseen engines powered row upon row of spindles while the mill workers, the spinners, supervised the creation of countless miles of cotton thread, destined to be made into cloth on other floors where the weaving took place. All about hung a haze of dust, on the ground and in the air, quite choking at times. Everyone, even the children, worked with a grim intensity under the eye of supervisors who strode about watching for any letup in the flow of production. Edward had told his son that the supervisors had the authority to fire a worker on the spot and no one would take that risk lightly.

Edward had passed Wharton over to a supervisor to conduct the boy about the mill until he had walked the length of the building several times over, had seen the spinning and the weaving floors, had seen the different machines and had had their purpose explained to him. It was a lesson unlike any that he would ever experience in a schoolroom.

He saw children all about, undertaking the simplest, the most menial and sometimes the most dangerous tasks. Watching them scrabbling about under the whirling, flying machinery for bits of cotton that had fallen to the floor was an unsettling sight.

'They are so young,' he said to the supervisor once. 'They look like me.'

'No, Master Wharton,' the man replied. 'They are older than you. There are none under twelve here. That's the law. I remember when they were your age here but we have better laws now. They go to school until they are twelve. They never used to go to school at all.'

'Well, some of them don't look any bigger than me.'

The supervisor gave a wry grin, strangely lacking in humour. 'You are a big lad for your age. You live in a nice home, you eat good food. These children don't live like that. They live five to a room and they eat whatever their parents can afford.' He glanced at his young charge. 'It's a very different life for them,' he added as if to make sure that the boy had not missed the point. He saw from Wharton's serious expression that the message had found its mark.

All this and more Wharton had learned from his father as part of an upbringing that Edward by now had honed almost to an education in its own right. Wharton had even been taken by carriage through a worker's area and seen at first hand the grim rows of brick tenements that housed the mill's employees. This too was a mill owner's responsibility, to see that the mill provided all these families with homes and a livelihood.

The worker's tenements were a far cry from Woodfield, the

mansion in which Wharton had grown up, a great house of many rooms, a house in which servants glided about like ghosts. The working classes, he had noted, whether mill workers or domestic servants, seemed devoid of humour, at least in the presence of their employers. He was learning that only by long hours of dedication to their labours could workers eke out a living and that living could be taken away from them in a moment, at the whim of those who held power over their lives.

Wharton was also aware of subtle differences in his parents' approach to life. Edward did not take his good fortune lightly but Emma, his wife, Wharton's mother, clearly felt a sense of entitlement and saw nothing to discomfort her in the established order of things.

Emma had firmly discouraged her son from questioning his place in life, in the society into which he was born. 'The poor will always be with us,' she would say. There were those who were born to lead and those who were born to serve. In this way, Britain had created a great Empire, one that spanned the Earth, and who would question the basis of such success? To Emma it was 'us' and 'them'. 'They only start drinking if they get too much time on their hands,' she explained to her son one day. 'It's better for everyone that they put their time to good use.'

Wharton found himself at the centre of a large and close-knit clan spanning a range of ages and personalities enough to fascinate any student of human nature. Dominating the clan was the formidable figure of Grandfather James. Even his children called him 'Sir' and to a grandson he was a larger-than-life figure. Though long retired, he had lost none of the drive that had made him one of Oldham's leading and most respected cotton barons. He had five children living and more than twenty grandchildren and all his descendants held him in awe.

James Collinge now lived a comfortable life on his Cheshire farm, surrounded by servants, farm workers and a hundred acres of prime land. Even nearing eighty, he was still a force to be reckoned with.

A visit by Grandfather James was always an event to remember, with servants scurrying about making preparations under Emma's watchful eye as though royalty was expected. James, long a widower, would be accompanied by his ministering angels, Mrs Parkes, his housekeeper of many years and his daughter Annie, his youngest child, born when he was nearly fifty years old.

Mrs Parkes was a kindly woman who had basically dedicated her life to the great man and was perhaps the only person who showed no fear of him. Annie, by contrast, seemed like a pale flower existing forever in the shade cast by her father's shadow. More than once Wharton's ears had picked up voices saying that James had robbed his daughter of a life of her own. She was in her thirties now, they said, and had never had a suitor. He should have pushed her out of his orbit before the shroud of spinsterhood had settled over her. She would remain forever the gentle lonely soul lacking any real personality of her own.

Wharton well remembered his grandfather's last visit. James was a tall man and strong, with a ruddy complexion and a hearty laugh. Even at his age he could pick up the boy and lift him into the air. Wharton heard the fondness in James's tone and knew that he was a favourite of his. 'Catch up with me later, my boy. Tell me what you've been up to, eh?' Wharton enjoyed his grandfather's attentions, appreciated that this was not a welcome granted to everyone in the family, certainly not the unsmiling William who received a cool greeting from the visitor.

Then they were all seated at the great table in the dining room while the best of Woodfield hospitality was bestowed on the visitors. Mrs Parkes sat at table with the family, a reward for a lifetime of faithful service that had in the end elevated her from the status of servant to that of companion, nurse and friend, all in one.

As they chatted, the plates of food were brought to them by the servants – Alice, the family waitress, aided by Emma and Sarah, usually laundress and nurse when not helping Alice. James's coachman would be eating with the other servants in the kitchen.

Mrs Parkes was not actually married but with time 'Mrs' came to be seen as an honorific more suitable than 'Miss' for people of significance in the world of servants. 'Miss' smacked of spinster-hood and lost lives and wasted opportunities – the fate that awaited

Aunt Annie. All this Wharton dimly sensed. He liked Annie and, as they all did, he pitied her. And somewhere in the recesses of his mind, a voice told him that it was only a fine line between pity and contempt, that Aunt Annie and brother William were two of a kind, however different they might seem. He saw how fortunate he was to be born into such a family. He saw a life ahead of him filled with opportunity, of chances to be seized. He must not waste those chances, as Annie and William had wasted them.

As these fragmentary thoughts passed through his mind, Wharton glanced across the table at his grandfather. The old man's gaze caught his. James had a knowing look in his eyes and for a moment Wharton had a strange feeling that his grandfather had been reading his mind. James smiled at the boy as though they had shared a private moment together and then inclined his head slightly and winked at his grandson, a wink that seemed to say, 'Go to it, my boy, the world is yours.' It was a moment of shared intimacy that Wharton would never forget. To know that he had James's respect, that his grandfather had faith in him, gave him more pleasure than any compliment could ever bring.

Grandfather James presided over a large family. Wharton found himself with a legion of cousins in addition to his six siblings. From an early age he had taken a great interest in his extended family and in its history. He would listen for new stories, new gossip, even eavesdrop on his elders' conversations. In such a large family structure, he saw shifting alliances, enmities, jealousies, close friendships and clashes of personality. James Collinge & Sons was not just a leading cotton milling company, a centrepiece of Oldham society, it was a dynasty. Understanding Collinge family politics became a source of endless fascination to an inquisitive child.

The oldest of James's surviving children was Richard Scott Collinge. Wharton did not like his Uncle Richard. In some ways Richard resembled James, his father, but Wharton saw crucial differences. As he well knew, Grandfather James was a patriarch, a formidable man, one who did not suffer fools lightly but to those who knew him there was a warm side. He had at least as many close friends and supporters as he did enemies.

Uncle Richard was formidable too, but he lacked his father's warmth. Wharton saw nothing endearing in Richard Scott Collinge. An astute businessman, he had amassed great wealth yet it had reached his nephew's ears that he was known as a hard master by the mill workers, indifferent to the actions of his overseers.

Richard's brothers Edward and Robert shared responsibility for the family company with him according to an arrangement that Wharton had never quite fathomed out. It seemed that Richard basically ran the day-to-day operations of Commercial Mills while the purchase of materials and the sale of the finished cloth was dealt with by the younger brothers. Thus it was not strictly their business how Richard ran the mill, but Wharton knew that his father for one was possessed of a softer heart. 'I told him this is not 1850; times have changed,' the boy had heard his father tell his mother one evening. 'The workers are human beings. They have rights. We have laws now. We cannot treat them like slaves. Their children can go to school. If they are sick or if a woman has a baby their jobs are held for them. Richard is living in the wrong age. My father understands that but Richard won't listen. If the inspectors catch him out, he'll know about it.'

As a family man too, Richard was something of a tyrant. He had six children, four daughters and two sons, but they were little seen at Woodfield. They were quiet, dutiful children, too lacking in spontaneity or high spirits to be of much use as playmates. Wealth beyond most people's imagining had brought little happiness to this household.

The youngest Collinge uncle was Edward's brother Robert. The two brothers were lifelong friends. When Wharton was little, their families had lived in adjacent mansions at Greenhill, a prestigious address indeed in Oldham. Four grand homes had been built there in the 1840s and Grandfather James had been one of the first occupants.

Edward and Emma had later sold up and moved to Woodfield. It was a pity, because Robert and his wife Hannah were two people who inspired a special fondness in Wharton, the ideal uncle and aunt, kindly and good-natured. Their brood of nine children were just the sort of spirited playmates that Wharton treasured as visitors. He never passed up a chance to go to their Greenhill home and always looked forward to their arrival at Woodfield.

Besides his Collinge relatives another group of people inhabited Wharton's life but their impact was much lighter. They could in fact be ignored altogether if one chose. These were the servants, the ubiquitous underclass who made the processes of everyday life in a stately home run smoothly – the cooking, the waiting on table, the laundry, the house cleaning, the endless unavoidable chores that had to be performed by someone. Emma had explained to her son that those blessed with wealth had no need to wash their own clothes or cook their own food when at an easily affordable price others could be employed to do it for them. After all, these people of the poorer classes were being provided with a home and with employment preferable to the grinding monotony of a mill worker's life.

Wharton was interested in people and servants were undeniably people, even if of lesser rank. Emma had warned her children to keep their distance from the servants lest they think them over-familiar and take advantage of this to offer a poorer standard of service.

Wharton knew that servants were instinctively trained, almost from birth it seemed, to have a constrained relationship with their employers. They knew to speak only when spoken to, to "give room" when passing a master on the stairs or in a corridor, to stand perfectly still when addressed. Even to say 'good morning' unbidden was not acceptable. Their hours were long, basically all day every day, except for time off granted at the whim of a master. They were all from distant places, it being thought best not to hire local people for fear that they might desert their post too readily to visit their relatives.

Edward had a less strict attitude to the hired staff than his wife. In fact, Wharton had come to realise that his parents had different attitudes to society in general and that this placed a strain on their relationship. While Emma was aloof and condescending at best to her inferiors, Wharton noticed that Edward would often nod and offer a passing greeting to a servant and the boy took his cue from that. A 'good morning' at the start of the day left servants free to reply with their own salutation.

Wharton had heard Emma referred to more than once as a 'snob' though he was not entirely clear what that implied. She was a loving mother but some instinct warned the boy that she had a perception of others that he should distrust, that judging people entirely by their station in life was a dubious measure.

The house servants were not the only hired staff. The grounds of Woodfield were ample enough to justify a gardener's cottage with a full-time gardener, Richard Taylor. He in turn had a wife and three children, the oldest ten-year-old Catherine, the same age as Wharton. Edward had explained to his son that in these more enlightened times, children like Catherine went to school, at least until they were twelve, and learned to read and write. They would not grow up illiterate like their parents and would have at least some chance to escape the life of a mill worker or a servant.

The limits of contact between the classes was brought home to Wharton one Sunday when he was idly strolling about the estate and encountered the gardener at his work, raking leaves on a path. 'Good morning, Mr Taylor,' he said politely, not wishing to address a grown man by his first name as others might have done.

The man leaned on his rake, smiled pleasantly down at the boy and responded, 'Good morning, Master Wharton, and a fine morning it is.'

At that moment, the gardener's daughter came up to them round a bend in the path. She was caught by surprise on seeing Wharton with her father and seemed flustered. Wharton had met her once before in the garden, a month or two earlier, and had spoken to her for a few minutes. She had been nervous in his presence but so eager to talk that he was somewhat flattered by her attentiveness to his words.

Wharton spoke to her now directly. 'Good morning, Catherine. I'm pleased to see you.' Always happy to meet other children his own age, he added by way of conversation, 'I have started going to St Martin's school on Riverhouse Lane. Where do you go?'

Catherine looked up nervously at her father and he replied for her in proud tones. 'She goes to the mill workers' school on Glodwick Lane.

She does well there. She reads and writes. She even teaches me and the wife.' Before the conversation could go any further, the man motioned past Wharton to the path behind. 'I think your mother is looking for you.' His voice took on a wary tone.

Wharton turned around to see his mother beckoning. He nodded a goodbye to the other two and returned along the path, following his mother wordlessly into the house. Once inside and alone with her son, she spoke sternly. 'Haven't I told you to keep your distance from the servants? They have work to do. I saw you talking to that girl before. There is no reason for you to speak to these people.'

'I was just asking Catherine what school she went to,' he responded defensively.

'You could have asked me that, you silly boy.' She was becoming angry now. 'She goes to the mill workers' school though I don't know what good it will do her. She will end up in the mill just the same or a maid in someone's house while you go to Uppingham. Now don't do that again or I will have your father speak to you.'

Wharton was not afraid of his mother nor did he have any great urge to please her. At that moment she seemed to him more petty than intimidating but he did not want to involve his father. 'Yes, Mother,' was all he was willing to say. The matter went no further but Wharton's distrust of his mother's values was sharpened. Surely a little idle talk to a servant girl was harmless enough.

The new year 1889 brought tragic news. Uncle Robert was dying and Edward was distraught. A pall of gloom settled over the household as word of his condition came in, each report worse than the one before. Robert had Bright's disease, kidney failure, Edward explained to his children, an affliction with no cure. On 17 February he died. He was only forty-six.

It was the first time someone close to Wharton had died. The fragility of life was brought forcefully home to him. How quickly death could come, how randomly it could strike. He was torn between grief for a loved uncle and compassion for a father who seemed to have suddenly aged. Edward himself had never had robust health and

Wharton felt an awful premonition that his father was not destined for a long life either.

The funeral was a major event for Oldham. The church was packed and Wharton listened to speeches extolling Robert's contributions to the city and his worth as a man. He was genuinely popular. Later, as the funeral procession began its journey down the main street to the cemetery beyond, Wharton was surprised to see many mill workers among the mourners, conspicuous in their drab garb. They had been given a rare day off for the funeral. No one could force them to attend but many had come to pay their respects.

Wharton walked with other family members near the head of the procession, following the carriage with the hearse and the grieving widow. He walked with heavy tread. He was surrounded by other children and young folk, cousins and family friends, but he felt too downcast to speak to anyone. The day was cold, bleak, overcast, a fitting setting for such a sad occasion. His uncle's face hovered in his mind's eye, haunting in its clarity.

Lost in his thoughts, Wharton started as a hand rested on his shoulder. It was his brother Robert, namesake of his dead uncle. Wharton had never seen him so upset, fighting back tears. Robert spoke first, in a low voice, for Wharton's ears only. 'I was always proud that I was named after him. He was a wonderful uncle. Poor father will never get over this.'

Robert was fifteen now, four years older than Wharton. He had always been a pillar of strength to the younger brother, someone to model himself on, someone with whom he felt an unspoken bond. Robert was tall for his age, confident, self-assured yet kind and warm, everything Wharton could have asked for in a brother. Robert never talked down to him, never assumed the big brother role. Wharton forced a sad sort of smile. A quote from an English classics class at school came to him. 'This too shall pass.'

Robert nodded in a weary way. 'Yes, I know.' He responded with a quote of his own. 'Time heals all wounds.' Then he added, 'I doubt if that is true though. Maybe some wounds never heal. It's damned unfair anyway. He was such a good man. Look at all these people. They all loved him.'

At that moment Wharton felt a small hand reach into his and he instinctively clasped it. He looked to his side to see the tear-stained face of little Marianne, all of six years old now. The brother and sister who walked beside him were very special to him and he felt uniquely blessed. He had six siblings but only with these two did he feel a powerful bond, a desire to keep them close to him always, to share his future with them.

Robert was laid to rest under the great tomb of the Collinges at Greenacres Cemetery. James had had the tomb built when a first-born son John had died. It rose in steps to a four-sided monument where Robert's name was now inscribed. How many more names would be added in the years to come, Wharton wondered. Would his own name be there one day?

Greater tragedy yet was soon to come into Wharton's life. His father did not seem to recover from the loss of Robert. He had not been well for some time but his condition worsened. He had stomach pains and difficulty in keeping his food down, sometimes being sick after a meal. By early the following year, 1890, it was clear that he was desperately ill. He was never strongly built but now he seemed to waste away before his family's eyes.

By the time summer came, his illness had forced Edward to give up work. Emma arranged for her husband to stay with his older sister Marianne at her country home in Bowness, in the Lake District, in the hope that the country air would do him good.

Wharton, still not twelve years old, could not come to terms with what was happening to the family. Life without his father was unimaginable. In so many ways, the boy had been inspired to win Edward's approval, to do the best he could. And now that guiding figure was being taken away and Wharton knew with grim certainty that a void was being created in his life that could never be filled.

Several weeks passed and then one day Aunt Marianne and her husband arrived at Woodfield. As their presence was announced by Alice the maid, Wharton and indeed the whole household knew immediately the purpose of their visit. Aunt Marianne's eyes were red-rimmed and tears glistened. Edward had passed away in his sleep on the Thursday past, two days before, the night of 21 August 1890. He was forty-nine. An autopsy gave the cause of death as a bowel blockage, an acute constriction.

The whole household lapsed into a state of profound sorrow. Aunt Marianne took Emma to another room to offer a sister-in-law's consolation while her husband stayed with the children. All seven children were home for the summer holidays and they reacted in their various ways. The older boys tried to be manly in their grief but the younger children gave way freely to tears.

Even as he put his arm around his little sister Marianne, it caught Wharton's eye that Alice the maid had tears running down her face. Edward had been a good master as well as a kind father.

A second carriage from Bowness had brought the coffin. Now the funeral process swung into action again, so soon after the death of Robert, with visits from the minister, the undertaker and others whose purpose was unclear to Wharton. It seemed a well-practised affair in which lots of people had roles and everyone knew what to do. As befitted a citizen of significance in Oldham, the flag over the town hall was lowered to half mast for the funeral; other flags too, the Commercial Mills and the Conservative Club, where Edward had been a popular member.

Once more the children walked in a procession that ended in Greenacres Cemetery. Another name had been cut into the granite face of the monument. As he stood there surrounded by siblings, cousins and family friends, Wharton could not stop thinking of his father lying in an unseen crypt below the monument, a room that no shaft of sunlight would ever reach. He saw his grandfather James standing alone nearby, a look of utter desolation etched into his face, another son lost before his time.

Wharton looked about for the faithful Annie but he could not see her. On impulse, he worked his way to his grandfather's side and touched his hand. James looked down at him. Tears were rolling down his face. Wharton had never seen his grandfather cry before, had not imagined that such a pillar of strength could cry. Softly, so that only his grandson could hear him, James said, 'Thank you, my boy, thank you.'

* * *

That year, Wharton left home for the first time to go to boarding school. Uppingham was one of the great public schools of England. It was situated in a small village of the same name in the countryside of the county of Rutland. Founded in 1584, it still had the original school house on the grounds, like a hallowed shrine.

Wharton enjoyed his school days. He liked the feeling of the place, of great age, of tradition. Discipline was strict and bullies had a free rein, it being felt that the boys should be toughened to face the adult world that awaited them. Wharton learned to defend himself and to gather like-minded friends around him. He came to enjoy the social life, the challenge of making his mark, of being an active participant whether in sport or class work or school life. It was indeed training for the life to come and he was to remember it fondly.

At Christmas time, he was back at Woodfield for a weeklong break. Wharton found his mother strangely calm, even cheerful, not the grieving widow at all. He did not wish to see his mother unduly upset but he had hardly expected her to make such a speedy recovery from her tragic loss. He would have thought the memory of such a good husband and father deserved more respect than this.

As always he sought out the brother he had come to regard as his mentor, never more so than now when their father was no longer with them. Robert did not disappoint him, always a source of comfort in troubled times. The four years between them never seemed to bother Robert and he treated his favourite brother as an equal. Wharton liked that.

Robert had something on his mind. They talked of school life and family matters for a while, then Robert approached a new subject warily. 'Have you spoken much to your mother?'

'Yes. She seems to have got over Father's death quite quickly.'

'Oh, she has indeed,' Robert nodded. 'Would it surprise you to know that she has a man friend already?'

This was all getting a little over Wharton's head. 'Well, is that such a bad thing? Would Father want her to be lonely?'

Robert showed a touch of exasperation at his brother's obtuseness.

169

'Our father has only been dead four months and she is already much in the company of Alfred Mayall. Have you met him?'

'Yes, he has been to our house. Father knew him through business. He seems a nice man. His wife is dead. He has a daughter.'

'He may well be a nice man but Mother is not after his company. He is rich, very rich. Mother likes rich men. She liked our Father's money and his position more than she liked him. She has probably had her eye on the wealthy Mr Mayall for some time.'

Wharton was surprised at the cutting edge to Robert's words. Robert and his mother had never seemed close, but Wharton had not seen him so openly cynical before. He responded to the other's words cautiously. 'Are you wondering what becomes of us if she marries Mr Mayall?'

Robert nodded approvingly at the reply. 'Now you are thinking. Well done. It's no use me talking to William or Edward. I need someone I can relate to.'

It was a role Wharton enjoyed. 'Well, you can relate to me anytime.'

Robert gave him a friendly clap on the shoulder and the matter was closed for now but it set the younger boy thinking. Life without Father was already becoming complicated and there were unpleasant aspects to it that he could not have foreseen.

Winter passed and summer returned and with it summer holidays. Again walks with Robert provided intellectual stimulation. His older brother was a constant source of surprise to Wharton. Something new could always be learned in his company.

'What are you going to do with your life, Wharton?' Robert asked one day.

'That's a big question.'

'Well, do you want to run a cotton mill? Do you want to be like Uncle Richard?'

Wharton could see a debate coming, some intellectual sparring. 'Not greatly. Well, I don't want to be like Uncle Richard. I don't want to work for him either. Do you have an alternative?' He looked up at the older boy. 'You have been thinking again,' he observed. 'I can tell.'

Robert laughed. 'Oh, I think a lot. I think all the time.' He gave

Wharton a penetrating glance. 'Have you ever thought of going to America – to the USA?' he added as if the younger boy might not have heard of the place.

Wharton grinned. 'Oh, I do know where America is. They teach Geography at Uppingham. And why would you go there?'

'Because that is where our cotton comes from. We send buyers over to Texas each year to get the best deals for us. Why not keep it in the family, eh?'

This was a novel thought. 'You want to be a cotton buyer?'

'For a start, yes. But after that, who knows? They call it the Land of Opportunity. I have talked to buyers who have been over there. There is a lot more happening there besides cotton. There is gold mining, cattle ranching, new factories – lots of things,' he finished airily.

'Well, when you have got it all sorted out over there,' Wharton responded flippantly, 'let me know and I will come and join you.'

He was surprised to see Robert take him seriously. 'Yes,' the older boy said thoughtfully. 'I just might do that.'

After they parted, Wharton shook his head in amusement. Time spent with Robert was never dull.

Rumours were already swirling of Emma's involvement with Mr Mayall. They were going beyond mere acquaintances to being regular companions. Mr Mayall was a frequent visitor and no expense was spared in providing him with the best dining that Woodfield could provide. It was becoming apparent to the older children at least that Emma was living an expensive life for a widow. She still had six servants to support, school fees for a growing number of boarders, indeed a way of life little changed from when a husband brought in a good income. Even William and Edward, neither noted for their powers of perception, were moved to comment. Robert's assessment of Emma's interest in Alfred Mayall was beginning to look shrewd.

That Christmas, 1891, the announcement was made. Emma Collinge would marry Alfred Mayall in February. Woodfield would be sold. Those of the Collinge children who wished to follow their mother and take up residence in the Mayall household could do so, at least for the time being. They were all well provided for by their father's will and could easily afford comfortable lodgings elsewhere if they chose.

Wharton took all this in with some trepidation. Not surprisingly, Robert was moving on. He would soon be eighteen and finishing school. He had negotiated a job with Uncle Richard in the office at Commercial Mills. William too was leaving the family but his interest in finding a job was less pronounced. Nevertheless, after some delay, stung perhaps by comparisons with Robert, he also found himself work in the mill office. The other Collinge children, all still at school, had little choice but to stay with their mother for now.

One unclear aspect in all this planning was the status of Jessie Mayall, aged twelve, the only child of Alfred Mayall. Wharton was kept informed by Robert who had a knack for tapping into servants' gossip. Whenever the owners of great homes visited one another, they took household members with them – at least the coachman who drove them about and personal servants if they were staying a day or two. Servants relieved the tedium of their existence with gossip about their masters and mistresses. Robert had found that a wealth of information stood to be gained with the aid of the odd cigar or knick-knack.

It seemed, Robert explained to his young listener, that Alfred was not a strong character, as well as being a rather distant father. Jessie had picked up an early dislike for Emma and the feeling was mutual. Jessie had a favourite aunt, somewhere in the country, and had announced her preference for living with her. When Alfred would have demurred, Emma encouraged him to accept the child's plan and he submitted to her will.

'And so,' concluded Robert, 'the Collinges move in and poor Jessie moves out. A fine state of affairs, I must say. I want no part of this whole business.' Wharton could only agree but some years of school lay ahead yet, so he would have to bide his time.

One more surprising piece of news marked the closing of the year 1891. Word spread that Aunt Annie, the sad lady condemned to a life in her father James's shadow, had married. When he heard this news from his mother, Wharton was at first incredulous, then delighted. She had married Piers Harry Leigh, from a manor house not far from

James's Cheshire farm. His family was active in the cotton trade and Annie had met him through her father, then conducted a romance beneath the old man's nose. She had slipped away from the farm one day to a quiet wedding in a nearby chapel. James was then informed of his daughter's altered status. A fait accompli, as Emma put it, and nothing James could do about it. 'Good for her' was the reaction of one and all.

The rest of Wharton's school years passed uneventfully. Life in the Mayall household in school holidays was pleasant enough. Alfred was an undemanding stepfather and Wharton knew how to stay out of trouble with his mother. She had her favourites among the children and he was certainly not one of them but it did not trouble him. He had no respect for Emma's values, including her desire to impress others by spending Alfred's money. Little of the fondness that he had felt for his father had attached itself to his mother, especially after her speedy remarriage, but he was living in her household so he should not be too ungrateful.

Robert had done well at Commercial Mills. He had learned the art of ingratiating himself with Uncle Richard who was glad to find that a bright and enterprising Collinge might be groomed to be his successor. Richard's own two lacklustre sons had shown little promise in the presence of their heavy-handed father, always quick to find fault and slow with praise.

All this Robert passed on to his younger brother and protégé. Wharton was learning a lot about success in the world of business just by allowing himself to be tutored by his worldly-wise brother. As the saying went, Robert was a young man who was 'going places' and Wharton was an eager pupil.

'You see,' explained Robert one day, 'Uncle Richard thinks I want to have a career like his and that I'll follow in his footsteps forever. I've raised the issue of going to Texas the next time he sends his buyer over there to negotiate with the cotton traders. The buyer usually goes once a year, in August. Austin is the city where the big cotton houses get together to sign contracts with the likes of us. I've said I want to learn all aspects of the business and it would be good experience for me. He has never been there himself.'

'So what did he say?' Robert's casual self-confidence always amused his younger brother. Now Robert was gulling the notoriously hard-headed Richard Scott Collinge, no mean feat.

'Oh, he thought it was a great idea. I think he is telling people he thought of it himself.'

Wharton laughed. 'And what will he think when you don't come back? He thinks you will succeed him one day – a Collinge running Commercial Mills. How are you going to do that from Texas?'

Robert smiled. 'With great difficulty, no doubt. But don't worry – I will be back.' He shrugged, then added, 'This time, at least.'

When Wharton came home for the summer of 1895 he had just turned seventeen and his school days were over. Sad news awaited him. Grandfather James had finally succumbed to old age at 85. Wharton had caught up with the grand old man at every opportunity during his school holidays and had seen his steady decline. He regretted not being able to attend the funeral and pay his last respects. He had learned a lot about life from his grandfather.

A note awaited Wharton from Robert asking for his brother to visit him without delay. He found Robert in a rare state of excitement. 'I leave for Texas in a week's time,' he exulted. 'I go on the *Germanic*, a real ocean liner, from Liverpool. Three weeks to New York, then the train to Texas. I'm going to see the world. Not bad for twenty-one, eh? I am going with Uncle Richard's buyer, James Beckett. He's about thirty. Good man. Lots of experience. He's been there before.'

Wharton had never seen his brother so stirred but he had more to tell.

'I have a job for you too. I have told Uncle Richard that you are a young man of great promise, and a Collinge to boot. He loves to keep the family name going. Those poor sons of his are scared witless of him. You can start at the bottom, like I did. I've told you a lot already. You must show Uncle respect of course but be prepared to stand up for your rights. He respects people who stand up to him as long as they do it the right way. No one in his family has ever worked that out. I hope you don't mind me organising your life for you but you weren't around to discuss it.'

Wharton moved to set his brother's mind at rest. 'No, no, that's fine with me. You make it too easy for me, following in your footsteps.'

Robert clapped his hand on the other's shoulder, his special gesture of comradeship. 'Plenty of time to show what you're made of. You know, Uncle doesn't think much of poor William. He really just tolerates him for the sake of the name Collinge. William hasn't got much going for him, and he doesn't even use what he has got.'

Early in August, the whole family, Emma and Alfred and all Emma's children, were at the Liverpool docks to see Robert off on his travels. Wharton had never seen an ocean liner before and the vast size of the SS *Germanic* awed him. They all had the opportunity to go aboard in the First Class section and visit Robert's cabin.

Emma was impressed. Luxury always fascinated her and this was a floating hotel, the First Class section at any rate – sumptuous furniture and fittings everywhere, a grand staircase; nothing was too good for the elite of society in their journey across the Atlantic.

Robert had one last quick word with Wharton before they parted. 'Give the job your best shot, Wharton. I'll be back in November. There's a big wide world out there just waiting for us.' His enthusiasm was infectious and Wharton felt the stir of adventure in his blood. He blessed his good fortune in having a brother like Robert.

Chapter 9

Wharton Rye Collinge: Preparations for a Journey
Lancashire: 1895–1897

Robert was expected to be away for about three months, returning in November. Half of that time would be travelling, getting to Austin and returning by train and ship. Wharton spent the time in a fever of anticipation. He had hoped for a letter from Texas and finally it came. In fact two letters came, one for his mother and the rest of the family and one for Wharton alone. He felt uniquely privileged. It was a measure of the special place that he had come to occupy in Robert's life.

The tone of the letter was positive in the extreme. Robert waxed lyrical about the USA. like a latter-day Columbus discovering the New World. He used the word 'dynamic' several times. The sheer unbridled drive that unfettered capitalism had brought forth in the American people, the pursuit of the American Dream, the vastness of the land – it had all combined to fire the ambitions of a young visitor used to the cloistered confines of the Mother Country.

Robert had enjoyed the voyage to New York and the long journey by train to Austin had been a great prelude to cotton business in Texas. He had talked to everyone he met and had amassed a wealth of information about the country before he even reached his destination. Learning about the cotton business in Austin would take more than one short visit but with James Beckett's help, he had already gained useful knowledge. The Commercial Mills was only one part of the process. Robert had seen a lot more of the cotton trade now than the spinning and weaving. It would help too, thought Wharton that James Beckett, as an employee of Uncle Richard's, would want to make the best impression on a young man who might be of great importance in his future. It must be obvious to all that Robert was being groomed for a management role, even eventually to succeed his uncle. Another generation of Collinges was on the rise and Richard would certainly want to keep the succession in the family if he could.

Dealing with Uncle Richard was an art in itself and Wharton had been carefully schooled by his brother. Richard certainly had little of the warmth that Wharton had found in Grandfather James but being Richard's nephew was clearly an advantage. Under Richard, the Collinge name opened doors but nevertheless Richard was no fool. Even a Collinge had to prove himself worthy of promotion as William had found, languishing now in much the same clerical position as he had started. The older brother had been easily surpassed by Robert in his rise through the ranks.

Wharton realised that although he had something of an unfair advantage over others, he must still work hard to exploit it. Though he found office work less than inspiring compared with dreams of travelling to Texas, he kept his feelings to himself. Instead he applied his best efforts to his first taste of paid employment and sought to learn all that he could about the business of running a cotton mill. It was all good experience. It would stand him in good stead for whatever the future might bring.

The day came when Wharton was once more standing at the Liverpool dock watching a tall ship berth in its ponderous way. Gangplanks came down and then an interminable wait for the brother he had said goodbye to from this same spot three months before. This time only Emma was with him. The others were all at school or at work. He would not have seen fit to take time off either but Uncle Richard in an uncommonly jovial mood had personally asked Wharton to go to welcome the travellers back from their journey on his behalf. By now Richard was quite convinced that it had been his idea for Robert to spread his wings on company business.

They were joined at the dock by James Beckett's wife and children, eager to see their husband and father again. As the two men were suddenly spotted coming down a walkway from the upper deck, their families rushed to greet them. Robert hugged his mother and brother simultaneously in an uninhibited way. As the two groups walked away together, Robert talked animatedly about his journey. He included James Beckett and his family in the conversation. The two were clearly good friends by now, more than just travelling companions. Wharton sensed a new maturity in his brother – a man of the world now, returning from his overseas adventure.

In the days that followed, Robert had the opportunity to tell his brother at length about his experiences in the USA. The New World had clearly not disappointed him. The energy, the drive, the boundless optimism of a young nation had had a powerful effect on the young Englishman. He had learned much about the American end of the cotton business but he had broader ambitions than that.

'There is a different feeling over there, Wharton. People are not so set in their ways as they are here. They're not all stuck in their damned classes like we are. Anyone can make it big there. It doesn't matter what your background is. Sure, it helps to be born rich, the same as anywhere, but you can make it on your own there if you're smart and you're ready to work hard. They love the "rags to riches" story. Abe Lincoln started in a log cabin and no one ever held that against him.'

It was fun just listening to Robert. The stilted life at the Mayall residence seemed less appealing than ever. The two agreed that after the younger ones came home on their school holidays, Wharton would leave home and share lodgings with his brother. But first Emma had planned a delayed Welcome Home dinner for Robert when all the family could be together.

It was a pleasant evening. Alfred proposed a toast to the returning traveller and they all joined in. It was plain that Emma and Alfred thought that Robert was destined for a long and successful career in the cotton milling industry, tutored by the vastly influential Uncle Richard. Only Wharton knew how far that ambition differed from Robert's real intentions.

After the meal, as they mingled in the sitting room, all in good humour, all family tensions put aside, Wharton felt a tinge of guilt that he took his family ties so lightly. He was looking forward to leaving home. He had not told anyone yet of his plans, other than Robert, and the effect of that decision on his mother and stepfather and siblings had not troubled him. Now he realised that he was leaving all this behind, leaving the bosom of his family forever, and he felt a tinge of sadness.

He had had little chance yet to speak to Marianne, now all of thirteen, growing up fast, a vibrant young lady with an easy self-confidence. She took Wharton by the arm. 'Come with me, Wharton,' she said imperiously. 'You and Robert have some explaining to do.' She drew him with her to where Robert stood, talking to others. She caught his eye and with a motion of her head signalled him to come to her.

'Now,' she said, 'I have the two of you together.' She looked up at Robert, a look of mock seriousness on her face and said sternly, 'I have a brother who goes all the way to Texas, the first Collinge to go anywhere that I know of, and he only sends two letters – one for his very special brother' – she poked Wharton in the ribs – 'and one,' she continued, 'for everyone else.' She let that sink in for a moment, then added, 'I didn't even get to see it until everyone else had read it. And so,' she continued, 'next time, I will have a letter of my own.'

Robert was enjoying his sister's performance. In a contrite voice, he responded, 'Very well – the next special letter I send from Texas, I promise, will be to you.'

'Be sure to tell me all I will need to know when I go there myself,' continued Marianne.

Before anyone else could respond to that, Ellen chimed in. 'You go there?' she said with a touch of scorn in her voice. 'Who would you go with? You can't go all that way on your own.'

Marianne replied lightly, 'Oh, you never know. I might just surprise you one day.' The others took it as a joke but Wharton was not so sure. He detected just enough seriousness in his sister's tone to make him wonder if there could be an element of prophecy in her words. Was she already planning for an adventure of her own? Perhaps he might not be the only one to follow in Robert's footsteps.

***

Life settled into a comfortable rhythm once more. Wharton joined Robert in his lodging house and Robert resumed his employment at Commercial Mills. The old year passed and the new one, 1896, came in.

The brothers discussed Robert's plans for the future at great length. Next time he would not return from Texas, at least not for a long time. He would seek to make his fortune there and work life out as he went. He had made useful contacts at Austin on his previous trip and he had many half-formed ideas but it was not possible to go with a detailed plan for his future. Nor did he want to – it would be up to him to make the most of opportunities as they arose. Sometimes Wharton would sit back and watch with amusement as Robert strode up and down and tossed ideas around. It was an exciting time in Wharton's life and the future seemed filled with promise.

Uncle Richard was entirely in agreement with Robert's plan to go alone to Austin this year. He would be his own buyer this time – no need for a James Beckett to provide leadership. It would be August again, once more on the *Germanic*.

'Will you wait till you get to Texas before you resign, Robert?' asked Wharton one day.

Robert had clearly thought this out already. 'No, that would be a rotten thing to do to Uncle Richard. He's been very good to me. I'll tell him of my plans to stay on in Texas. I'll offer to arrange the contracts for the year, as he expects, then leave his employ and move on.'

'What if he takes it badly? What if he says he will send someone else? He will certainly be disappointed in you.' Wharton was playing devil's advocate now but in any case, Robert's plans were of critical importance to him personally. He had come to accept beyond question that his future was bound up with Robert and with Texas. He had had enough of office work at the mill by now to know that, like Robert, it was not for him.

Robert reflected a moment. 'Well, I'll go anyway. I will just have to pay my own way. Maybe not First Class in that case. Maybe I'll go Steerage and see how the other half lives.' He shrugged. 'Anyway,

180

I don't think it will come to that. There is more to Uncle Richard than people see. I think he wishes he had done more with his life than just work and get rich. His brothers' dying was a great shock to him. I think he really envies me, being young and going overseas.'

Wharton nodded. One did not usually think of Richard Scott Collinge in such human terms but Wharton had seen enough of him by now to see that the man was more complex than others appreciated.

More months passed and the time approached when firm arrangements for Robert's voyage needed to be made. Robert requested a meeting with his uncle.

This was a major milestone in Robert's life, and by extension in Wharton's. When Robert returned after what seemed like a rather long time, even for such a complicated discussion, he had an odd expression of bewilderment on his face. Wharton had been ready for either elation or disappointment but he gathered instinctively that something unexpected had happened.

He had to wait till they arrived home that night to have his curiosity satisfied. As soon as they had thrown down hats and coats, Wharton asked somewhat breathlessly, 'Well, what happened?'

Robert shook his head in a distracted way. 'Tell me, have you ever heard of Alice Cover?'

'No, I don't know anyone called Cover. Does her family live in Oldham?'

Robert smiled in amusement for the first time that evening. 'No, her family lives in Surrey, on a farm. In fact her father is a farm labourer, almost certainly illiterate, and Alice is a maidservant at the Cleggs.' The Cleggs were a leading cotton milling family with close ties to the Collinges.

Wharton was becoming a little exasperated. 'Robert – will you please stop being mysterious and get to the point.'

Robert spoke the words slowly and deliberately. 'Our brother William claims to have fallen in love with a servant girl and plans to marry her.'

A stunned silence followed. 'My God,' said Wharton finally. 'What does Mother think of that?'

'Needless to say, she is horrified.' Robert mimicked his mother, throwing his hands up and proclaiming, 'What will people say? We will be a laughing stock. We will never live this down.'

Wharton gave a wry grin. 'Probably true too. So how does this affect you?'

Robert poured them both a glass of claret before settling into a chair. Clearly he had a lot more to tell. 'Uncle was very gracious about my intention to leave his employment. He said he envied me the chance for adventure in the New World and he would appreciate me making the buying arrangements for him for the next year before I left his employ.'

'So far, so good,' interjected Wharton.

'Yes, but then he said this was dependent on me performing a favour for him. That is when he told me about William and Alice Cover. It seems Mother has been around crying on his shoulder and our scheming uncle hatched a plot. After all, he doesn't want the Collinges embarrassed either and William is an employee of his so that brings it closer to home.'

'Go on then. What's the plot?'

'I take William to Texas and make a buyer out of him. He hopefully comes back from overseas all fired up with ambition for his new career and by then has forgotten all about Alice Cover.'

Wharton looked at his brother incredulously and then burst out laughing. 'So you will be William's mentor – or is it nursemaid? Does Uncle expect you to perform a complete personality change on William?' He reached for his glass as the humour of the situation continued to grow on him. 'I think you would be better off paying your own way on the ship and going Steerage. You never know. You might meet a nice servant girl of your own to marry.'

In mock-serious tones, Robert responded, 'Master Wharton, sir, your sense of levity does you no credit.'

But Wharton's sense of levity was not to be stifled. 'Oh this is priceless,' he continued. 'Marianne will love it.' Their sister's contempt for William was well known. Then he became more serious and added, 'Has anyone met this Alice Cover? Is she a beauty, a new Helen of Troy?'

'I don't know. I don't think Mother has met her either but she has already decided she is a scheming little bitch trying to get her hands on a piece of the Collinge family fortune.'

Wharton was still trying to absorb this extraordinary turn of events. 'Could they be genuinely in love? You know, Romeo and Juliet and all that?'

Robert's tone turned cynical. 'Money aside, what does William have to offer to set Helen of Troy's heart a-flutter?'

Wharton conceded the point. William's mental laziness was apparent to even the most casual acquaintance. His vague, detached personality seemed hardly likely to fit the role of romantic suitor.

Robert had one more thing to say. 'Here is a good saying to remember. Uncle Richard said of William that 'weak men are stubborn because they mistake stubbornness for strength'. In other words, William will not give Alice up lightly. He will think he is being strong in persisting where a better man would back down.'

Wharton turned the words over in his mind appreciatively. He and Robert were both keen wordsmiths. 'That's good,' he said. 'Very fitting.' A thought struck him. 'I take it William has agreed to go to Texas?'

'Yes – and your next question is: Why does our stubborn brother not just refuse to go?'

Wharton nodded. 'And the answer is...?'

'Because he buckled under the combined pressure of our mother and our uncle. Those two are pretty formidable together. It would take a lot stronger person than him to withstand that. Oh, and by the way, the Cleggs will be packing Alice Cover off back to Surrey without delay. Poor William didn't realise what he was up against when he threatened Mother with a scandal.'

'No, indeed,' murmured Wharton, marvelling at the extent of the plan that had been concocted to thwart William's romantic ambitions.

The next few weeks passed swiftly and then it was the night before Robert's departure once more on the *Germanic*. Wharton was apprehensive. Robert was so much a part of his life that it did not seem possible that he was off overseas once more and this time with no intention of returning in the foreseeable future.

'I'll miss you, Robert,' he said with evident sincerity.

'I'll miss you too, brother. Come and join me soon. I'll need a partner out there in the West. It's a tough place.' His tone too was serious.

Then Robert held out his hand. Wharton clasped it and said, 'Partners it is then. I won't keep you waiting long, I promise you.'

At the dock with Robert next morning, Wharton was surprised to see not only William and Emma waiting for them but Uncle Richard as well. As they prepared to depart, Robert shook Richard's hand and said with conviction, 'Thank you for everything, Uncle. You've taught me a great deal.'

Richard's reply held a tone almost of wistfulness. 'It's been a pleasure, my boy. And if you ever come back, there will always be a job for you at Commercial Mills.' Wharton knew just how much of a compliment this was for Robert. The much feared Richard Scott Collinge was not known for the human touch and here he was seeing his nephew off in person even though Robert was leaving his employment.

Richard shook William's hand too but the feeling was different. The sulky look on William's face boded ill for his mother's plans and for William as a travelling companion for Robert. This was not a partnership with a future, Wharton judged prophetically.

It was only a few weeks before the first letter came from Texas for Wharton. It contained an assurance that a letter had also gone to sister Marianne, as well as one to Emma for the family. As expected, William was proving a poor companion, lacking both talent and conviction for the task at hand. Otherwise, the cotton buying was proceeding and as Uncle Richard's agent, Robert was signing the necessary contracts with the company's best interests at heart. He would write again after he had discharged his duties for his uncle and sent Richard the final details.

As it happened, other letters followed soon after. A brief note to Wharton told how William had not wasted a day in Austin after the contract signing but had already departed post haste for New York en route for home and Alice.

William made no contact with his family and they were not even aware of his return to England until invitations arrived in the mail from London to each family member for his wedding to Alice in two weeks' time, on 5 December 1896 at St Luke's Parish Church at Chelsea. Wharton marvelled at the speed of William's actions. Scarcely three months had gone by since his departure from the Liverpool dock and already he had returned to England from Texas, tracked down Alice and rushed her to London for marriage. Everyone, Wharton included, had underestimated William's determination. If this was stubbornness, William had certainly taken it to extraordinary lengths. Then again, Wharton mused, maybe it really was love, on William's side at any rate.

Emma called a meeting of the family, consisting only of Wharton and Edward, the younger children being still away at boarding school. Edward still lived at the Mayall residence. He had by now found himself employment in a publishing house, free of the cotton business and any entanglements with Uncle Richard.

Edward had always been closer to William, to some extent sharing his lacklustre personality. He volunteered to represent the family at William's wedding and the others agreed with some relief. Edward even promised to arrange a letter of introduction for William to the London head office of his publishing house. William would need employment sooner or later. He was not used to life as a member of the working class but eloping to London with a servant girl was not the best way to endear himself to the mother who held the purse strings.

It was to be many years before Wharton would meet his eldest brother again but the whole affair set him thinking about the nature of life partner he would hope to find one day. From the few girls his own age with whom he had had a passing acquaintance, he had formed some sour impressions. The shallow type, well-bred and very proper, with limited interests beyond showing off to her peers, was not for him. Nor was the eager social climber, fascinated by titles and wealth. He decided that he wanted a wife who had a mind of her own, someone who would not be afraid to challenge him, someone he could respect as an equal. It occurred to him that the description fitted his own sister Marianne's personality, that she was something of a role model for him, a standard to measure by. It was an interesting thought.

Meanwhile, Wharton's own immediate plans were developing quickly. Much as he admired his brother Robert, he was beginning to feel a little tired of living in his shadow and following in his footsteps. Would he take passage in the SS *Germanic* and travel by the direct route to New York and then train to Austin, as Robert had done? Or would he find a more original way to get to Texas?

He began making inquiries into more roundabout ways of getting to the USA, such as travelling via Portugal and Brazil, but he wanted to bring an element of adventure into the journey, not merely take a longer voyage. He began to investigate merchant shipping that took fee-paying passengers. One caught his eye. The SS *Louisianian*, a small merchant ship of the West India and Pacific Steamship Co Ltd, was setting off from Liverpool for New Orleans via the Caribbean early next year, 21 January 1897.

Wharton's curiosity was aroused. He made further inquiries. The cost was very reasonable, less than Steerage on the *Germanic*. That was a consideration, for Uncle Richard would certainly not be paying his way.

The cost suggested that conditions might be even more dire than the *Germanic's* lowest class but he could not expect to go adventuring in comfort and the list of ports that the *Louisianian* planned to visit was enticing; Trinidad, Panama, Jamaica, Cuba en route to New Orleans and potentially other stops if required for cargo or passengers along the way. It would take six or seven weeks for the *Louisianian* to reach its namesake state in early March.

Here was the opportunity for a bold move indeed. He felt a thrill of excitement, and a shiver of fear. He was only eighteen. Leaving Oldham and setting off for Texas was a big enough step as it was, without wandering the Caribbean on an old tramp steamer on his way there. And then he would have to make his way from New Orleans to Austin. He noted the tonnage of the *Louisianian*, 2385, less than one tenth that of the *Germanic*. His family would think he had taken leave of his senses. Probably Robert would too. Well, if he wanted to show his family that he was capable of some originality, of thinking for himself, this would certainly do it.

He steeled himself to take the necessary steps. First he made his way to the Liverpool office of the West India and Pacific Steamship Co Ltd. It was an amiably musty place manned by salty old sailors retired from the sea. Clearly cargo was the lifeblood of the company, passengers merely an extra. Usually about a dozen passengers left Liverpool but more would likely be picked up in the Caribbean. The ship had six passenger cabins with bunks for four in each. It had not occurred to him that he would be sharing a cabin with strangers. He had a lot to learn, he realised. This was going to be a far cry from First Class on the *Germanic*.

He was not going to turn back now. He paid a deposit to hold a place for him, the balance to be paid two weeks before departure. Before that, he would have a chance to visit the ship at the Liverpool dock and could still change his mind but by now the prospect of embarking on an adventure that was uniquely his own had stirred his blood. He had never even been on a ship, except the *Germanic* at anchor, but nevertheless the die was cast.

Wharton had not told anyone of his wild plan, too afraid of the realistic objections they would surely raise. He waited until the first night the family was together again for the Christmas holidays before making his announcement. As he spelled out the details, he saw a range of predictable expressions, beginning with a mother's concern that her son was embarking on a dangerous mission. Alfred was befuddled that a person would give up a promising career so needlessly, Edward and Ellen were unable to comprehend a spirit of adventure that they entirely lacked. Arthur, thirteen now, seemed simply puzzled by it all, unsure how to react. Only Marianne, predictably, showed enthusiasm.

'That's wonderful, Wharton. What fun.' Her eyes sparkled. 'You must write to me from every port and I will save the stamps in my collection.' He did not know that she had a stamp collection but she was a girl of many interests.

He nodded agreement. 'Very well.'

'And not just Marianne,' chided his mother. 'We would all like to hear from you. And if you fail to write we will assume that you have been kidnapped by pirates and will notify the authorities.'

Wharton grinned. 'I think this is blackmail, but I'll do as you say.'

Having negotiated one hurdle, he now faced the next, informing his uncle. The departure date was only a month away and Christmas Day came in between. He had better get it over with quickly. Next day he applied to Richard's secretary for a meeting with his uncle, the manager, and was given a time the day after.

The morning of the meeting arrived and Wharton felt apprehensive. Uncle Richard was never a man to be taken lightly and resigning from his employment after such a short period of work made him feel guilty. He had been well looked after in the office of Commercial Mills. A promising career had clearly been in store. Even Robert had stayed for several years. Richard was entitled to feel cheated.

By the time he was ushered into the manager's office, Wharton felt decidedly ill at ease. Richard gestured to him to sit in a chair facing his desk and gazed at his nephew a moment before speaking. 'I suppose you are here to tell me you're off to join that brother of yours in Texas?'

'Yes, sir.' Wharton was caught off guard by his uncle's insight.

'The *Germanic* doesn't leave till February. Do you have some other ship in mind?'

'Yes, sir, the *Louisianian*.'

'Never heard of it.'

Wharton explained about the ship and the roundabout route that he would be taking to get to his destination.

Richard paid close attention to his words and there was a note of approval in his tone when he responded. 'Well, well, the impetuosity of youth, eh. You're really out to do Robert one better, aren't you? And what does your mother think of this?'

'She says that if I'm kidnapped by pirates, she will notify the authorities.'

Richard gave a hearty laugh. 'And what then? The Royal Navy

will send a gunboat to the Caribbean? Even the Collinges don't have that much influence.' Wharton had never seen his stern uncle so amused before. Then the mood passed and he became pensive. 'You know they call me a heartless old devil and I suppose they're right but if I had my time over again I would do just what you're doing. Get out and have an adventure while you're still young enough to do it. I'll tell you what I'll do for you. I'll write you a letter of introduction to a couple of the main cotton houses in Austin. I did the same for Robert. You'll need a job to get you started. Collect them from my secretary tomorrow.'

Wharton stood to leave. 'Thank you, sir. I really appreciate all you've done for me. I have learned a lot working here.'

'Pity it wasn't longer. You've got a good head on you, Wharton.' A thought struck him. 'I expect a letter now and then – let me know how you're getting on. I'm still your uncle, you know. Haven't heard from that brother of yours yet, so I expect better from you.'

Wharton smiled. 'It will be my pleasure, sir. I won't let you down.'

The weeks passed quickly, Christmas came and went, and then two weeks before departure, the *Louisianian* was in dock. Wharton had his first chance to see the little steamer that would be his home for the next six weeks or more. He would have another day to make up his mind, then either pay the balance or bow out and lose his deposit.

Marianne accompanied him to Liverpool, having delayed her return to school by several days. She was determined, she said, to see "Wharton's banana boat" as she had christened it. The unbridled enthusiasm of a fourteen-year-old was a tonic to her brother who was plagued by moments of doubt. At eighteen, he was taking on a journey that would daunt an older man and at the end of it, what then? What would he do in Texas? How would he even get there from New Orleans? He could see a lot of major unknowns in this course that he had set for himself.

The ship did not disappoint. It was old, rusty, cluttered, with six small cabins even more cramped than Wharton had feared. Most of the ship was cargo space. It was clearly everything Marianne hoped for, even if the sight did nothing for her brother's peace of mind. 'Oh, Wharton,' she breathed. 'It's like something out of *Treasure Island* – my favourite book. Oh, if only I could come with you.'

'I wish you could too,' he responded. 'I could do with the company.'

When they met the captain, the analogy with *Treasure Island* seemed even more apt. Captain Tost was a leathery, weather-beaten man of entirely indeterminate race, a classic sea dog from an adventure novel. He seemed a jovial type, shaking hands with them both and playfully suggesting to Marianne that she sign up for the voyage there and then. As he assured her, 'You'll learn more about the world on this ship than you ever will at school.'

Wharton asked how many passengers there would be.

'Supposed to be twelve, but three dropped out.' The captain laughed. 'Probably took one look at the old girl and lost their nerve. Well, better off without them, eh?'

Marianne was entranced. As they walked away, she bubbled with delight. 'Oh Wharton, what an adventure. Oh, I do envy you.' Not for the first time, Wharton blessed his good fortune in having a sister like Marianne. It would be a long time before he saw her again. He would miss her.

Wharton had already written to Robert in Austin telling him of the unorthodox route by which he would be travelling to Texas. He had no house address for Robert, only the cotton brokerage, and he hoped that the letter would reach him. He had not heard from Robert for a while now and was unclear about his movements.

The day came at last, 21 January. The younger siblings were away at school. His mother and Alfred were there to see him off, and Edward, his brother. Without an adventurous bone among the three of them, they clearly all thought he was a little mad to embark on such a voyage, especially after they had seen his cabin. Still, he appreciated them taking the time to come. How long would it be before he saw another familiar face?

The other passengers, all eight of them, were saying their own goodbyes on the dock. Wharton would have plenty of time to meet them later.

The ship's whistle blew. The time had come. One last round of hugs from his family and then he turned away to walk the rickety gangplank to the slightly heaving deck. He would not have firm ground under his feet again until the other side of the Atlantic. The gangplank was pulled back and the *Louisianian* slowly drew away from the dock. It was with very mixed emotions that Wharton waved goodbye to the distant onlookers until he could see them no more.

Chapter 10

Wharton Rye Collinge: Southern Hospitality
Texas / Lancashire: 1897–1905

Wharton leaned on the rail of the *Louisianian* and gazed out at the flat expanse of water. Nearly three weeks into the voyage and the novelty of shipboard life had well and truly worn off. He wondered how Columbus's sailors must have felt after many weeks of this and no sight of land. At least the age of sail had passed. On windless days like this the ships of Columbus would be becalmed, no further forward, while the *Louisianian* with its sturdy engines could press on regardless of the wind, or lack of it.

He was joined at the rail by Margaret Lewis, a missionary's wife, en route to Jamaica to join her husband. She had returned to Liverpool to attend her dying mother. She was quite some years older than Wharton but pleasant company.

'Looking forward to land, Wharton?'

'Oh, yes.' His reply was heartfelt. 'I've finished *Treasure Island* that my sister loaned me, and *Moby Dick*. I'm running out of literature.'

'I can loan you *The Last of the Mohicans* if I can borrow your *Moby Dick*.'

It was a deal. Passing the time each day was becoming more difficult and boredom was setting in. The passengers were a mixed lot. The McIver family, mother, father and ten-year-old son, were going all the way to New Orleans. Mr McIver was taking up a position as manager of a branch of a major British bank. To his credit, in Wharton's eyes, he had chosen this unorthodox route to show his family a different view of the world than they would see from an ocean liner or a cross-country train. The son, Michael, had accepted the role of only child on a ship full of adults manfully and never complained.

Dr Ken Kaiser was an expert on tropical diseases on his way to do field work in Cuba. He was an interesting person but little given to conversation, content to pass the time with his medical journals. Of the remaining three, two were on their way to Jamaica – a Mr Roxburgh and a man whose name sounded like Grettian. Wharton's conversational approaches brought little response so he took the hint to mind his own business.

The last passenger was a mining engineer, Len Jerrard, on his way to Panama in connection with the ongoing dream of a canal to link the Gulf of Mexico to the Pacific. He told Wharton of the disastrous French attempt of 1889. The Americans were known to be planning another try at the task. Jerrard's company was out to gain information that could enable it to play a part in such a venture. He proved to be an agreeable companion.

As for the dozen or so crew, they were a polyglot group drawn from the seaports of the world and to a man appeared to speak no English or to show any interest in the passengers. Captain Tost was a genial type but generally busy with his work. He was half Jamaican, half European, child of a sailor of unknown nationality who "went native" as the captain put it and settled down with a local woman in Kingston. In due course, he moved on, never to be heard of again, leaving behind a mother with two small children. Tost had gained some schooling and worked his way up from deckhand to captain – no mean feat. Not for the first time, Wharton blessed his own good fortune in being spared the challenging task of fighting his way out of poverty.

The meals were basic in the extreme but plentiful. At least hunger was not an issue but a bland diet centring on potatoes and salted meat and oily soup made mealtime a less than exciting prospect.

Captain Tost had one pastime to offer his passengers to while away the evening hours. After dinner, he would produce a deck of cards and offer a game of poker. Bets were in pennies and limited to three pence maximum. The captain had a large jar of pennies and halfpennies which players could purchase with their own larger value coins. It was harmless fun since even with the least skill or the worst luck no one could make more than a small loss. Wharton became captivated with the game and had soon learned a new skill.

At night he shared a cabin only with Dr Kaiser. He knew the ship would become more crowded after they reached the Caribbean but for now he had room to spare. The McIvers had a cabin to themselves, as did Margaret Lewis.

At last Trinidad, a British colony and their first port of call, was only a day away. Captain Tost had a word of advice for the passengers – stay on the main streets where the crowds were and beware of pickpockets and prostitutes. The latter, he assured them, carried a variety of diseases to pass on to the unwary. This was Dr Kaiser's area of expertise and he echoed the captain's words, adding a warning to be careful what food they ate away from the ship. The captain ended with another warning, that anyone not back for the scheduled sailing time would be left behind and their possessions taken on to the New Orleans office. The prospect of being stranded in a Caribbean port alone with only the money he had in his pockets was not a threat that Wharton took lightly.

Next day the passengers crowded the railing to see their first land in what seemed like a long time. It was a colourful scene at dockside, a chaotic mix of small craft and canoes jostling for position and beyond the dock could be seen palm trees with parrots flying about. All around were black people in brightly coloured clothes. It was as exotic a picture as Wharton could have hoped for, as far removed from the Liverpool dock as if he was on another planet. Home already seemed a long way behind.

He went ashore with Len and Margaret, the missionary's wife and the mining engineer, a strange pair of companions for an eighteen-year-old, both in their thirties, but they were the two with whom he felt the most comfortable. The town, Port of Spain, may have been desperately poor but it was still a fascinating blend of the tropics and black culture, as alien a society as he could have asked for and it entranced him. The beggars and the prostitutes were indeed out in force but he quickly learned to ignore their approaches and to enjoy the myriad of strange goods and merchandise for sale in the markets and the little shops that fronted the winding street leading up from the dockside. He had written letters in advance to his family, Marianne, Robert and Uncle Richard and these were now posted with colourful stamps on the envelopes, sure to please his stamp-collecting sister.

By the time the three returned to their floating home, Wharton was well content with his day ashore. It surprised him to realise how his cramped shipboard cabin had become his home away from home. Indeed where was home now? Was it a lodging house in Oldham? Was it the Mayall residence? It really did not matter. The future was everything now and the prospect was exciting and intimidating in equal measure. But for now the *Louisianian* was home.

The next port of call was the Dutch colony of Curacao. It was an unscheduled stop but Captain Tost had been asked in Port of Spain to deliver some machine parts to Willemstad, the port of Curacao, and he was not one to miss a profitable diversion.

Willemstad proved to be a neat little town with Dutch style houses lining the main street, a quite enchanting place, and once again Wharton had a pleasant day ashore with his two companions.

The next port would be Colon in Panama. Len Jerrard would leave the ship there. By now several new passengers had joined the *Louisianian* on its meandering journey from port to port but they were Spanish-speaking and of little interest to an eighteen-year-old without a word of another language except some Latin and Greek he remembered from Uppingham. Useless languages, he reflected. Why couldn't modern schools teach modern languages?

Colon proved to be a depressing place, more grim than exotic. Margaret and Wharton had said goodbye to their engineer friend and Len had gone his way, intent on a journey into the interior. After taking in the port scene, Wharton admired the man for his courage in tackling the place alone.

The ports that Wharton had visited so far had at least a veneer of European civilisation bestowed on them by their colonial masters but Colon seemed a lawless place. With Margaret beside him, he took a short cut down a narrow alley connecting two streets. He sensed something vaguely sinister about the grim-faced onlookers at the doors of the tenement homes. As they emerged from the alley, a black man in a nondescript uniform stopped them.

In halting English, he asked, 'You from the ship? You walk down that street?' He pointed back the way they had come. They nodded. 'That is dangerous place,' he continued. 'You follow this street and go back to the ship.' He pointed the way. 'Go on now.'

'Thank you,' replied Margaret and to Wharton, 'I think we had better do as he says.' That was as much of Colon as he saw, or cared to see. It was a reminder that his safety was not something to take for granted in foreign ports.

The next stop, a couple of days away, would be Kingston, Jamaica, Margaret's destination. The two had become good friends. Margaret's husband Dan belonged to a Protestant missionary society that specialised in setting up schools in deprived communities to bring literacy to children who would otherwise have no education. Jamaica, an English colony, presented no language barrier. The Lewises had two children who attended their parents' school with the local children. It sounded a noble enterprise and Wharton showed interest. This clearly put an idea into Margaret's mind.

The day after leaving Colon, she asked, 'Wharton, why are you going to New Orleans when your destination is Texas?'

He could see she had something in mind. 'Well,' he replied, 'that's where this ship goes. There weren't too many choices if I wanted to see something of the world on the way. You don't see much just crossing the Atlantic on the *Germanic* like my brother did.'

'So,' she continued. 'Here is an idea. Stop off at Kingston and stay with us a week or two. You could tell the school children about your life in Oldham and the cotton mills. It's all good learning for them. Then catch a ship direct to Galveston. They go from Kingston.' She let that sink in for a moment then added, 'You would have to pay for another ship passage but you would save the train trip from New Orleans so it wouldn't be much extra.' She smiled as a thought came to her. 'Anyway, if your family owns Commercial

Mills at Oldham, money should not be a problem.'

The prospect of such a drastic change to his plans took his breath away for a moment. Then he shrugged and smiled. A new adventure beckoned. Why not? 'It sounds wonderful. Thank you very much.' And so another twist was added in his circuitous route to Texas.

Wharton explained the change of plan to Captain Tost who he knew felt some responsibility for his young passenger. The captain approved. 'I'm glad to know you'll be in good hands. I'll be catching up with my family too in Kingston. I won't see much of them this trip but I get a few months off in the hurricane season when the ships don't run.'

What a bizarre world the captain inhabited, thought Wharton. Imagine taking your holidays in the hurricane season – what better reason for a break could there be than that?

When the ship docked at Kingston, Wharton collected his bags and said goodbye to the captain and the other passengers. He shook hands warmly with Captain Tost, as unlikely a friend as he could have imagined, as far removed from the cotton mills of Oldham as anyone he was ever likely to meet.

Dan Lewis and his children were waiting for Margaret at the dockside. He was a tall lean man of about forty, the children two boys about eight and ten. The reunited Lewises hugged without inhibition – a close knit family. Then Margaret introduced her companion. 'Dan, this is my good friend Wharton Rye Collinge. He is on his way to Texas to join his brother. I said he could stay with us a week or two.' She gave her husband a meaningful look and added, 'The Collinges own Commercial Mills.'

As he shook hands with the youth, Dan raised an eyebrow. 'Commercial Mills in Oldham?'

Wharton grinned. 'That's the one.' He was beginning to feel as if he belonged to some sort of commercial royalty.

Dan turned to his wife. 'You do have expensive tastes in friends. What is this young man doing on the *Louisianian*?'

'Looking for adventure,' she replied.

Dan's face broke into a broad grin. 'Oh well, we'll see what we can do about that. I'm afraid our humble abode will not pass as a mansion but it should compare favourably with the *Louisianian*.'

Wharton already felt comfortable with his new host family. For now it was impossible to plan ahead. He would just have to see what the future brought. He had made no plans for meeting Robert in Austin, though his brother would surely worry if a long time passed without word.

A carriage was waiting with a black man at the reins. Wharton was introduced to Luther, the coachman. As they travelled in the carriage, Dan explained that the education they gave was free, their wages being funded by the missionary society. A small number of otherwise unemployed men like Luther were hired for a few necessary tasks. It was clear that money was short and a simple life for this family was a necessity.

A week with the Lewises passed quickly. He met the two other teachers and was introduced to the three classrooms for different grades up to twelve years old. The children they taught were bright and eager to learn and it humbled him to reflect on how lightly he had taken his right to an education. Even the mill workers' children had some schooling but the students here in Jamaica, only a few generations removed from slavery, would receive none at all without the missionaries.

The Lewises encouraged Wharton to tell the children of the world outside, about his own life in the great mother country that had colonised so much of the Earth. He told them of the cotton industry and of his journey to Texas. He could not have asked for a more attentive audience in each classroom and he felt that in a small way he had brought a little extra knowledge into their lives. He tried his hand at a few English classes, teaching spelling and grammar for the small children.

The time came to leave. Wharton was welcome to stay longer but the SS *Augusta* was leaving for Galveston and he knew he must seize his chance. He had written to everyone, bringing them up to date with his news, but he did not want to disappoint Robert with another long delay. With no telegraphic service in Kingston, he had to rely on the Royal Mail. At least all the stamps in the colonies were pretty – Marianne would not be disappointed.

Before he left he offered to pay for his accommodation but, as he expected, they would not take money from a guest. He had an alternative in mind, a donation to the missionary society, and this was accepted gladly.

In no time it seemed, his stay in Jamaica was over and he was saying dockside goodbyes, a familiar ritual by now. Once more he was waving a sad goodbye from a ship's railing as a chapter in his journey ended and another began.

The voyage to Galveston was unexciting. It was a straightforward passenger ship with none of the character of the *Louisianian*. The day came when Galveston appeared on the horizon. Wharton had mixed feelings. A life at sea had begun to appeal but it was time to move on.

After a night in a waterfront hotel, he found his way to the main train station and was soon on his way to Austin. As he watched the Texas countryside pass by, he had time to reflect that he was at last in the United States, the country that had occupied his plans for the future for so long. Was Robert even in Austin now? The only address he had for him was care of the General Post Office. However, in his last letter Robert had said that he had taken up employment with Fraser & Sons, one of the cotton brokers for whom Uncle Richard had provided a letter of introduction.

Wharton could only make his way to the cotton brokers' office and work it out from there. When he arrived at the address, it was a more imposing building than he had expected. Fraser & Sons was no small enterprise. His name seemed to mean nothing to the secretary in the front office and she asked him to wait while she took his letter to a manager. As he settled into a waiting chair, he felt decidedly ill at ease. What if no one had ever heard of Robert Collinge?

He was soon ushered into a manager's office, a Mr Clyde. The man had already read the letter from Uncle Richard and Wharton explained that his brother had preceded him in Texas and was believed to be with this company. Mr Clyde grinned. 'Well, we'll have to see what we can do for you,' he said in the Texas drawl that still sounded so unfamiliar to Wharton's ears. The manager pressed a bell to summon an assistant. 'Get Mr Collinge for me, will you?'

Wharton could not believe his good luck. When, a moment later, the door opened again and Robert walked in, a cheerful smile on his face, a wave of relief swept over Wharton. He walked towards Robert with his hand extended.

'Oh, don't give me that stiff upper lip stuff,' responded Robert. 'You're not in Oldham now. This is Texas.' He enveloped Wharton in a bear hug, unconcerned about their presence in the manager's office.

Mr Clyde spoke up. 'Take an hour off, Robert. Buy the lad a coffee. He's come a long way to see you.'

Moments later, the two were seated in a coffee shop nearby. Robert was eager to hear about his brother's journey through the Caribbean. After Wharton had told his story, Robert explained his own circumstances. He had been six months with the company now and was content to stay a while yet while he planned his next move. His experience at Commercial Mills was prized here and he had settled in easily. He was confident that, with a letter of recommendation from Uncle Richard, a place would soon be found for Wharton. The names Richard Scott Collinge and Commercial Mills carried a lot of weight in Fraser & Sons.

And so once more, Wharton settled into a role prepared for him by his enterprising brother. As before, Robert had found lodgings with Wharton in mind and within days a home and a job had been provided for him.

Wharton found Austin to be an attractive city with parks and gardens and, as capital of Texas, a magnificent Capitol building only recently completed. He saw a growing number of motor cars in the streets, vying for place with the horse-drawn carriages of old. Robert had been in Austin long enough to have developed a circle of friends and life soon settled into a comfortable pattern. One thing Wharton did not like about Texas was the fierce summer heat, and that, coupled with a vague sense of homesickness for the familiar world he had left behind, made him realise that he would in the end return to England. He did not think of himself as a migrant then but rather a visitor enjoying an adventurous interlude in his life. He turned nineteen that July. He had plenty of time yet to continue the unplanned life – the future could take care of itself.

Robert's mind had not been idle in his brother's absence. He had looked into various forms of investment and with a couple of the other young cotton brokers was considering buying shares in a gold mining venture in Gillespie County, some seventy miles to the west, a day's journey by stage coach. Gold had already been found in the area, not enough to spark a gold rush but in commercial quantities nonetheless. The gold was found in leads in the local quartz deposits and the crushing machines needed were expensive items, beyond the reach of businessmen in Fredericksburg, the county capital.

Robert and two companions from Fraser & Sons had bought shares in a venture to buy the quartz-bearing land and supply machinery. Robert had travelled to Fredericksburg to weigh up the situation personally and returned convinced that it was a sound proposition, based on contracts drawn up by a reputable firm of local solicitors.

Wharton was only too conscious of the risks of being caught up in a fraudulent scheme designed to swindle the unwary. The local papers often ran cautionary tales but Robert assured his brother that these were usually 'get rich quick' schemes that promised huge rewards. The Gillespie County venture was a sound investment promising comfortable returns but no more. It would not leave them so rich that they would never need to work again.

As the months went by, and the investment costs were recovered, returns began to come in. In due course Wharton made his own modest investments and some way into the new year, 1898, he joined Robert on a trip to Fredericksburg.

It was a pleasant town, a string of shops and office buildings lining a modest main street. There was a strong German flavour. Fredericksburg had been founded fifty years ago when a wave of German settlers brought over by a short-lived immigration company had created settlements in the area. The company had then gone bankrupt leaving thousands of settlers to fend for themselves. A cautionary tale, thought Wharton.

Robert took his brother to see the site of their holdings, a rather desolate place of diggings and machinery, where workmen laboured in the heat to break up the rock for crushing.

A trip to the lawyers' office followed. Wharton had already viewed all the relevant contracts. He saw little point in the visit and voiced this feeling to Robert, who responded, 'I have something to show you.' Robert enjoyed a touch of mystery. Wharton realised something was afoot. Robert had made quite a number of trips to the town at weekends in the past few months, more than seemed necessary. His interest in the place had begun to seem a little odd. He generally stayed overnight when a day trip might have been practical. A frequent coach service ran between the two counties yet even this time they were booked into the local hotel.

The secretary at the front desk was an uncommonly pretty young woman. She had fair hair, blue eyes and a complexion that seemed little affected by the Texas sun, all of which Wharton took in in an admiring glance. The lady welcomed Robert with a smile and a familiar greeting. He was clearly known to her. 'So this is your brother,' she said, 'the one who sailed around the Caribbean.' Her accent added to her fascination, part Texas drawl, part European, a recent immigrant perhaps.

Wharton stared. Suddenly it was all falling into place. Robert's secret was out. He was courting a country girl and he had more in mind on trips to Fredericksburg than checking on quartz leads and crushing machinery.

Robert was enjoying the moment. 'Elsa, meet my brother Wharton, come all the way from England to keep me out of trouble.'

She laughed. 'Oh well, he has obviously failed at that, hasn't he?' Wharton was fascinated. She was quite delightful. Robert had struck gold in Fredericksburg in more ways than one.

'Wharton,' Robert continued, 'meet Elsa Eisfeld.' They shook hands, such an American gesture, so much more friendly than the nod of the head that would pass for recognition between the sexes in England.

Wharton looked at his brother. 'I take it we didn't come here to check the contracts?'

'No,' he replied, 'we came to have dinner with Elsa's family tonight. I told them all about you so naturally they were keen to meet you. And now,' he added, 'we must let this lady get on with her work. We will see you at seven,' he said to Elsa by way of goodbye.

As they strolled off down the main street, Wharton could hardly believe what he had just experienced. 'You sly dog. How long has this been going on?'

'Oh, six months or so. I didn't know if anything would come of it. It's hard to get a romance going when you are seventy miles apart but we both want to pursue it to wherever it leads.'

'Sorry to be practical,' persisted Wharton, 'but what do her parents think of her having a beau from far away who is hardly likely to settle in Fredericksburg?'

An explanation followed. 'She lives with her married sister and the sister's husband and their children. He is the town doctor, Dr Keidel. Elsa came out from Germany about eight years ago to live with the Keidels. The mother is a widow. She came out three years ago but she hardly speaks any English. Elsa has lots of brothers and sisters. Some are in other parts of Texas and some still in Germany.' Wharton had lost the thread about halfway through this account but he gathered Elsa was part of a large extended family and by no means a treasured only child. That would help if Robert was to take the fair Elsa away, perhaps far away.

Dinner that evening was an outdoor feast, all seated at a long table laden with food. It was more German style than Texan. Wharton ate bratwurst sausages and schnitzel and dumplings and strudel and other foods whose names he had never heard before. It was an introduction to a way of life that was quite new to him and he enjoyed himself enormously. The Keidels were gracious hosts and it was plain to see that Robert was already virtually one of the family. Always gregarious and party loving, he fitted in easily. Elsa sat between the two brothers and saw to it that the new guest was made to feel at home. She had a charm and an elegance that left him envious of his brother's good fortune.

Steins of beer loosened tongues. At one point, Dr Keidel stood up and called for silence. 'I would like to welcome Wharton Rye Collinge to our household. He arrived in this country on what his sister,

I am told, refers to as "Wharton's banana boat".' They all laughed at that. 'So now, Wharton, would you like to tell us something of your journey?'

Wharton stood and gave an account of his voyage, ending with thanks to his hosts for their welcome. A round of applause followed. By the time the two of them retired to the hotel, Wharton was tired but happy after a remarkable night. 'Robert,' he said in a slightly slurred voice, 'you have found me the perfect sister-in-law. You are a lucky man.'

Robert grinned. 'I haven't proposed to her yet.'

'Well, you had better hurry up or I will,' were Wharton's last words for the night.

Life returned to its steady rhythms and Robert's weekend trips to Fredericksburg continued. The day came when he told his brother that proposal time had come. On this visit he would ask for her hand in marriage and seek the agreement of her family. The latter was only a courtesy as Elsa had no father and was quite capable of making her own decisions as an adult. Robert returned to Austin exultant. He had been accepted. Next he would find an engagement ring in Austin, there being little of choice in Fredericksburg.

'So when is the wedding?' asked Wharton in his forthright way.

'Well, we all thought a long engagement was best. In all honesty we don't know each other as well as a couple should to take such a big step. Being so far apart is a problem. We will marry in a year's time and get to know each other better in the meantime.'

This seemed a curious line of logic to Wharton, still only twenty and used to short time horizons, but he assumed that mature people of twenty-four had a better understanding of these matters.

As time went by, marriage plans fell into place. The ring was obtained and the engagement was announced at a party in Fredericksburg to which Wharton was invited. The church was selected, the Evangelical Church in Fredericksburg and the vicar who would officiate, Pastor Roehm. The date was set, 6 August 1899.

'Next,' announced Robert one day, 'I need a best man to attend me at the wedding, someone who knows me well and in whom I have complete faith.'

Wharton could see where this was leading but he feigned ignorance. 'So did you have someone in mind?'

'Who else but you, brother?'

Although it was hardly a surprise, Wharton was still touched. 'It will be my pleasure.' They shook hands on it as they had on that now distant day when Wharton had committed himself to following Robert to Texas. He would be just turned twenty-one at the time of the wedding. He had packed a lot into his life before he had even reached adulthood.

Robert had broached the issue of where the married couple would live. A temporary home in Austin would be a start but for the longer term he had come to the same conclusion as Wharton, that England was home. This caused some concern to Elsa's family but in truth she was an adventurous person with no great attachment to outback Texas and no ties to her relatives that she could not break, if with some reluctance.

One day it occurred to Wharton to ask Robert, somewhat tongue in cheek, if the bride would have a best woman, equivalent to the best man.

'She is called the maid of honour,' explained Robert. 'Elsa has a brother, Hale Eisfeld, in San Antonio, who works for a merchant called George Koerner. Through Hale she met Mr Koerner's daughter, Ella Theodora Koerner. The Keidels and the Koerners have got to know each other. They often visit. Elsa wants Ella to be maid of honour. She is going to San Antonio soon to see her brother and will ask her about it then.'

Wharton turned the name over in his mind. 'Ella Theodora Koerner. Interesting name. It has a sort of ring to it. I would like to meet someone with a name like that. How old is she?'

Robert shrugged. 'About eighteen, I think, younger than you.'

Wharton was surprised. 'Why so much younger than Elsa? I thought she would get a friend her own age.'

Robert seemed not to have given the matter much thought. 'A maid of honour is meant to be a young person, I think. Anyway it is more an issue between the two families. It's a nice touch. The Koerners will see it as an honour to be involved. They've been good to Hale so Elsa's family wants to acknowledge that.'

And there the matter rested for the next few months but the name of Elsa's prospective maid of honour continued to intrigue Wharton and he was oddly pleased to hear that she had accepted the role in Elsa's wedding.

Robert's involvement in the Gillespie County gold venture continued to grow and he bought out some of the less committed shareholders. Now that returns were coming in, he told Wharton, he felt more confident in re-investing some of the money. With his double involvement in Fredericksburg he was finding it difficult to maintain a full-time job in Austin. Still, he reasoned, after the wedding he would bring his wife to Austin and perhaps wind down his investments. Then he could think about what to do next.

Wharton too was beginning to think about his future. His close bond to Robert must inevitably be weakened when his brother had a wife. He was in no hurry to return to England but he needed to decide his next move. He was beginning to get restless in Austin. He had friends here but no real commitment. First though he would see out his role as best man.

Some three months before the August wedding Wharton travelled to Fredericksburg to be instructed in what was expected of him. He and Robert were to stay the night with the Keidels. The maid of honour would be there too and they would learn how to work together in their supporting roles. He was curious to meet the owner of the name.

It would be something less than a full rehearsal – more a training course in the details, the protocols, the etiquette of what he gathered was being billed as "the wedding of the year" for Fredericksburg. It was all becoming quite overblown, Wharton thought, with Robert described as an English entrepreneur with large mining interests – even some talk of him being titled.

The Koerners it seemed were high society in San Antonio and their involvement guaranteed the presence of a reporter from that city. Well, if people wanted a show, the Collinges would give them one. They were not short of money and were willing to spend it in a good cause. Wharton was quite looking forward to the whole event.

He arrived at the church with Robert in the early afternoon. They were dressed in casual clothes now, to be replaced by rented wedding finery when the big day came. Elsa and Dr Keidel had met them at the coach station nearby. At the church he saw more people than he had expected – some he knew, most he didn't. Smiling broadly, Elsa took Wharton's arm. 'Time to meet the maid of honour.' She led him and Robert towards a group conversing nearby. 'Ella,' she called. A young woman with dark hair turned at the sound of her name. Without hesitation, she broke free from the group and walked towards them.

Wharton saw a tall attractive girl in her late teens with large brown eyes. She smiled at him and he felt there was something cool about her gaze, oddly penetrating, faintly quizzical, as though they had met somewhere before and she was trying to remember the occasion. He felt suddenly at a loss, like an actor who had forgotten his lines.

Ella held out her hand and he took it, embarrassed that she had had to move first, still unable to think of what he had meant to say. She spoke then, the soft southern accent sounding almost musical to his ears. 'I'm pleased to meet you, Mac. I've been looking forward to this meeting.'

Elsa intervened. 'Ella, his name is Wharton Rye – or just Wharton.'

He realised he had forgotten to let go of her hand and did so awkwardly.

Ella grinned now, an impish grin. 'Well, he's from Scotland, isn't he? Why can't I call him Mac?'

Before Elsa could correct her again, Wharton finally found his voice. 'You can call me Mac if you wish. I like that name.'

'Well then,' she said in soft tones with a little tilt of her head, 'Mac it is then.' Her self-confident air was quite captivating and Wharton was instantly charmed. She had a way of focussing herself totally on the object of her attention, as though she could read his thoughts.

For the moment, he had forgotten the others around him, the

other introductions waiting to be made. 'And do I call you Ella Theodora, or is Ella enough?'

She laughed and the saucy expression returned, as if they were old friends sharing a private joke. 'Oh, if I can get away with Mac, I'm sure you can get away with Ella.'

At that moment, Robert intervened. 'Now that you two have met, Ella, can you introduce Wharton around? Elsa and I have to see about the wedding plans.'

'Sure. No problem.' And to Wharton, 'Come with me, Mac. Let's meet some home folks.' She guided him over to the group with whom she had been standing before.

The centre of the group was a stocky middle-aged man with a broad intelligent face and alert eyes, a commanding presence, as Wharton was immediately aware.

'Wharton, meet my father.'

'George Koerner. Glad to meet you.' Wharton's hand was enveloped in a powerful grip. 'This is my wife, Elfrieda.'

The lady beside George Koerner seemed possessed of the same cool self-confidence as her daughter, the image of the Southern family matriarch, intent on setting the guest at ease. 'We've been looking forward to meeting you, Wharton. Robert has told us all about you.' And then as if sharing a private confidence she added, 'We all love your brother. Elsa is just one lucky girl.'

'Well,' responded Wharton, 'I love him too. I've followed him all the way to Texas. He's been a great influence in my life.' He was feeling relaxed already in the company of the Koerners.

More introductions followed; Ella's uncle Benno Goldbeck and his wife, younger sisters Lillian and Elfrieda Jr and others, too many names to be remembered all at once, and then Elsa's own relatives whom he had meet at their home on the previous occasion.

Some time was passed in conversation and then the wedding organisers proceeded to explain to the key participants the roles they would be playing, especially those of Wharton and Ella. The afternoon flew by for Wharton in Ella's company. That evening, dinner was held at the Keidel household, a larger group than before with the Koerners added, all the women joining in to help.

Wharton sat next to Ella at the table. As they waited for the meal to start, she rested her chin on her hand and gazed at him in the cool, poised way that was beginning to cast a spell over him. 'Tell me about your boat trip, Mac. It sounds like a lot of fun.'

It was another memorable Texas night for Wharton. By the time he and Robert retired to their hotel room, his mind was full of the Southern belle who had so charmed him with her strange combination of poised sophistication and mischievous spirit, of the way her eyes sparkled when she teased him and melted away his English reserve.

All this had not passed unnoticed by others. Robert gave his brother a knowing look. 'A real charmer, don't you think? I thought you would like her.'

More time passed before the wedding rehearsal, a week before the event itself. Meeting Ella again had come to seem in Wharton's mind as big an issue as his role in the ceremony.

At the rehearsal, he found much of a practical nature to be learned, a role to be practised, but reunion with Ella did not disappoint. They still had time to converse and when he left for Austin, he was more determined than ever to pursue the relationship by whatever means he could.

The wedding morning, Sunday, 6 August, came at last and Wharton and Ella and all the others with roles to play were gathered at the Keidel home. Shortly before 9 o'clock, Wharton entered the waiting carriage with Robert, who by now was unusually silent, clearly nervous as the big moment approached. They were both wearing the black frock coats obtained for the occasion. At the church they walked up the aisle together, between the ranks of seated guests and stopped before the altar. Wharton then stood to one side and watched, as the organ music rolled out and Elsa entered on the arm of Dr Keidel. She carried a bunch of white carnations that matched the wedding dress and was followed by Ella and two small flower girls. Ella also carried flowers.

As Wharton later read in the San Antonio *Daily Express* under the headline 'The Most Fashionable Wedding of the Year – In Society

Circles', the bride 'was dressed in white duchesse satin, had a sprig of myrtle in her hair and carried a beautiful bouquet of white carnations. Miss Koerner, the maid of honour, was dressed in white organdie and carried a magnificent bouquet of pink carnations.' The *Daily Express's* reporter in Fredericksburg was clearly impressed by the town's big day. The description of Robert as 'holding a controlling interest in the most valuable mining properties in Gillespie County' was certainly an exaggeration. He had without doubt done well out of his mining venture but above all, it had brought him Elsa – a strange twist of fate, Wharton reflected.

After the ceremony, the carriage was ready to take the married couple to Austin and the start of an eight-week tour through the United States and England, where Elsa would meet the rest of the Collinge family. As they rode away, Wharton felt a touch of wistfulness, almost of loneliness. For the first time he was in Texas without Robert. Life would be different now.

He felt a hand take his and looked to see Ella beside him. 'You'll miss him, won't you?' she said, quite serious now.

'Yes, I really will. He's been a part of my life for so long I can't imagine life without him.'

'Well, my family and I hope we will see you in San Antonio soon. You aren't alone in Texas, you know. You have friends here and friends in San Antonio. Come and visit just any time.' She smiled then and added, 'I wouldn't like to think of you lonely.'

A few weeks later, Wharton took up the invitation and spent a weekend at the Koerner home, a grand old mansion in a tree-lined street in a wealthy part of San Antonio. He was shown the downtown office of "George Koerner, Wholesale Grocer and Commission Merchant, Dealer in Fine Cigars and Tobaccos", as the signs on the windows explained. His company also dealt in coffee, cheese, rope, fruits, rice and a host of other merchandise, much of it brought in from Mexico. He was the classic self-made man.

George Koerner showed a keen interest in Wharton's background and his experience in the cotton industry. The discussion ended with a proposition. As he sat back in his armchair and drew on one of his cigars, he said, 'I could use a man like you, Wharton. Cotton is a commodity, like any other. There would be a bit of travel, a bit of office work, more variety than just nothing but cotton.' He described the role in more detail and finished with the words, 'Think about it a couple of weeks, then let me know.' Then he lowered his voice, smiled and in a confidential tone added, 'I think my daughter would like you to say yes.'

Wharton laughed. 'Oh, Mr Koerner, you really do know how to sweeten an offer, don't you?'

The older man grinned. 'Well, that's my job.'

It did not take Wharton long to decide to leave Austin. His life there was not going anywhere. It was time to move on, even without the inducement of living in the same city as Ella and being able to visit her freely. In late September he left Austin for the last time and took up residence in a pleasant lodging house recommended to him by the Koerners. His working life began anew and he applied himself once more to learning the art of running a business. One day he would have a business of his own, he promised himself.

Romance with Ella now blossomed, unimpeded by the tyranny of distance. By the time Robert and Elsa returned from their honeymoon travels, tired but happy, much had changed in Wharton's life.

Robert needed employment for now while he and Elsa decided on their future. It seemed to be agreed that would mean a move to England in due course. In the meantime, he had given up his job in Austin to take his extended holiday and, like Wharton, had no special reason to return to Austin.

Once again, George Koerner had an offer of employment, an unusual one. He offered Robert the task of taking over his Mexican office in Monterrey and setting it up as a reliable source of the goods he needed to sell in San Antonio. Success had eluded two previous managers and the Mexican end of George's operations continued to function poorly. A nine-month contract was agreed on. The terms were generous, contingent on success, the experience priceless. Elsa would stay in Fredericksburg, an unfortunate side of the deal, but Mexico was no place for her.

On New Year's Eve, Wharton was a guest of the Koerners. They all stayed up late to see in the new year, the dawn of the Twentieth

Century. As bells tolled throughout the city, Mrs Koerner rested her head on her husband's shoulder and said, almost to herself, 'What changes will this century bring, I wonder.'

'More than we can imagine, my dear. Life is changing fast. Motor cars, telephones, electricity – they say flying machines will be next. Here we have a telephone at home and one at the office. Soon we will have electricity instead of gaslight and candles.' He reflected a moment, a faraway look in his eyes. Wharton knew that modern technology fascinated George. 'I reckon I'll trade the horses in on a motor car one day,' he continued. 'Moses can learn to drive us around.' Then as an afterthought, 'In fact, dammit, I may just learn to drive myself around.'

George Koerner stood up and gazed around at his family and their guests. He looked down at his wife, his hand on her shoulder. 'What better way to start the Twentieth Century than with a happy announcement, before anyone else knows?' His wife smiled her approval. He motioned to the youngest child, George Jr. 'Get Moses; let him hear this too.'

The boy headed off to the kitchen to find Moses Johnson, the Koerners' black house servant. When the two returned, George Koerner came straight to the point. 'Wharton has proposed marriage to our Ella, she has accepted and Elfrieda and I have given our blessing.'

The news brought happy smiles. Sister Lillian clapped her hands in delight, then jumped up and impulsively hugged her sister.

Events moved swiftly. The date was set, 8 May 1900, and the place, St Mark's Episcopal Church in the downtown, not far from the historic heart of the city, with the Alamo and the Menger Hotel nearby.

One disappointment for Wharton came when Robert declined to be best man. Sorting out the situation in Mexico for his employer was proving a challenge indeed and the journey to and from San Antonio was long and arduous. He would be there for the wedding but that was as much as he could promise. Wharton chose instead a recent acquaintance, Paul Schmidt, one of the Koerner circle of friends. The maid of honour would be Ella's sister Lillian, at eighteen only a year younger than Ella.

Once more Wharton went through the rounds of parties, rehearsals and all the planning that went into a Texas society wedding where money was no object. It was to be bigger and better than Elsa and Robert's in Fredericksburg. Wharton began to feel as if he was being carried along on a flow of events that was slipping out of his control. Just three years after arriving in Texas, knowing no one, he was now the centre of attention for San Antonio society, the star at another "Wedding of the Year" as it was already being billed in the local newspapers. And he was still only twenty-one.

On one issue he decided to take a stand. Texas had been a great adventure, beyond his expectations, but England was home and he saw no point in stretching out his time in San Antonio. He took up the issue of taking his bride to England to meet his family and left the prospects of returning to Texas, as Robert had done, deliberately unclear. Ella was an independent girl and she seemed to understand that in marrying a Collinge, she was transferring allegiance to another clan, one bigger and wealthier than her own, and based across the sea. The Koerners had the wisdom not to interfere. George had left his family behind at seventeen when he came to Texas. He respected spirit. He did not admire those who took the easy life but losing Ella, not knowing even when they would see her again, was still hard for parents.

The wedding day approached. On the night before the wedding, Wharton had been encouraged to hold a "Farewell Bachelor's Dinner". He had booked a private dining room at San Antonio's most prestigious address, the historic Menger Hotel, haunt over the years of presidents, Civil War generals and famous names of every type. He was especially gratified to greet Robert, arrived that day from Mexico, and staying at the Menger. It was a night of wining and dining and toasts and responses and it seemed to pass for Wharton in a happy daze, a blur of unreality. Was this all really happening to him or was Texas an elaborate dream? Perhaps he had just responded to too many toasts.

* * *

The wedding ceremony at St Mark's Church was a grand and lavish affair, more guests than at Fredericksburg, more bridesmaids, more flowers, more of everything; 'No expense spared' as the *Express* noted later. And afterwards the bridal suite at the Menger awaited the married couple.

Two days later, 10 May, Wharton and Ella boarded the train for New York. A week later, after taking in the sights of Manhattan, Wharton found himself once more on the high seas, but this time he was travelling First Class on an ocean liner, just as Robert had done years before.

Would they stay in England or would they some day return to Texas? Wharton was content to let his life continue to work itself out for a while yet before making firm decisions about the future. On the last day of the ten-day voyage, however, the unplanned life suddenly became less practical when Ella found that she was pregnant. A family was on the way. This was something for which Wharton was quite unprepared.

At the dockside, forewarned by telegram, was a gathering of Collinges, all eager to meet the newest addition to the clan. They were all there – Uncle Richard, older and slower now, looking forward to retirement, with his wife Sarah, Emma and Alfred Mayall, Ellen, engaged now with her fiancé, brothers Edward and Arthur, a scattering of cousins, and Marianne, the one Wharton missed most.

Wharton could see it was bewildering to Ella, already feeling unwell with the onset of pregnancy, and he was grateful for his mother taking charge. 'Don't worry,' she told her new daughter-in-law, 'you will have plenty of time to work out who they all are.' The couple were to spend the first week at the Mayall house while they decided on their next move. When told of Ella's condition, Emma assured her, 'You can stay as long as you like, my dear. Let Wharton sort things out. That's what men are for, you know.' Ella smiled wanly. Wharton was glad of Emma's welcoming warmth. They had had their differences in the past but in the role of family matriarch, she was a reassuring presence.

The welcome reception over, the group disbanded and the couple departed in the Mayalls' coach. In the next few days, they received a stream of visitors, some Ella had met at shipside, others new, a mixture of relations and family friends.

Marianne's visit was especially pleasing to Wharton. With Robert still seeing out his contract in Mexico, he was glad to be reunited with the sister who held such a special place in his affections. She was eighteen years old now, a grown woman. He felt a pang of regret that the fun-loving child of memory had vanished forever in his absence, to be replaced by a poised and charming young lady.

Marianne was only a year younger than Ella and she talked animatedly to her new sister-in-law, asking all about Texas, and to her brother, fascinated by his adventures in the years since she had last seen him.

'I want to go to Texas some day,' she announced to Ella. 'Would I be able to stay with your family, do you think?'

Ella was reassuring. 'Oh, they would love to meet you. First Robert, then Mac, then you. They would be delighted.'

Marianne gave her a curious look. 'Why do you call him Mac?'

'Oh,' replied Ella casually, 'it's just my pet name for him.' She did not care to allude to the ignorance of geography that had given rise to the name.

Wharton spoke up. 'Ella had everyone in San Antonio calling me Mac. I like it. "Wharton Rye" sounds clumsy and "Wharton" sounds incomplete. Mac is fine.'

Marianne raised an eyebrow and gave Ella a saucy look. 'Well then, Mac it is,' she announced.

Ella's baby was born on 10 February 1901 and named Edward George after its two grandfathers. By now the couple had purchased a home they called San Antonio on the Lancashire coast, in the little village of Freshfield, adjacent to the larger town of Formby. It was a large roomy home with space for servants – a nurse, a cook and a housekeeper acquired in quick succession.

Wharton found that he had no need to trouble himself unduly over his finances. He had incomes from both his father's and grandfather's estates and shares in James Collinge & Sons, still thriving years after its founder's death. He had also made a tidy profit from Robert's gold mining ventures in Texas. All in all, he had no need to work at all and for some months he was a gentleman of leisure, "living on own means" as he told the 1901 Census taker, enjoying his new home and family.

The unproductive life was not in his nature however. He was waiting for Robert to return from Texas at last with Elsa and then to pursue a plan that he had lately devised, a plan to form a company called Collinge Bros Cotton Brokers. It would comprise Robert and himself, along with Edward and Arthur. When he broached the possibility with Edward, the reaction was positive. Edward was by now seeking a purpose in life and Arthur, his schooling coming to an end, was delighted to have an offer of employment waiting for him.

Robert returned to England later that year and with Elsa took up residence in Freshfield in a house called Pearcedale, not far from Wharton and Ella. In one crucial respect, Wharton had now surpassed his brother. He had become a father only nine months after his wedding while Robert and Elsa were beginning to wonder if parenthood would ever come their way.

With the brothers' combined expertise, Collinge Bros Cotton Brokers prospered and ultimately provided a good living for four families. In 1902, Wharton sold up and moved his family to a grand two-storey mansion nearby called Lawswood. Although neither he nor Ella was in any hurry for more children, it was always a possibility and more space for the servants and perhaps a governess in the future would not go to waste.

In 1903, the couple received distressing news from Texas. George Koerner had become bankrupt. Problems in Mexico, some bad investments and a local downturn had combined to overwhelm him with debts that he could not pay. His home had to be sold to satisfy his creditors.

Ella was distraught and Wharton offered to go to San Antonio to see what he could do to assist her father with his financial problems and get him launched again, perhaps in a new direction.

Wharton set off on 13 January 1904 on the *Cedric*, the latest liner to take up the New York run. He returned in June, happy to report that he was able to help the Koerners find their feet again and see George set up in business as a share broker, once more with his own office. In November that year, at the Koerners' invitation, Marianne took ship for New York on the *Cedric* and beyond by train to Texas, fulfilling a dream of travel that had been born many years before. She was just twenty-two.

One evening, a few weeks after his return from Texas, Ella greeted her husband at the door with the words, 'I think I must have overdone the welcome home, Mac.'

On 1 March 1905, a second son was born to the couple and was named Robert, after the brother who had had such a profound influence on the course of Wharton's life.

Chapter 11

Wharton Rye Collinge: In Flanders Fields
France: 1917

As midnight approached a hush had fallen. It was disturbed by the muffled boom of a heavy gun, some distance away – a British cannon, an 18-pounder, once, twice. The faint sound of high explosive could be heard landing somewhere behind enemy lines. Silence again and then suddenly the crack of a sniper's rifle, quite close now. Some British sentry was passing his time firing at any glimmer of light that caught his eye. No response came from the German lines.

Lieutenant Wharton Rye Collinge looked down at his wrist watch, trying to pick out in the moonlight the moment when the month passed and the new one, April 1917, came in. The sounds of war were never still for long but he enjoyed the silence while he could. He knew that behind the Front, miles back, the movement of soldiers and trucks and horses and wagons never ceased, ensuring that the titanic duel of men and machinery would go on as it had all through the past year and the year before that.

At the moment of midnight several heavy guns off to right and left roared defiance at the enemy and the crump of their shells landing came seconds later. Flares rose into the sky from the enemy lines, green and weirdly beautiful. Again the Germans did not fire back, perhaps less wasteful of their firepower than the British.

It was cold sitting there in the dark, the dirt wall hard and slimy, an alien feel, but after six weeks of life in the trenches Wharton was already inured to discomfort. Be thankful it was not raining. To be still in one piece, with all his limbs still with him, to live another day, that was all one could ask for in this hell of death and suffering. Never in all his early years of good fortune, years blessedly free of poverty and hardship, could he have imagined the life of unrelenting horror that would one day be his. The lines of a popular poem came to him.

In Flanders fields the poppies blow
Between the crosses row on row

He couldn't remember the rest. He thought a moment, frowning in the darkness, but the missing words would not come. That piece of verse had been around a long time and yet the guns still roared and the rows of crosses extended on and on. He could see no end in sight to the war, no end imaginable. The two sides were so evenly matched that progress was impossible and every attempt brought more rows of graves for no perceptible gain. As for poppies, they were long gone. No trace of Nature remained now except the odd shattered tree stump among the shell holes.

A form appeared beside him in the gloom and Wharton started.

'Hey, Mac. What's on your mind? Planning the next attack?' It was Eccles, Lieutenant Thomas Eccles, fellow officer and keen card player, a good comrade for bad times.

'Don't make me jump like that. You could have been a Hun for all I knew.'

Eccles laughed. 'I'm lucky you didn't run me through then, eh?'

Wharton grinned in the dark, his spirits lifted momentarily, then shrugged resignedly. It was impossible to stay light-hearted for long in the world of the trenches, even on a quiet night like this and the moment passed as quickly as it came.

Still, the mix of boredom and depression that filled in the time between bursts of activity was certainly preferable to the naked fear that came with action, with the vicious little trench raids that filled in the gaps between major battles. He had survived two of these murderous affairs already. His sleep was sometimes haunted by the memory of the German he had once confronted and killed, a youth hardly older it seemed than his own son Edward George. He lost three of his men that night but they killed a dozen Germans and seized a stretch of opposing trench. It was what passed for a successful raid by the standards of the Western Front, though this tiny salient was soon lost to the inevitable counter-attack.

Eccles spoke again, using Wharton's nickname. 'And what's April going to bring us, Mac? More of the same?'

'Or worse. They say Russia's falling apart. They're having a revolution over there. If we can't beat the Huns when they're fighting on two fronts how the hell will we beat them when they only have us to deal with? Tell me that.'

Eccles lowered his voice and spoke in mock-serious tones. 'Spreading defeatism, Lieutenant? You know there are penalties for that. Your men might hear you.' They could see the huddled shapes around them, hear the occasional cough, see the glow of a cigarette. There had to be a guard in the forward trenches at all times in case of a night attack.

The man's humour was infectious and Wharton chuckled. 'Oh, get away with you. I'm going back and get some sleep. Are you here to stay?'

'Yes. Go on. See you in the morning.'

Wharton turned towards the approach trench and set off back to the officer's billets behind the lines. He crouched instinctively as he walked, wary always of a sniper's bullet, the price of a moment's carelessness.

It had taken Wharton a surprisingly long time to find himself in the war zone. He had enlisted in July 1915. Given his position in society, he had been promised an officer's rank. The King himself had signed the commissioning paper and shaken his hand. True, he was only one of a long line of officers-to-be that day but a ceremony to remember all the same, one intended to imbue them all with the spirit of loyalty to King and Country. The commissioning paper spoke of Duty, Order and Discipline and more – all the key words had capital letters. He was now Lieutenant Wharton Rye Collinge of the King's Liverpool Regiment, 6th Rifle Battalion (Territorial).

The Collinge fortunes had all but vanished with the onset of war. The submarines sank the merchant ships that brought the cotton to Lancashire. The mills closed, the men went off to war and the source of the Collinge family wealth seemed to vanish before Wharton's eyes. The servants had to be let go, his sons taken from their expensive schools and then finally Lawswood itself sold for a poor price, far less than its pre-war worth. Only the London apartment in Maida Vale remained. Ella Theodora and the boys had gone to Abbots Brow, the home of Wharton's sister Marianne and her husband Alexander Pearson up north at Kirkby Lonsdale.

At this low ebb in the family fortunes, a belated sense of patriotism spurred Wharton to enlist. What was there to lose, except his life? And when one so high in society had been brought so low, that life had come to seem less precious. At thirty-six, with a wife and two young children, he did not need to fear the white feather of cowardice but many a man his age and older had enlisted and been accepted by a War Office desperate for manpower. What was the alternative after all – to go to Abbots Brow and live on the charity of his relatives, the Pearsons? He still had his pride, if no longer the fortune to go with it.

To Wharton's surprise, the journey to the battlefield had been a long time coming. Routine gunnery training had showed him to have a keen eye for a target. To be a crack shot was a skill much in demand. He had graduated into the role of Musketry Instructor and had spent the better part of a year and a half teaching others to aim and fire the rifle with precision. He learned too, the complexities of siting and firing the big guns, the artillery with which enemy positions were destroyed and enemy soldiers blasted. Bombing Officer was added to the list of capabilities in his officer's record – a title as far removed from that of Cotton Broker as it was possible to imagine.

It was with very mixed feelings that he received word at last that he was to apply his officer's training to the real world, the world of the battlefield, of the trenches that snaked five hundred miles from the Channel to the Swiss border. Many of his pupils and his fellow officers had gone to war while he stayed safe, far from the sound of shot and shell. He felt no sense of heroics in preparing to go to the Front. He had seen too many desperately wounded soldiers returned to the home country, maimed and blinded, heard too many stories of men dying in No Man's Land. The zest for adventure that had inspired legions of volunteers in 1914 was long gone. No one had any illusions now about the nature of modern warfare.

It was the 13th day of February 1917 when he said goodbye to his wife at Paddington station for the journey to Dover and the Channel crossing. By unhappy coincidence, it was Ella Theodora's birthday. She was thirty-six. With some of his remaining money he had bought her a brooch, a simple thing compared to birthday presents of the past but she wore it proudly on her coat lapel as she hugged him one last time. He was in his officer's uniform, so neatly pressed, the insignia of the Liverpool Regiment on each lapel.

He saw tears in Ella Theodora's eyes but she kept a brave front. 'Have you got my photograph with you? The one of me when we got engaged. The one with the mink stole you gave me.'

'You know I have, dear,' he reassured her. 'In my wallet. It's always with me, wherever I go. I'm sure I will have looked at it a thousand times before I see you next.'

'I have yours too, Mac. In your uniform, just like now.'

The train gave an anxious hoot. Men all up and down the platform were saying their goodbyes, stretching out the last moments.

He had his hands on her shoulders. 'Remember me to the boys. Tell them how much I miss them. And Marianne and Alex too.' It was time to go. The great locomotive wheels were creaking into action. The station master's whistle was blowing. 'I love you Ella. I've always loved you.' He released his grip, turned swiftly and climbed the steps into the carriage. He heard her voice behind him. 'Goodbye, Mac. Goodbye.'

A moment later he had found a window seat and was leaning out, longing to touch her again, but already the slim tall figure in the dark winter coat with the brooch on the lapel was receding away from him. She was calling to him. The noise of the engine and the hubbub all about drowned out her words but he could read her lips. 'I love you, I love you.'

The platform slid past as the train moved ponderously out of the station. The last he saw of Ella Theodora was a distant figure still waving bravely. He felt suddenly more lonely than ever before in his life.

Major Morrison was a grizzled old veteran with a permanent scowl. He sat at his desk looking up at Wharton and muttered in a disapproving tone, 'Looks like you're getting out of the action again, Lieutenant.' He glanced down at the piece of paper in his hand before adding gruffly, 'So, musketry instructor, eh? Isn't that what you were doing all that time before they sent you here?'

Wharton disliked the man. He had had dealings with him before. The Major seemed to think that anyone surviving the trenches was somehow betraying the memory of those who had died there. You were sent here to fight and you stayed at your post until you had fulfilled your duty to King and Country and could fight no more. The Major's left arm was missing below the elbow and one eye was permanently closed. Well, no one could accuse him of not doing his duty, unlike the armchair generals who kept a safe distance from the Front while they plotted the next attack.

Military courtesy in the face of a superior officer must prevail. In even tones, Wharton responded, 'Yes, sir. I was eighteen months with the Territorials. Rifles, artillery.' He kept it brief but his heart leapt. Another spell of instructing, a rescue from the trenches.

Morrison was reading the paper again. 'Etaples.' His pronunciation was all wrong but Wharton knew the name. 'Where the hell is that?'

'Gunnery training school,' Wharton replied. 'On the coast, near Boulogne.'

Morrison shrugged. 'Well, I suppose someone has to do it. Can't win the war if we can't shoot straight, eh? Here – copy for you.' He handed over the form in his hand to Wharton. 'Make sure Captain Miller knows what's going on. Wouldn't want you shot for deserting, would we?'

Wharton forced a smile at the man's humour, then saluted and left. His step was lighter as he walked from the Major's command post. He felt a twinge of conscience that he would have to pass the men in his command over to others. He would be leaving his brother officers, Eccles, Huntley, Jordan and the rest to their fates too. The bond he felt to these men was something only wartime could forge.

Still he was going to safety far behind the lines, where the roar of the cannons and the crack of rifle fire would no longer be heard to shroud his every waking moment with the shadow of imminent death. No relief could be greater than that.

Three months of gunnery instruction, or musketry to use the War Office term, seemed to pass all too soon. In mid-July the dreaded instruction came. Major Morrison and his like did not care to see individual officers enjoy the security of training school for too long while others less fortunate faced death on a daily basis.

Wharton found himself being pulled by opposing forces. He could see that the Morrisons of the world would have everyone in the trenches until they were killed or invalided out but wiser heads would see the need for training soldiers to outfight the Germans. For this there must be men to instruct them. Wharton had developed some well-placed supporters. The idea had been floated that his services would be valuable in the future to help train the American forces that would soon be arriving in great numbers. He could see that the USA was the great hope now, the counterbalance to the loss of Russia. The raw forces of this new ally could learn much from the battle-hardened British and men like Wharton would be needed to pass on their experience from the Western Front.

Wharton had begun to hope that he might have escaped from the Front indefinitely but he heard the rumours that swirled about of a great battle planned for the near future. General Haig, leader of British forces, was planning another of his great pushes that for all their meticulous planning never seemed to achieve their objectives. Haig would try to break out from the salient at Ypres where his men were exposed to murderous fire from the enemy. There would once more be enormous loss of life for minimal gain. Wharton shared the general lack of faith in army leadership to be found throughout the ranks of the junior officer class.

He felt that if he could not avoid one more stretch at the battlefront, then he must stay alive until the call came that he was needed to train the new American units. But that date was maddeningly elusive and in the meantime the powers that held sway over him wanted him at the Front.

With a feeling of great foreboding he headed once more for the trenches. A different section of the Front this time but little else had changed. Jordan had been invalided out, Eccles and Huntley were still alive. The war ground on. In the absence of a major battle, hundreds still died every day all along the Front from "normal wastage" to use the repellent phrase of the War Office. The endless shelling of each other's lines, the relentless rifle fire, the silent ghostly gas clouds – it all combined to create a world of random death that left no one in the forward trenches safe by day or night.

Wharton's 6th Battalion was presently situated before Armentieres at the southern end of the Ypres salient, guarding the approaches to the shattered town behind them. Heavy shelling had reduced the town to rubble and the reek of gas clung to the stonework, enough to make him feel sick at times. In his first few days back with his regiment, random bombardments tore into the town and its defences at any time, sometimes for hours at a stretch. The salient was exposed on three sides and the Germans took full advantage of this to kill as many of the defenders as possible from a distance. Return British fire never seemed to have any discernable effect on the enemy.

The strain on Wharton's nerves of the endless shelling and gunfire left him feeling shaken and depressed, sleeping fitfully. He had a mortal dread of the nightmare world of which he was once more a part, the vast implacable slaughterhouse that was the Western Front. Shattered remnants of one-time forests, gaunt and blackened, protruded from the mud of No Man's Land, surrounded by shell holes filled with polluted water reeking of poison gas. Arms, legs, traces of bodies were everywhere, remains of comrades who had simply vanished, never to know even the final dignity of a marked grave. As batteries on both sides roared unceasingly, some men were reduced to gibbering idiots, the notorious "shell shock". At night one might hear the screams of wounded men trapped in the barbed wire of No Man's Land, victims of the last abortive raid on the enemy lines, beyond reach, doomed to a lingering death. Life, it seemed to Wharton, had been drained of all meaning, reduced to its very essence, the desire to live, to remain whole, for one more day. And yet if one survived the daily lottery of life and death in the trenches, Haig's next all-or-nothing push would make the losses of "normal wastage" seem trivial by comparison.

One of Wharton's first tasks on his return to the Front was to put together a map of the trench lines of both sides in this sector, near the southern end of the Flanders line. He was not told the purpose but he knew well enough. It was his tiny contribution to the planning for the coming Third Battle of Ypres – or was it the Fourth? It hardly seemed to matter any more.

Wharton made his own observations of the local situation as best he could, without inviting a sniper's bullet. Then he interviewed as many trench raid survivors as he could find, men with hard-won knowledge of the enemy positions. A key feature was Chard Farm, a handful of almost destroyed buildings around which the Germans had established machine gun positions. That would have to be taken, no doubt at great cost, in the early days of the coming battle. He marked the enemy artillery positions and any natural features that still showed themselves above the mud. Over a couple of days and after several false starts, he produced the best compromise he could, based on all the information available to him.

He made several copies of the map on blank pages torn from a journal. He folded one copy and put it in his breast coat pocket. He might need it himself – who could tell?

In a pensive mood he took out his wallet with the photograph of Ella Theodora and gazed at it thoughtfully. He had performed that action countless times before, always with a sense of sadness and longing. This time, however, it served to raise his spirits, for some rare good news had recently come his way. Against all odds, his application for home leave after six months in France had been approved. Perhaps someone at Battalion HQ did not know of Haig's plans and was still issuing passes. Perhaps they thought to lull the suspicions of spies that would be aroused by the cancellation of all leave. Whatever the explanation, he was able to write to Ella Theodora at Abbots Brow that on Wednesday, 1 August, he would be arriving in London for ten days' leave. She should come to the Maida Vale apartment the day before and be ready at Paddington station to meet him. They would spend the night there before going to Abbots Brow. He would see his boys again. He would see Marianne and Alex. How precious such simple pleasures seemed now, the very thought of them a ray of light in the darkness.

The morning of 28 July dawned warm and sunny. Birds still flew overhead and their twittering could be heard occasionally over the rumble of gunfire. Wharton knew what many only suspected, that the great offensive was only days away. It was ironic that he would be home on leave when the push began, unless his leave was cancelled at the last minute. He would be only too relieved to miss the first days. Such thoughts no longer aroused any feeling of guilt in him. Staying alive was paramount now, returning some day to his wife and his children, becoming a human being again, freed of the fear of imminent death. Training American forces in gunnery and artillery skills would give him an honourable exit from the battlefield if he could stay alive until the call came. He had seen how little an individual life was worth in this place of death and he had no desire to see his own life wasted, traded for the price of an enemy bullet.

The morning passed uneventfully enough with limited action from the German guns – a blessed lull in the storm. Wharton made a routine check of the billets where his men lived their off-duty time behind the front lines and wrote in a note to the adjutant that they were "in a clean and sanitary condition". He dated and signed the note and put it in his pocket to be passed on later. In another note, he drew up a careful list of newly arrived stores, including thirty Mills No.5 grenades, twelve rifle grenades, ten thousand rounds of SAA ammunition and, more prosaically, nine dixies and a meat safe. This note too was dated, signed and placed in a pocket.

Around midday, checking the forward positions, he heard a shout. It was Lieutenant Huntley, rushing along the communication trench towards him. Wharton caught the urgency in the man's voice.

'Mac, our billets, the officers' billets – they're on fire. Take some of your men with you and help out. I'll get some more.'

The incongruous nature of Huntley's mission struck Wharton. 'What, are we firemen now?'

The irony was lost on Huntley. 'We're going to lose all our gear, Mac. You want to sleep in the open?' He hurried on and Wharton quickly rounded up a dozen men and set off for the back trenches.

Early on, army engineers had set up officers' billets dug into the trench sides, partly below, partly above ground. They used wood planking to build a series of dank, dark caves. They smelled of unwashed bodies and cigarette smoke and leaked badly in the rain but they were a home of sorts nonetheless, a place of retreat from the horrors of the forward trenches. It was in no officer's interests to have them burn down and Wharton lost no time in reaching the scene.

Shellfire had ignited one end of the row of billets and he could glimpse flames dancing up from the roof and out of the dark interior. Thick clouds of smoke obscured his view. Other men were rushing up now but he was one of the first there. A couple of men had found buckets but seemed wary of getting too close. An officer had to show initiative. He seized a bucket from one of the soldiers and scooped it through a pool of stagnant water nearby, where past shelling had gouged away part of the trench.

He shouted to the others to find more buckets and, leading by example, ran into the smoke to throw the water on the flames. As he did so, the acrid reek of the smoke seemed to sear his lungs. Too late he realised the danger and retreated. Gas – these were gas shells. The smoke was all around him. Hands seized his shoulders and dragged him away but already he was gasping for air. His sight was blurred and his eyes were hurting.

Wharton still tried to assist the others but he could no longer see and breathing was painful. Suddenly he was afraid, very afraid. He heard Eccles' voice, urgent, commanding. 'For God's sake, Mac, get away from here.' Others had arrived by now and were taking the situation in hand. Eccles held Wharton's arm firmly, guiding him to a safe distance, seating him carefully. 'Wait, Mac – I'll be back in a minute.' He returned soon after with the news that the fire was out. 'You look bad. I'm going to get you lying down and then see if I can find you a doctor – get you out of here.'

Wharton felt strangely helpless. By now his eyes were burning and his breathing was laboured and painful. 'Thanks, Tom,' was all he could find to say.

Eccles led Wharton to an undamaged part of the billets and made him lie down while he went for a doctor. 'I'll be a while, Mac. I'll do the best I can.' They both knew it would not be easy to get help quickly. Even on a quiet day like this, "normal wastage" ensured that doctors were kept busy. Hours passed while Wharton lay in growing agony, by now almost blind. Well into the afternoon, Eccles arrived with a doctor and an ambulance, brought along the supply road that ran to within a short distance of the billets.

By nightfall, Wharton found himself in a field hospital at Merville. As his breathing grew ever more painful, black despair overtook him. He could hardly believe his misfortune; three days away from taking leave, from seeing his wife again. She would be waiting for him by now in London, unaware of tragic news.

He had been so close to escape from the trenches, success within his grasp, but an implacable Fate had intervened.

Lieutenant Wharton Rye Collinge lived for ten more days before dying of gas poisoning on Tuesday, 7 August, 1917. He lies buried in Merville Communal Cemetery, near Armentieres.

Part 3

A Search for Answers

Chapter 12

Rob Collinge: Out of the Wilderness
England: 2004

I walked along the quiet lane, checking off the house numbers as I went, seeking the address that might resolve a lifelong mystery. I had come to this picturesque Cornish village in the south west of England on a quest, to find a relative whose name had been familiar to me all my life and yet about whom I knew absolutely nothing – my cousin Gerald.

It struck me that I should remember this date, 6 August 2004. It could be a day of discoveries or one of great disappointment. Uncle George's will was over 20 years old but the address it gave for Gerald was still listed in the telephone book against his name, so I had reason to be hopeful. At the age of 60, would I at last unlock the secrets of my father's unknown family?

I stopped outside the house and looked up the driveway. I saw a tidy-looking single-storey home with a neat garden. It was a warm summer's day and a lady was seated on the verandah, taking in the sun, reading a book. As I approached, she heard my footsteps and looked up.

I had had plenty of time to plan my words. 'Good morning. I am trying to locate Gerald Collinge.'

'Well,' she replied, 'you have come to the right place but he is out playing golf at the moment. I'm his wife. Can I help you?'

Her words were music to my ears. 'My name is Rob Collinge. I believe Gerald's father was Edward George Collinge.'

She gave me a puzzled look. It must have seemed a strange introduction. 'Well yes, that's right,' she responded.

'And,' I continued, 'Edward George had a younger brother named Robert.'

She began to realise where this was leading and the puzzled look gave way to one of astonishment. 'Yes,' she said, almost to herself, 'yes, he did.'

'Well, I'm his son,' I concluded. Simple words but they conveyed an extraordinary message. My father, Gerald's uncle, had vanished without trace over fifty years ago and this was the first word of him in all that time.

She gazed at me for a moment and I heard her say under her breath, 'Well, I never.'

And then suddenly she was all activity. 'Please, have a seat. Can I get you something to drink?'

Moments later I was seated comfortably, a glass of fruit juice in my hand. She introduced herself, Joan Collinge. And now it was her turn to astonish me.

'Did you know,' she began, coming straight to the point, 'that you had a half-brother and a half-sister?'

Taken totally by surprise, I could only reply, 'No. No. I had no idea at all.'

All my life I had known three names, the three 'G's – my Uncle George, who was my father's only sibling, and George's children Gerald and Geraldine. My father had lost track of George long ago in England, when I was a very small child, and he said that he had never met George's children. He had last seen his mother, Ella Theodora, about the same time. The Collinge side of my family had always been a closed door to me, an enigma.

My parents had emigrated to Australia with me in 1951 when my father was forty-five. I was then seven years old. They settled in a town called Orange in the New South Wales countryside, about 150 miles inland from Sydney. I left home at seventeen to go to university in Sydney and never lived at home again. I had a much younger brother, born when my father was almost fifty, but he was only six when I left Orange and I hardly ever knew him. With his usual sense of self-importance, my father had named my brother Robert, after himself.

I had a very distant relationship with my father. To me he was a pompous man, a product of the British upper class, though this meant nothing in egalitarian Australia, and my parents fitted in poorly in their adopted country. My father's profession was always described as accountant, though I discovered eventually that he had no qualifications at all. A compulsive gambler, he was cursed with an addiction to betting on the horses, the "sport of kings" as he called it. He would have been a poor provider at the best of times and for a man of limited business skills and largely unfounded faith in his own abilities, it was never the best of times. Only my mother's eternal gratitude for what she saw as her marriage into the upper class prevented her from realising what a bad choice of life partner she had made. In her eyes, my father had rescued her from her working class origins, like a knight in shining armour, and nothing could matter more to her than that.

Being possessed of a lively sense of curiosity, I had established from an early age the basic facts of my father's origins. He was born in a grand house named Lawswood, the mansion owned by his father Wharton Rye Collinge, a member of a very wealthy Lancashire family involved in the cotton trade. As a young man, Wharton had sailed to the USA, presumably on cotton business, and there he had met a young Texas belle, Ella Theodora Koerner, from a prosperous merchant family in San Antonio. They had married and the bride, believed to be still in her teens, was transported back to Lawswood for what she no doubt expected to be a life of ease and luxury.

And so it was for a while. My father's earliest memories were of a great house, a house with servants in the attics employed to provide all the attentions expected by members of the ruling class – a cook, housemaids, a governess, whatever it took to maintain the lifestyle that distinguished the elite few from the toiling masses. It was not to last but it coloured my father's expectations of life to his dying day.

The cotton trade was a victim of the Great War as German

U-Boats sank shipping, but Wharton did not live to see the financial ruin of the Collinges. He died of poison gas on the Western Front in 1917, when my father was twelve. His mother, Ella Theodora, cast adrift in a foreign land, bereft of husband and fortune, embarked on a life of aimless wandering, a life with a past but no future.

When my father was eighteen, in 1923, his mother set off back to Texas, taking her youngest son with her. His brother George remained in England. My father was to spend ten years in the US, first in Texas and later in New York. He married a Danish immigrant girl in New York but it ended in divorce and at the height of the Depression he drifted back to England, accompanied or followed by his mother.

By the start of the 1940s, my father had found work as an accountant in the Castle Bromwich Aeroplane factory in Birmingham where the Spitfires were made with which the beleaguered country fought the Battle of Britain. In this dramatic setting, punctuated by nightly bombing raids, he met my mother, Dorothy Cleaver, working in the typing pool. In January 1942, in the darkest days of the war, they married in a brief registry office ceremony. I was born in November 1943 and was named Robin Christopher but later opted simply for Rob by preference.

Some years later, after the war, my parents moved to London where my father built up a modestly successful accounting practice before emigrating to Australia in 1951.

One curious story that I knew from an early age concerned the last contact with my father's mother, Ella Theodora. It seemed that she lived briefly with my parents when I was a baby. She was, I was told, haughty and difficult. With war widow and cotton industry pensions, she was relatively well-off financially and reputedly fed her dog better food than my parents could provide for me on wartime rations. My father suggested to my mother that they get her out of their lives by a ruse. They told her that they were going away for a brief holiday and would see her shortly. They did not return, however, and she was never heard of again. Even as a child, it struck me as a cowardly way to deal with the situation.

On what proved to be one of the last opportunities I ever had to speak to my father before he died in 1983, I asked him to tell me what he could of his family and his ancestry. It was a moment of inspiration that I could never explain, and for which I would one day be extremely thankful. Given my lifelong reluctance to discuss any matter of substance with him, lest he use it as an occasion to show off to me, it was for me an uncharacteristic action. By now though, so late in life, the pomposity and the desire to impress others had all but vanished and he told me all he could, or so it seemed at the time, openly and frankly. I wrote it all down on a single piece of paper and put it away, to remain unseen for many years.

It was sometime in 2003 that my interest in trying to track down my lost Collinge relatives crystallised into a determination to do something about it. The curiosity had always been there but where was I to start? My father genuinely, it would seem, had no idea what had become of his mother or his brother or his brother's children. I studied the page of notes that I had taken down in that long ago conversation. Wharton was one of seven children but my father knew little of the six siblings. One brother was named Robert and my father had been named after this uncle who had managed factories in England, France and New York. Ella Theodora had siblings too but my father knew even less about them. He had no idea who had originated the Collinge family wealth. Supposedly a family crest existed and a Latin motto, *Fidelis in Omnibus*, meaning Faithful in All.

None of this gave me a point from which to start. By now I had been living in Melbourne with my wife Helen for many years and we were the parents of three adult sons. Our middle son, Stuart, was living in London. He had always taken a keen interest in the family tree, so far confined mainly to my mother's relatives. Though at opposite ends of the world, we both read what we could of genealogy, the investigation of one's past, and we traded ideas.

Initial explorations of the Internet and searches of genealogical databases yielded little at first but then I found that English Census records up to 1901, the last so far published, could be accessed on various sites. Slowly a picture of the Collinges of the Nineteenth Century, Wharton Rye Collinge's siblings and parents and uncles and aunts, began to emerge, as if I was unearthing the secrets of a lost civilisation. A world of wealth and privilege could be discerned, with servants sometimes outnumbering children and numerous idle rich whose only occupation was "living on own means" or even just "gentleman". But while I learned about the Collinges of long ago, I was no closer to finding out about the recent past, my own near relatives.

One day, Stuart alerted me to a database covering births, marriages and deaths complete for England back to 1837, when systematic record-keeping began. One could search for specific records then order copies of the actual certificates. Stuart had found that he could even obtain the wills of people for whom death certificate details were known.

An idea seized me. Could I find out when Uncle George died, get Stuart to obtain his will and see if it referred to Gerald and Geraldine? Might I discover some clue to the whereabouts of my mysterious cousins?

The search took longer than I expected. Starting in the 1940s, I had to access the name Collinge in a separate record for each quarter of each year. In my talk with my father about our ancestry over twenty years before, he had given me a priceless tip. George's full name was actually Edward George Collinge. I was saved from the disappointment of a fruitless search, but even so it took a long time. My uncle had died in 1982, a year before my father, at the age of eighty-one. Along the way I found Ella Theodora, my grandmother. She had died at the end of 1961, aged eighty, when I was eighteen. If only I could have known. I had never met a grandparent, the other three having died before I was born.

I passed on the details of Uncle George's death to Stuart who applied for the will, if one existed. A couple of weeks later, I received an excited telephone call. Like my father, George had left very little but fortunately he had made a will. He left all he had to his son Gerald – at an address! Suddenly we had an address. A clue at last – from twenty years ago perhaps, but a clue nonetheless.

By chance, my wife and I were planning to go to Britain shortly for an entirely unrelated reason, a Welsh wedding. The eldest son of close friends had met a Welsh backpacker in Melbourne and romance had flourished.

I decided that I would travel to Cornwall to visit the address given for Gerald in the will. I would not write a letter as I would not know what to make of a failure to respond – had he left or was he not interested? By now, Stuart had located Gerald's telephone number on the Internet, suggesting that he was still at the address. This was promising but I resisted the temptation to call the number. No – I would arrive in person and just take it from there. I would at least meet my cousin, or give it my best attempt.

I spent only half an hour with Gerald's wife Joan on our first meeting. I had left Helen and Stuart in the town centre and I did not want to keep them waiting too long. Joan invited the three of us to come for dinner with herself and Gerald the following night.

In that half hour, I had caught up with a lifetime's worth of family information. Gerald was seventy-six, a retired schoolteacher. They had three married sons and eight grandchildren scattered across southern England. Geraldine had died long ago of breast cancer, leaving two daughters, both married but only one with children.

Of even more direct concern to me, my father had had two children before he met my mother. My highly strung, over-emotional mother could never have known that about her "darling Bob". Such knowledge would have provoked a nervous breakdown at least. The move to London and then to Australia, the sudden rejection of his mother and brother from his life, it must all be connected. He must have been running away from his past, from the possibility that my mother might some day learn the shocking truth.

And shocking it was. George's wife Lena, the mother of Gerald and Geraldine, had had a sister Lily. My father had been introduced to Lily after his return from New York and soon began an affair with her. They had a son who my father, with astonishing gall under the circumstances, named Robert after himself, a practice to be repeated many years later in the case of my younger brother. Less than a year later, Lily was pregnant again. My father seemed to have decided that this was becoming a habit.

The novelty of domesticity and parenthood having worn off, my father abandoned Lily and Robert and vanished. Poor Lily was forced to return to her parents in Manchester for the birth of a daughter, Maureen. My father never set eyes on his only daughter.

Before long, the luckless Lily was stricken with TB. A lonely death followed ultimately and the two small children ended up in an orphanage where they were to spend the rest of their childhood. Meanwhile my father had married my mother and moved on with his new family, putting the past behind him.

Robert and Maureen grew up and made lives for themselves in Manchester. They married and each had two daughters. Tragically, Robert had poor health and died of an asthma attack at the age of fifty-five. Brother and sister were always haunted by the loss of their childhood and by the mystery of the father they had never known. As Robert's daughter was to tell me later, her father never spoke of the past except with great sadness.

Maureen set herself the task of finding out about her father but years of searching had ended in frustrating failure. She had always known about Uncle George and his family since George's wife Lena was Lily's sister but George had no idea what had become of his brother either. My father had disappeared without a trace and no clue to his whereabouts had ever been found.

I returned to my wife and son in a state of sensory overload. Never did I dream that my visit to Gerald's house would provide such a treasure trove of information. The dinner the following night and meeting with Gerald was an event to remember with over fifty years of family history to be filled in on both sides.

I learned later that as soon as I left the house after our initial meeting, Joan telephoned Maureen in Manchester and told her (or words to this effect), 'Maureen, it is Joan Collinge of Cornwall here. I have just had a visit from a stranger from Australia. His name is Rob Collinge – and he is your father's son!'

Maureen told me later that when she heard that a person had appeared from nowhere who had all the answers to the questions of a lifetime, it was 'like coming out of the wilderness'. Her immediate fear was that I would disappear again as suddenly as I had arrived. She had no way of transporting herself on short notice to Cornwall. She could only ask Joan, when she saw me at dinner, to prevail on me to contact her and, best of all, visit her in Manchester. And that is exactly what I did.

I was as keen to meet Maureen as she was to meet me, and I was a lot more mobile. I rang her at the first opportunity. We were both overjoyed at having made contact and I promised her that after the Welsh wedding, Helen and I would come to Manchester to meet her and her family.

And so, two weeks later, I met my new half-sister, her husband Jimmy and daughters Vicky and Anna. Stuart had changed his plans in order to accompany Helen and me to the historic meeting of families. At the dinner that followed, in a local old English pub, we traded stories of the man who had let so many people down. He had been a poor enough father to me but at least he had not abandoned my mother.

Vicky had taken up the search for my father where her mother had left off. Between them they had scoured the Internet, pursued birth, marriage and death records, placed messages in genealogy databases, in fact left no stone unturned. In one case, Vicky had contacted a Robert Collinge in East Africa and received the memorable reply, 'I would love to help you, but I'm not your grandfather.'

After all avenues of investigation had been exhausted and the search at last given up as hopeless, I had arrived on the scene, a breakthrough as welcome as it was unexpected. No one had had a clue that my father had gone to Australia.

And so, laden with new information, still stunned by the knowledge that I had gained, I returned with Helen to Australia. One basic question of Maureen's was quickly answered – what did he look like? I sent her a dozen photos of my father spanning a thirty-year period. The man of mystery was unveiled at last.

I still had matters of interest to investigate in my ancestry, particularly my grandmother Ella Theodora's Texas background and my father's time in the U.S., but the big discoveries seemed to have been made. How wrong I was.

Chapter 13

Rob Collinge: Take Care of Billy Boy
Maryland: 2007

When trying to unravel the secrets of one's ancestry, various analogies come to mind. One is of the jigsaw puzzle, a puzzle with an unknown number of pieces and no picture to show the final product. Even after months or years of searching, some key pieces remain tantalisingly elusive and what you have before you is open to different interpretations. Some pieces will never be found and parts of the picture will remain forever veiled in mystery. And yet sometimes the picture you have pieced together will reveal to you facts that you had never suspected, stories of which you had no knowledge, and that is perhaps the greatest reward of all.

Another analogy is the chain, the series of discoveries that takes you step by step, link by link, ever further back into the times of your ancestors. Sometimes the links are so fragile, the vital piece of information so trivial and obscure, that it is as though Fate has taken a hand, has decreed that this window into the past should be opened just for you. You may shine a candle into the darkness and rediscover information that had been lost long ago, facts unknown even to your grandparents.

So it was in the years that followed my discovery of my half-sister Maureen and my deceased half-brother Robert and my cousins and all their children and grandchildren. Almost at a stroke, some thirty new relatives had been found scattered all over England and I was soon in touch with a number of them.

It was now apparent why my father had chosen such a deceitful way to eject his mother from his life. In simple terms, she knew too much. She had the power to destroy his marriage with a sentence or two. There may even have been an element of blackmail. Could Ella Theodora have been saying or implying, 'Look after me, Bob, or I will tell your wife things you don't want her to know.'? If that was the case, she underestimated her opponent. As if in a game of high stakes poker, she thought she had a winning hand, but her opponent's was better.

I obtained Ella Theodora's death certificate. Whoever filled in the certificate did not know her deceased husband's name or even that Ella Theodora was a war widow. Husband's name and occupation were simply 'unknown'. The woman who had had the world at her feet at twenty, who had lived in a mansion with a nurse, a cook and a housekeeper to attend her every need, had died penniless among strangers and now lies in an unmarked grave.

The original wealth of the Collinges was truly vast. Wharton's grandfather, James Collinge, had died in 1895. Wharton's father Edward and his brother Robert had predeceased their father. All three had died in a six-year period leaving a total of £400,000 or some £30 million at today's values. How ironic that after World War I and the demise of the cotton trade, James's many grandchildren were left with only their threadbare upper class pretensions and memories of the wealth and power that had once been theirs.

One of my cousin Gerald's sons, Martin, proved to have been the final inheritor of all Lieutenant Wharton Rye Collinge's battlefield possessions, beginning with the wallet with his initials on it. It contained the photo of Ella Theodora that he carried with him throughout those last terrible months. She looked very young and the trappings of wealth were apparent in the velvet jacket with the ermine collar that she wore, the folded fur stole held close to her with her left hand, the pearls, the ring. She was young and she was rich and her life was full of promise.

The dying Wharton's pockets held other treasures for posterity, most of all a detailed hand-drawn map of the trenches, presumably those that he and his men would be facing in the next attack. With

243

the map was the pen that he had used to draw it. The map was a single page of cross-hatched drafting paper, torn from a journal of numbered blank pages and folded twice to fit in his pocket. The zigzag trenches were clearly marked and landmarks such as Chard Farm were shown. Numerous features were identified by initials explained in a list at the bottom of the page. B.P. was Bombing Post, V.G. was Vickers Gun and so on.

Lieutenant Collinge also had a 'Bomb-Throwing Instructor's Certificate' from the Aldershot Command Bombing School. My grandfather was a licensed bomb thrower!

Two especially poignant items were notes dated 28/7/17 and signed WR Collinge attesting to the sanitary condition of his men's billets and listing a quantity of war material and provisions taken over from another battalion. He must have written these notes hours or even minutes before the incident that was to take his life. He put them in his pocket to pass on later. Instead they were passed on to eternity, mute witness ninety years later to his tragic end.

Martin also had a photograph of Wharton in his officer's uniform, head and shoulders, handsome and proud, and the commissioning paper signed by King George making him an Officer of the British Army. Then came a harrowing handwritten account by Ella Theodora of Wharton's death from poison gas, of the ten days it took him to die and of her anguish that she could not be with him one last time.

Two main areas of investigation came to fascinate me now. One was my father's first marriage to the Danish immigrant woman and the other Ella Theodora's Texas origins.

I had an early breakthrough with the first marriage. By chance, the 1930 US Census, the latest published, had entries for my father and his bride in Manhattan. They had apparently married only the month before, in March 1930. Her name was Anna. She was eighteen and he was twenty-five. And for the next two years, that was all I knew. The next link in the chain was maddeningly elusive.

I had more success with the Texas connection. Not for the first time, everything depended on one tiny clue. In my single conversation with my father about his family tree, he had been unable to remember the names of either of Ella Theodora's parents, the Koerners. As we moved on to other areas, a chance thought struck him. She had had a brother Theo. As I jotted that down, I could not have imagined the significance that fact would one day hold for me.

Koerner is a common German name and my best hope in searching the US censuses of the late Nineteenth Century was to locate Ella Theodora but she was nowhere to be found. I was later to discover that she had been born too late for the 1880 Census and had left the country after her marriage just before the 1900 Census. As for the 1890 Census, it had been destroyed long ago in a fire in a basement in Washington DC, to the eternal regret of generations of genealogists. I was getting nowhere.

And then I remembered the tip about brother Theo. After some searching I found a Theodore Koerner in the 1900 Census. The parents were George and Elfrieda Koerner. They had two daughters and two sons, plus Moses Johnson, a black servant. Columns in the Census record showed that the mother had had five children and that all five were still living. One child was missing. It had to be Ella Theodora. George Koerner was a 'wholesale grocery merchant'. He sounded wealthy and successful enough to fit the part of Ella Theodora's father. George was an immigrant, born in Germany, but Elfrieda and both her parents were born in Texas. On the mother's side at least, Ella Theodora's ancestry must go back to the early days of pioneer Texas. My curiosity was aroused.

The next breakthrough was another lucky chance. Someone had taken the trouble to enter into a database the names of all the people buried in the San Antonio General Cemetery. In Plot 7A was George Koerner and various family members, including his wife Elfrieda. She was named as Elfrieda Koerner nee Goldbeck. Her maiden name must be Goldbeck. Then it caught my eye that Plot 7B was full of people called Goldbeck. The Koerner and Goldbeck plots were side by side with Elfrieda the link between them. Without the entirely unnecessary 'nee Goldbeck' on the gravestone, I would never even have noticed Plot 7B – a fragile link indeed.

The jigsaw puzzle pieces now came in thick and fast. The Goldbeck patriarch was clearly Theodore Goldbeck (1826–1890). US census records for 1880, 1870, 1860 and 1850 tracked the Goldbecks back to the days of the early pioneers. Elfrieda was the fourth child of Theodore and Bianca Goldbeck. Theodore and his mother Judith were in the first group of German founders of New Braunfels, north of San Antonio, in 1845, the first of a series of German settlements in Texas.

A diary kept by Elise Tips, another original New Braunfels pioneer, contained frequent references to her friends Theodore and Bianca. She even attended their wedding. An even more remarkable document was known to all present-day Goldbecks as 'the Robinson Book'. It was the product in the 1970s of a man named Robert Robinson, now deceased, one of Judith Goldbeck's many descendants. Unable to pursue a normal working life due to ill health, he took on the self-imposed task of documenting the story of Judith Goldbeck, her ancestry and her descendants. The book, obviously a labour of love, spanned 1500 pages in two volumes. It was extremely rare but from various Goldbeck clan members I tracked down, I received precious pages.

In March 2008, Helen and I attended a Goldbeck Family Reunion, headquartered in the historic Menger Hotel in San Antonio, next to the Alamo. Descendants of Theodore Goldbeck and their spouses from far and wide, over fifty in all, attended the Reunion and it was a great success. The programme included a trip to the original cabin in the town of Comfort built by Theodore Goldbeck in 1854. The highlight, at the gala dinner that ended the festivities, was the unveiling of a recently acquired oil painting of Judith Goldbeck dating back to 1832, when she was twenty-eight and still living in Germany.

One special side trip that we took in Texas was to find the grave of Judith Goldbeck. We were aided in this by one of the Goldbeck relatives at the Reunion, Dan Adams, who had followed a cryptic map in the Robinson book and with admirable persistence had tracked down the last resting place of the great pioneering matriarch. With his instructions to guide us we did indeed find the lonely gravesite, contained within a wire fence, overlooking the Guadalupe River. Her husband Heinrich was there too and his second wife, all together in death. It was a moving experience.

Completing the story of my ancestors in old Texas filled in much of my free time in the years after my 2004 discoveries in England. On the quest for my father's first wife, Anna, however no breakthrough came. I was up against the proverbial brick wall.

I did discover one curious fact from the 1930 Census. My father's Uncle Robert, Wharton's older brother, was living at that time in a town called Bainbridge in Chenango County in upper New York State. He had a wife Elsa and he was a factory manager. This was the uncle after whom my father was named. Perhaps my father had left Texas in the hope of getting assistance from his uncle in relocating to the Big Apple. Perhaps he had tired of the Deep South. Interesting though this speculation was, it didn't get me any closer to solving the riddle of Anna and my footloose father.

One day while driving in the vicinity of my home in Melbourne, I noticed a church of the Latter Day Saints, the Mormons, in a nearby suburb. They were famous for their genealogical research. I found that they had a Family History Centre with microfiche listings of tapes of genealogical records from all over the world. For a modest fee, one could order in any tape of interest.

An idea came to me. Could I obtain marriage records for New York City for 1930? Indeed I could and in due course tapes for all five boroughs of the City for 1930 arrived. It was all for nothing. Not a single Collinge was to be found.

It was certainly a disappointment but not altogether a surprise. The explanation was obvious enough. Anna and Robert had most likely married in Anna's hometown, where her parents lived. And where was that? It could be anywhere in the surrounding area. New York State alone had over fifty counties with hundreds more in other nearby states and each had its own birth, marriage and death records. No one, it seemed, had ever tried to get all this mass of information into an accessible form. The brick wall still stood. I was no further forward.

One day I had an inspiration. Could my father have met Anna through Uncle Robert? Could Anna have come from Bainbridge? This was a long shot indeed. I went back to the Mormon Family Centre. On a microfiche index of New York State tapes I found little relating to Chenango County but miraculously I discovered one tape with marriages from 1928 to 1932 – exactly what I needed. It was as though Fate had decided to reward me for my persistence.

It still seemed a case of clutching at straws and I was not hopeful. It took many weeks for such an obscure tape to be sent from its storage place somewhere in the US but eventually I received the call. It had arrived. As I mounted it on the tape reader at the Family Centre, I prepared for another disappointment.

The tape began with an index of the marriage certificate photocopies that it contained. And there it was – Robert Collinge and Anna Nymann, the name that had eluded me for years. I was so excited that I told everybody in the room. I asked if I could get a copy of the certificate. I could, for a cost of 20c. I only had $5. I told them to keep the change and left the Centre in triumph.

It was a big step forward but I wasn't there yet. Letters sent to every Nymann in the US on the Internet brought no replies. I returned to the 1930 Census and located the Nymann family. Anna was the oldest of three children. She had a younger sister Ellen and a brother Svend. A record of the immigrant ship on which the family arrived from Copenhagen in 1928 gave a description of Anna as having blond hair, blue eyes and a fair complexion. The effect on my father of such a combination was not hard to imagine. Was there anyone still alive who knew of Anna and her ill-fated marriage to Robert Collinge?

Searching for a way forward I signed on with a California background search company specialising in credit references. I checked their Nymann listings, hoping for better luck than I had had on the Internet. One entry was for Svend Nymann of Florida. Could it be the original Svend? He would be ninety years old. Careful to keep my hopes in check, I rang the telephone number provided and asked the woman who answered if Svend Nymann was available. She asked why I wanted him.

How to explain? 'Well,' I began, 'my name is Rob Collinge. I believe Svend may have had a sister Anna who married my father Robert Collinge in 1930. I was trying to find out about their marriage.'

It took her a moment to swallow this sudden onrush of information but from then on it was all systems go. 'Yes, that's right. Oh yes, I know all about that. And your father was Robert Collinge, you say? That's amazing.' A pause, and then the big one. 'Did you know they had a son?'

A feeling of déjà vu swept over me. The old devil had done it again. Another family abandoned. He had left a trail over three continents. How greatly I had underestimated the man. Far from being merely a pompous snob, he was actually a scoundrel of the highest order. Never could I have imagined that he could be so much more interesting in death than he ever was in life.

My new half-brother was William Alexander Collinge of Baltimore, Maryland, aged seventy-six, retired chartered accountant, married, wife Lois, three children, eight grandchildren. Stunned, I jotted it all down, plus address and telephone number.

Bill, as he was known, was on a cruise at the moment with Lois and would be back late Sunday. I could get him on Monday.

I thanked the lady for all this new knowledge. Her name was Eileen, Svend's step-daughter and carer. I even spoke to Svend himself, my father's brother-in-law, as fascinated with my story as Eileen had been. It was with a feeling of unreality that I finally put down the telephone.

This was too much to keep to myself, even briefly. It was Saturday morning. My wife Helen was at that moment on a shopping trip to the Melbourne city centre with her friend and neighbour Ursula. Helen did not have a mobile phone but Ursula did. I rang the number and heard Ursula's voice.

'Can you put Helen on? Tell her I've got something that will blow her mind.'

I told Helen the news. She shrieked to Ursula, 'He's got a half-brother in America.'

Ursula had followed the Robert Collinge saga from the start. 'Another one. Oh my God.' They were in a teddy bear shop, an interest they shared, and they told everyone in the shop. It was a memorable day.

Given the time difference with the US and my work week, it was not practical to ring until the following weekend. When I reached Bill, he was waiting for the call. Eileen had phoned him as soon as he and Lois returned home and told him the dramatic news. My father had left the country when Bill was two years old. And now, seventy-four years later, I was here to tell him all about the man. He was deeply touched. All his life, like Maureen, he had been haunted by the mystery of his unknown father. Where did he go? What did he do with his life? What sort of a person was he? What did he look like? When did he die? And I had all the answers. I had brought another person "out of the wilderness", to use Maureen's memorable phrase.

I told Bill, and Lois, listening on an extension, many things. And I told them about Maureen. Bill was gaining not one but two half-siblings in a single telephone call. As soon as the call was over, I emailed Maureen: 'He's waiting to hear from you. Go for it.' Now there were three of us, on three continents, the children of Robert Collinge, surely the world's most exclusive club. Then I gathered the same photos of my father together that I had sent Maureen three years before and set off to get copies.

In the weeks that followed, many facts came to light. Amazingly, Anna was still alive at ninety-six, in a nursing home near Bill and Lois. She had lived in Bainbridge, New York, and had been the housemaid of my father's Uncle Robert, the factory manager. My father had indeed met her through his uncle.

Another notable fact was that Anna had not divorced my father until eighteen months after he married my mother. So an act of bigamy could now be counted among his exploits. My trusting mother had died in 2003, too soon to learn that the man to whom she was married for forty years was not legally married to her at all. And then came the matter of Lily and two children in an orphanage. And two-year-old Bill in Baltimore. Death had spared her nightmares beyond comprehension.

I thought of the Collinge family motto of which my father had been so proud: 'Fidelis in Omnibus' – 'Faithful in All.' Could any motto have been more wildly inappropriate for such a man? I wondered if the irony had ever occurred to him.

On Christmas Day, 2007, Bill rang Maureen and heard her voice for the first time. The Christmas card from the Collinges of Baltimore to the Collinges of Melbourne said, 'What a beautiful Christmas it is this year. God has given me my lost family. It makes me feel complete.'

In March 2008, after attending the Goldbeck family reunion in San Antonio, Helen and I journeyed on to Baltimore. Bill and Lois awaited us at the airport, along with daughter Nancy. It was an emotional meeting. Unknowingly, we had waited all our lives for it.

Over the next few days we met all three of Bill's daughters, his sons-in-law and eight grandchildren, warm and welcoming families like Bill and Lois themselves. A whole new family structure, a sturdy new branch, had been grafted onto the family tree.

Even after two more failed marriages, Anna had kept all the love letters my father had sent her in their courting days, while he worked in Manhattan and she was in Bainbridge. I counted forty-five letters in all. It was extraordinary to see my father's distinctive handwriting from long before I was born. More surprising still was the content of the letters. The stiff and distant man I had known as a child rattled on, page after page, to his 'dearest little girl', 'the prettiest, dearest, sweetest, most lovable girl in the world', like a lovesick schoolboy. In one letter he even waxed philosophical and declared how much he hated 'lies and deception', two skills for which he would demonstrate mastery in the years to come. The word "hypocrite" hardly seemed adequate.

Anna had even kept the final letter my father had sent her after leaving her forever and returning to England. From an address in London, he apologised for being a bad husband, reminisced about the good times they had shared together and closed with the words 'Take care of Billy Boy' – the son he would never see again. How those words must have rung in her ears over the years that followed. She replied to his letter but her reply was returned "Not at this address". He had already moved on to new addresses and new horizons.

I had followed my father into the darkest corners of his past, a past that he had tried so hard to erase from view. Pieces of the jigsaw puzzle were missing still but the broad outlines were clear at last, more than twenty years after his death.

My father had brought so much heartache to those he had abandoned and betrayed and yet his ultimate legacy had been the coming together of families on three continents and the joy of forging new and lasting friendships.

I could take satisfaction in the thought that in this final act of closure, my father's ghost had at last been laid to rest.

Lightning Source UK Ltd.
Milton Keynes UK
UKOW040746250413

209724UK00001B/22/P